"In an age that sees too many therapists and counselors writing in strings of buzzwords and trendy movements, the contributors to this book remind us there are deeper currents that bind us in our common work. From time to time, artist/therapists need to rejoice in the human, and in the soulful nature of making art in the service of healing. This book may provide opportunities for many to pause, take stock, and rejoice."

—Bruce L. Moon, PhD, ATR-BC, Professor,
Art Therapy Department, Mount Mary University

"Expressive arts therapy is rapidly emerging as a mainstream approach in psychotherapy and healthcare. This volume vividly illustrates leading-edge expressive arts applications while providing important historical foundations of this field. Readers will be inspired by the authors' wisdom and insights on theory and practice of expressive arts in mental health, education, research and community work."

—Cathy Malchiodi, PhD, LPCC, LPAT, ATR-BC, REAT,
Executive Director, Trauma-Informed Practices and
Expressive Arts Therapy Institute

"Ellen and Stephen Levine have given birth to an anthology of breadth and depth, of ideas and revelations. The writers are carefully chosen to open up the boundaries and conversations regarding expressive therapy, a discipline more needed than ever in a broken world in denial of history and in need of direction. The Levines offer a blueprint for repair, a *poiesis* in itself, something new and playful and powerful."

—Robert Landy, PhD, Professor of Educational Theatre and
Applied Psychology, Founding Director,
Drama Therapy Program, New York University

by the same authors

Art in Action
Expressive Arts Therapy and Social Change
Ellen G. Levine and Stephen K. Levine
Foreword by Michelle LeBaron
ISBN 978 1 84905 820 9
eISBN 978 0 85700 270 9

Principles and Practice of Expressive Arts Therapy
Toward a Therapeutic Aesthetics
Paolo Knill, Ellen G. Levine and Stephen K. Levine
ISBN 978 1 84310 039 3
eISBN 978 1 84642 032 0

Foundations of Expressive Arts Therapy
Theoretical and Clinical Perspectives
Edited by Stephen K. Levine and Ellen G. Levine
ISBN 978 1 85302 463 4
eISBN 978 1 84642 185 3

Poiesis
The Language of Psychology and the Speech of the Soul
Stephen K. Levine
ISBN 978 1 85302 488 7
eISBN 978 0 85700 074 3

Trauma, Tragedy, Therapy
The Arts and Human Suffering
Stephen K. Levine
ISBN 978 1 84310 512 1
eISBN 978 0 85700 193 1

Play and Art in Child Psychotherapy
An Expressive Arts Therapy Approach
Ellen G. Levine
ISBN 978 1 84905 504 8
eISBN 978 0 85700 919 7

NEW DEVELOPMENTS
in EXPRESSIVE ARTS THERAPY

The Play of Poiesis

EDITED BY ELLEN G. LEVINE AND STEPHEN K. LEVINE

Jessica Kingsley *Publishers*
London and Philadelphia

Cover image credit of Rowsea Gordon

First published in 2017
by Jessica Kingsley Publishers
73 Collier Street
London N1 9BE, UK
and
400 Market Street, Suite 400
Philadelphia, PA 19106, USA

www.jkp.com

Copyright © Jessica Kingsley Publishers 2017

All rights reserved. No part of this publication may be reproduced in any material form (including photocopying, storing in any medium by electronic means or transmitting) without the written permission of the copyright owner except in accordance with the provisions of the law or under terms of a licence issued in the UK by the Copyright Licensing Agency Ltd. www.cla.co.uk or in overseas territories by the relevant reproduction rights organisation, for details see www.ifrro.org. Applications for the copyright owner's written permission to reproduce any part of this publication should be addressed to the publisher.

Warning: The doing of an unauthorised act in relation to a copyright work may result in both a civil claim for damages and criminal prosecution.

Library of Congress Cataloging in Publication Data
A CIP catalog record for this book is available from the Library of Congress

British Library Cataloguing in Publication Data
A CIP catalogue record for this book is available from the British Library

ISBN 978 1 78592 247 3
eISBN 978 1 78450 532 5

Printed and bound in Great Britain

CONTENTS

Acknowledgments 8
Preface 9
Stephen K. Levine

Stuhl-leben 16
Brigitte Wanzenried
The Poietics of Alterity 17
Stephen K. Levine

PART I THEORY
Pasture 6. 19
Shaun McNiff
After 20
Sally Atkins

1. Cultivating Imagination 21
   Shaun McNiff

2. The Essence in a Therapeutic Process, an Alternative
   Experience of Worlding? 31
   Paolo J. Knill

3. Longing for Beauty and the Work: An Interview with Paolo Knill   48
   Stephen K. Levine

4. Modality: A Phenomenological Concept for Expressive Arts . . . 66
   Jacques Stitelmann, Translated by Jackie Beaver
   Translated by Jackie Beaver

5. The Poietic Basis of Being: Thoughts on Expression
   and the Other Person Based on the Work of Merleau-Ponty . . . 82
   Majken Jacoby

PART II THERAPY
Nutcase Alarm 97
Rowesa Gordon
Practicum on the Eating Disorders Ward: Sonnet 1 98
Shara Claire

6. The Arts Work: The Process of Intermodal Decentering
   in Professional Conversations 99
   Herbert Eberhart

7. The Question of Quality Art in Expressive Arts Therapy 113
   Shaun McNiff

8. A Tango in the Ruins: Encounters with Beauty
   in a Harm Reduction Environment 128
   Sabine Silberberg
9. Stepping into Locked Space: An Algorithmic Dialogue
   between Choreography and In-Patient Work 137
   Rebekah Windmiller
10. The Garden of Praise and Lament: Expressive Arts
    Group Psychotherapy with Trauma Survivors in Exile 145
    Melinda Ashley Meyer DeMott
11. Play, Art and Ritual: Working Therapeutically
    with Children and their Parents 158
    Ellen G. Levine

Part III Education
Untitled 175
Judy Nisenholt
CHANGE in the AIR 176
Elizabeth McKim

12. Aesthetic Education: Learning through the Arts 177
    Stephen K. Levine
13. Aesthetic Responsibility in Expressive Arts: Thoughts
    on Beauty, Responsibility and the New in the Education
    of Expressive Arts Professionals 181
    Margo Fuchs Knill and Paolo J. Knill
14. Education on the Edge: Acts of Balance 184
    Elisabeth Hösli and Peter Wanzenried
15. Art Asylum: Exploring Otherness through Play and Art-Making . . 194
    Ellen G. Levine
16. Artists in Community: The Black Mountain College
    and the White Mountain Graduate School 196
    Sally Atkins

Part IV Social and Ecological Change
Degradation and Preservation 209
Ellen G. Levine
Cedar Fire Fragment 210
Judith Greer Essex

17. Community Art: Communal Art-Making to Build
    a Sense of Coherence 211
    Paolo J. Knill
18. The Pulse of Humanity 234
    Carrie MacLeod

19. What Do You Care About? Arts Therapies in Support
    of Civil Courage in a "World Gone Slightly Mad"   244
    Rosemary Faire
20. Why Eco-Philosophy and Expressive Arts?.   258
    Per Espen Stoknes
21. Nature as a Work of Art: Towards a Poietic Ecology   261
    Stephen K. Levine

PART V RESEARCH

ROCK, from 4 perspectives (2004)   273
Kelly Lycan
AMONG.   274
Elizabeth McKim

22. The Open Space of Art-Based Research   275
    Shaun McNiff
23. Crafting Maps, Attuning to Flesh, and Dancing the Radicant
    Mobilizing the Expressive Arts and Arts-Based Research
    to do a Conceptual Translation of "Science as Usual".   281
    Kelly Clark/Keefe, Jessica Gilway, and Emily Miller
24. Knowing Not-Knowing: Research as an Art-Analogue Process. . .   301
    Sabine Silberberg
25. Playing with Auschwitz: A Liminal Inquiry into Images of Evil . .   311
    Lisa Herman
26. Per-forming Home: Spinning New Scripts for Re-Search.   318
    Cold Spell   329
    Isabel Hayeur
    Two Poems   330
    Margo Fuchs Knill

LIST OF CONTRIBUTORS   331
SUBJECT INDEX   336
AUTHOR INDEX   343

ACKNOWLEDGMENTS

This volume could not exist without the contributors to all the issues of the *POIESIS* journal, both those who are represented here and those who wrote equally valuable pieces which could not be included for lack of space. The European Graduate School, a unique educational institution, supported the publication of the journal throughout. The founder and first Provost, Paolo Knill, was an enthusiastic supporter from its inception, as was Shaun McNiff, one of the pioneers in the field of expressive arts.

Particularly helpful throughout the years were our poetry editor Elizabeth McKim, associate editor Shara Claire, managing editor Sarah Farr, and production manager and art director Kristin Briggs, without whom the journal could not have been possible.

Ellen G. Levine and Stephen K. Levine are jointly responsible for the editing of this volume, including the articles, poems, and visual images. We greatly regret that we could not include many other interesting and significant contributions, but we had to respect the limits within which this book was possible. All *poiesis* takes place within limits or frames. We hope we have found enough freedom within this frame for a meaningful work to emerge.

PREFACE
Stephen K. Levine

The essays, images and poetry in this volume are drawn from the journal, *POIESIS: A Journal of the Arts and Communication,* a publication of the European Graduate School (EGS), from 1999 to 2015. EGS consists of two Divisions: Philosophy, Art and Critical Thought (PACT) and Arts, Health and Society (AHS). Although the *POIESIS* journal included contributions from both Divisions, the essays published here are all drawn from AHS, in which the focus of study is the field of expressive arts in all its forms. As well as discursive writing, poetry and visual art were included in accordance with the title of the journal. As editor of *POIESIS*, my intention was to emphasize a poietic approach to the expressive arts, rather than a social scientific one. In this way, I hoped to promote work that was in keeping with the artistic essence of the field rather than to search for legitimacy through imitating the methods of natural science, which are drawn from and appropriate to a quite different domain.

The subtitle of this book, *The Play of Poiesis*, has a double meaning: on the one hand, "play" refers to non-purposive activity pursued for its own sake. On the other hand, we speak of the "play" of a device, whether it has room to expand and contract. Expressive arts (EXA) is a field in which both meanings apply. EXA is based on play and retains that free and spontaneous character even when it takes the form of art-works, and the field has also expanded from its therapeutic origins to aesthetic approaches to education, social and environmental change, and even to research, as the sections of this book indicate.

In this Preface, I have tried to think through the meaning of *poiesis* in a way that applies to all of its different manifestations. Each of the essays in the book, however, has its own character, stemming from the particular perspective and style of its author. Rather than attempt to make a forced unification, I see them all as different expressions of a totality that can never be grasped in itself, just as each art form can only show itself through the individual style of the artist. The essays, poems, and visual art that are included represent this aesthetic dimension to be found in a multiplicity of forms. We hope the reader will appreciate the unity in this diversity, the creative spirit that animates us all.

EXA is based on *poiesis*, the act of bringing something new into the world. *Poiesis*, however, is understood in a different way for us than in the philosophical tradition. At the beginning of Western thought and throughout most of its history, the human being was conceived of as a conscious agent who acts in accordance with what he knows in order to control what is around him. (I use the male pronoun here advisedly, since the classical conception of *poiesis* is in accordance with the traditional image of masculinity.) In this perspective, consciousness and will are seen as the primary characteristics of human action, including creative action. Taken to their limit, these are also conceived of as attributes of God, the divine being who is omniscient and omnipotent.

For Plato, then, at the beginning of Western philosophy, the arts are lacking in these characteristics. Artists do not know what they are doing, but act according to an inspiration which is out of their conscious control. Consequently, their works can only appeal to the emotions; they stir people up and foster that disorder which is the greatest danger to the *polis*, the political state. For this reason, Plato would ban most artists from the just society, one which should be ruled by philosophers, those who know what is good and act in accordance with it.

Of course, Plato's works themselves exhibit all the characteristics of the arts: they are constructed in dramatic form, contain many metaphors and resort to myth when reason reaches its limit. In fact, Plato is one of the most poetic of thinkers. He may have banned poetry from the state, but he was unable to ban it from himself.

This conflict between poetry and philosophy in early Western philosophy shows the ambiguous relationship that *poiesis* has had with scientific thinking since the beginning. On the one hand, *poiesis* is seen as having little to do with knowledge. On the other hand, the power of the arts in human existence cannot be denied, and even science has to acknowledge the importance of the creative element in scientific discovery.

Aristotle, following Plato, attempted to account for the power of the arts with his concept of catharsis, a term from both medicine and ritual, indicating either purgation or purification. The emotions of pity and fear, dangerous to the social order, can be eliminated or purified through identification with the fate of the hero. The artist, for Aristotle, creates in accordance with a certain kind of knowledge, a knowing by making (*poiesis*), to be distinguished from knowing by acting (*praxis*) and knowing by observing (*theoria*). Of these three forms of knowledge, however, *poiesis* is the lowest for Aristotle. Only theory, which can see what is without being directly affected by and involved in it, can deliver what was later called objective truth. Knowledge is attained through taking a distance from emotion and interest. It is a vision of the truth, attainable in its pure form only by the divine being, itself unmoved but moving all else through the power of attraction and emulation.

Poiesis itself was understood by Aristotle according to this model, in which a particular form is thought to be imposed upon matter, itself chaotic and formless. The tradition of aesthetic thought in the West follows this way of thinking, conceiving of art-making from a theoretical perspective in which disinterested knowledge is considered the highest form of understanding. "Aesthetics," in its traditional sense, presupposes this framework.

Expressive arts, on the other hand, comprehends art-making from a phenomenological point of view, attempting to grasp the way it is understood in itself, rather than from a perspective which presupposes *theoria* as the basis of all knowledge. Nor does an expressive arts perspective conceive of pure inspiration as the source of creative action. "Inspiration" only makes sense as a basis if all knowing is reserved for science, understood from a theoretical perspective. *Theoria* comes from a root, meaning "to see." Vision, grasped only as objective and disinterested, is taken as the sensory mode at the origin of knowledge. When we see, we look at what is displayed before us. However, we do not usually take account of our situation in the field, where we are located, and the movement of our body that makes vision possible. Further, we are not normally aware of the fact that what we see depends upon what we focus on, and that itself depends upon our interest in what is to be seen.

In fact, theory is grasped from a theoretical point of view, as pre-existing and given to us, not as something that we make. However, we are not in the world as disinterested observers, although we can take that stance for specific purposes. Nor are we ourselves separate from the world in which we live, nor from the others who are there with us. We cannot impose our will upon the world and those others without disastrous consequences, as human history shows.

Rather, we exist in the world. We find ourselves at every moment with others in a world that is already there, and we can only respond to what is given to us.

The concepts of "response" and "responsibility" are central to an understanding of *poiesis* and to our work in the expressive arts. To say that we respond to the world that is given to us implies that we are caught up in it, situated in it. We are "thrown" into the world, to use Heidegger's term (Heidegger 1962, p.174), at a certain point of history, with a particular body, gender, class, ethnicity and other qualities that are given to us. Even in the arts, we must take account of the materials that have been handed down, the traditions of making, and the history of styles. We never create *ex nihilo*, as the Creator was thought to do, but always with the possibilities that are given to us in our situation.

Nevertheless, we do not have to repeat the tradition that lies before us. Rather, we are always free to modify it and to create new pathways for others to follow. *Poiesis is always possible* (Levine 1999, p.11). Everything can be re-formed. We can even turn what is given around, make a revolution, and produce altogether new forms; but whatever we make will always bear the marks of what has come before. I can change, for example, my religion, my class status, the beliefs and attitudes that I have inherited, I can even change my gender, but whatever I change I cannot escape my origins. The present, as Leibniz has said, is laden with the past and pregnant with the future. It is our role to assist with the birth of what is to come.

If then, *poiesis* is a response to what is given, what is the responsibility of those of us who try to help others become able to respond to their difficulties in ways that are creative and life-affirming? In expressive arts, we think of this as an "aesthetic responsibility." Aesthetics here is not conceived of in the traditional way as the knowledge of beauty, a knowledge of that which stands apart from us and is presented to us without our involvement or interest. Rather "aesthetics" is taken as a bodily response, in accordance with its original meaning of having to do with the senses. Beauty is what moves or touches us. It strikes us and takes our breath away. Only afterwards, in a reflective stance, can we analyse it and know it objectively.

It is the responsibility of expressive arts practitioners to help the other or others have this aesthetic experience of beauty. This then is the practitioner's aesthetic responsibility, to facilitate an aesthetic response in others, to guide them in such a way that their experience moves them and moves them to change in productive ways. To do this, the participant must be able to incorporate their aesthetic experience into their daily lives, to make a bridge between what we call a "decentering" from everyday life, a moving away from focusing on the difficulty and instead stepping into the alternative world of the imagination, and their literal experience of everyday life. Without this return, there is a danger of isolating the aesthetic response as a special experience that is only valuable for the "high" that it offers.

Many other change agents take this step back into daily life in cognitive ways, through explanatory frameworks that account for aesthetic experience in terms of concepts and theories which derive from different realms of knowledge, whether psychological or other. In expressive arts, we try to "stick to the image," in James Hillman's phrase (1983, p.54). We begin by taking a phenomenological approach to the "decentering" phase of an expressive arts session, letting what appears show itself as it is in itself. Phenomenology is the study of what appears to us, and the arts are the realm of appearance par excellence. They show themselves insofar as they are as they appear to be. We might even say that the arts *are* phenomenological. Thus phenomenology is the appropriate response to them, rather than an attempt to explain them in other terms. We call this phenomenological phase of our work the "aesthetic analysis."

During the aesthetic analysis, we stick with the image and carefully speak about what we see, what we felt and what we imagined. Only then do we ask for the meaning of the experience. Meaning comes from the senses, as the French word "*sens*" and the English "sense" indicate. It is only from a reflective position that the separation of thinking and sensing is seen as a radical one. "The symbol gives rise to thought," the French philosopher Paul Ricoeur wrote (1967, p.247). Sensing leads to thinking. What we sense makes sense, if we can pay attention to it without putting it into another framework. In fact, there is a pre-reflective element of thinking in our sense experience. We not only see but we know that we are seeing; sensing only appears as divorced from cognition when we step back and take a reflective or theoretical attitude that separates us from our experience. What we call the aesthetic analysis refers to the careful attention that we pay in expressive arts to the experience we have in a decentering process, both what we experience and how we experience it. The meaning will come from the experience, not the other way around.

What kind of relationship can foster the aesthetic response we are speaking of in those with whom we work? This question has come into greater prominence as relational perspectives have been foregrounded in psychotherapy and other disciplines. Is art-making enough? Why do we need the other to help us have an aesthetic experience? First of all, we must recognize that all experience is with others. Even solitude is a being-apart-from-others. We are born, as Heidegger says, in a world with others (Heidegger 1962, p.149). Human existence itself is a being-in-the-world-with-others. It is only in philosophical reflection or in pathology that we appear as isolated egos outside of the world. What then is the relational character of expressive arts? Winnicott speaks of the holding environment which is necessary for a child to flourish (Winnicott 1974, p.130). In psychotherapy today, the role of the therapist is often seen as that of holding. The therapist, then, is likened to the maternal figure who gives the child a basic sense of trust by providing an environment in which they feel held. She does this through an accepting non-judgmental attitude of empathic attunement. Expressive arts practitioners would agree that holding is essential in any helping relationship. The client or participant must feel safe or no act of *poiesis* will be possible. However, holding is not enough. The client must also be able to respond to this sense of security by taking a step away from it, by feeling safe enough to take a risk. We speak of "shaping" as well as of "holding" as the two-fold essence of the relationship in expressive arts. The therapist or other expressive arts practitioner not only tunes into the experience of the other in an empathic way, he or she also intervenes when necessary to help the participant shape their experience.

Obviously this must be done with great sensitivity. The participant must never be forced into an experience. Force destroys trust, but it is not the only alternative to a purely receptive attitude on the part of the practitioner. This is why we speak of guiding as an appropriate way of being-with. Elizabeth McKim, the Poet Laureate of EGS, says in performance, "An agile guide's good/when you cross a fragile bridge/from here...to here...here!" (unpublished haiku). The practitioner must take an attitude that we can describe as being like the Taoist *wu-wei*, non-action that nevertheless leads to a result.

This attitude is not restricted to the therapeutic relationship. Rather the field of expressive arts has expanded, as we indicated, to all relationships which are based on facilitation. Thus we can speak of an expressive arts approach to education, but also to social and environmental change, and even to research, as this volume attempts to show. In each of these fields, *poiesis* is considered as central. Education helps the student to draw out their capacities for knowing, as the origin of the term indicates (*educare*—to draw out). It is not a matter, then, of imposing knowledge on the other but of helping him or her learn to learn, to be able to shape their own way of understanding appropriate to the given field of knowledge. Similarly, social change cannot be meaningful if it is carried out according to a plan on the part of the change agent. Rather, community members must become aware of their own capacity for poietic action in order to shape a world that is satisfying for them. Finally, even research can be reconceived from an expressive arts perspective. Research is always an act of *poiesis*, it discovers the new. This means that research itself is something in the making. Recently, the use of arts-based ways of doing research has come into prominence in the expressive arts, as is appropriate, but we should remember that all research worth the name originates in *poiesis*. It is always a question of bringing something new into being.

Expressive arts is based on the play of *poiesis*. It is a special field of activity that draws upon the basic human capacity of creativity. As we shape the world, we shape ourselves. Suffering comes when we are unable to create. We suffer when there is no room to play with what is possible, when our play range is too restricted to imagine the new. "Imagination," Einstein said, "is more important than knowledge" (Einstein 1929, p.117), but it is not opposed to knowledge. Rather imagination is the vision of possibilities in our situation that can lead us to new understandings, new ways of acting and being that bring freedom to a restrictive situation. As we shape the world, we shape ourselves. Therefore, change the world. Only then can we be free.

References

Einstein, A. (1929) "What Life Means to Einstein: An Interview with George Sylvester Viereck." *The Saturday Evening Post,* October 26. Philadelphia: Curtis Publishing Co.
Heidegger, M. (1962) *Being and Time.* New York: Harper.
Hillman, J., with Pozzo, L. (1983) *Inter Views: Conversations with Laura Pozzo on Psychotherapy, Biography, Love, Soul, Dreams, Work, Imagination, and the State of the Culture.* New York: Harper & Row.
Levine, S.K. (1999) "Poiesis and Post-modernism: The Search for a Foundation in Expressive Arts Therapy." In S.K. Levine and E.G. Levine (eds), *Foundations of Expressive Arts Therapy: Theoretical and Clinical Perspectives.* London: Jessica Kingsley Publishers.
Ricoeur, P. (1967) *The Symbolism of Evil.* New York: Harper & Row.
Winnicott, D.W. (1974) *Playing and Reality.* Harmondsworth: Penguin.

Stuhl-leben Brigitte Wanzenried

The Poietics of Alterity
Stephen K. Levine

You to whom I write,
are you really a brother to me,
a compadre born of the same familial spirit
to carry the body of words?

Do we speak the same language?
When I say "I," do you agree?
Or are you foreign, alien, an other,
one to whom this message is naught,
an empty page with unintelligible marks.

I conjure you out of the silence.
We share a birth into speech.
Listen to me, O my brother.
Be you man or woman,
I address you fraternally as Walt did,
closer to me than my own skin.

Let us have our conversation.
Respond to me in your reading,
and speak the name that is your own.

Out of doubt and unbelief,
we will build this republic.
And in the dark days will make
our darkness shine with light,
as we finally read
the writing of our lives.

Part I
THEORY

Pasture 6   Shaun McNiff

After

Sally Atkins

for Majken

We have cracked the categories
Analyzed the knowing
Decentered, deconstructed

                  The world
                  Art and beauty
                  Ourselves
                  And knowing itself,

Can we stay in that place of unknowing,

                  The uncertain, quivering,
                  Strange, mysterious
                  Dark and also beautiful
                  Place where the story
                  breaks down,

         The space between paradigms?

And what does the artist say to us?
She says
Something calls

                  There is more, open the door
                  The art
                  The other person
                  The tiny blue flower
                  In its green grass bed
                  Beside the path,

And what does it mean to be human?

                  To respond to that call?
To say: Yes, I am here,
And to stay there
Not knowing

                  Yes, I am still here.

1

CULTIVATING IMAGINATION

Shaun McNiff

As the popularity and relevance of expressive arts therapies continue to expand, we are on the verge of becoming a mainstream discipline. The realization of this opportunity will depend upon our ability to understand and articulate what we can offer the world. Our discipline is based upon the activation of the medicines of the creative imagination that operate in ways that cannot be explained by the linear paradigms and the analytic narratives which have characterized psychological thinking during the past century. In addition to articulating the healing function of the creative imagination, we need to realize that this "intelligence" has few limits in terms of what it can become. The expressive arts therapies have powers unrealized and applications yet to be imagined.

What is the creative imagination?

The lack of appreciation for the intelligence of the creative imagination originates largely in the dualistic world views that have for so long cast complementary elements—reason and intuition, science and art, the real and unreal, subjective and objective, empirical and imaginal—into polar camps which enjoy few possibilities for reciprocal creation. Imagination is an "integrative" intelligence that includes reason, intuition and many other contributors in keeping with the nature of reality. It is time to move past dualities of mind and to appreciate the complete "*participation mystique*" of imagination.

Imitating nature, the creative imagination operates by making connections between all things. In *Art-Based Research* (1998), I document how the expressive arts therapies can do much more in utilizing the creative imagination as a mode of discovery.

The literature documenting the process of creative discovery in science and industry speaks often about the process of imagination. We have heard many accounts of how creative scientists make their most important discoveries while pondering some aspect of nature outside the context of the laboratory or while relaxing in a state of reverie. Discovery frequently occurs during periods when the linear thinking of a particular experiment is suspended, and this allows the various aspects of a problem to take on a different relationship with one another. The relaxed reverie of imagining generates a new "integration" of the participating elements.

It seems that areas of life which are driven by the need to innovate and change embrace the creative imagination, whereas those sectors striving to justify themselves according to prevailing concepts of reality are less likely to acknowledge its existence as a primary intelligence. When we plan and assess everything that we do according to what we already know and accept imagination is apt to suffer.

The presumption that imagination is "only" idle fantasy and make-believe has been a serious deterrent to its growth. When cast as a trivial activity, imagination loses the benefit of energies focused on realizing its full potential and its capacity to work closely with reason and science in solving problems and creating new life.

It might be asked whether there is an "unreal" aspect to the working of imagination. For those who see imaginative reverie as simply another form of reality, a distinctly imaginative presence that can be distinguished from the structure of physical things, there is a constant need to differentiate the varied types of reality. The conventional view of "reality" is limited to "facts" and "hard data" as verified by the perceptions of reasonable people. In my work with psychiatric patients in the 1970s, I observed how the person labeled psychotic or schizophrenic was caught in a bind when it came to self-expression. Contents that they presented in their art or in their conversations that deviated from the most literal definitions of the external world were often viewed as confirming that they were out of touch with "reality."

It seemed natural to me to view a person's inner experience as simply a form of reality that differs from what exists in the material realm of consensual experience with others. When a patient made a painting or a poem expressing personal feelings, they were creating reality within the context of their individual relationships with the media. The experience of psychosis, approached as a disorder of imagination, involved an inability to distinguish amongst the different aspects of reality that might be interacting with one another in a particular situation.

The mind is disoriented by psychosis and unable to move from one type of experience to another in a way which is congruent with the experiences of other people. A person experiencing this condition no longer makes the subtle distinctions between inner and outer experiences that characterize healthy relations with the world. In psychosis the purely imaginal, and nevertheless real, phantoms of the inner world are experienced literally, as though they were material beings existing in the external world. It can be argued that the one-sided belief that only "hard data" are real is equally out of touch with reality. The phenomena of the creative imagination contribute in a productive way to improving the quality of life when inner visions take shape within the physical world.

How does imagination operate?

Creative vitality can be viewed as a condition in which all of a person's or a community's resources simultaneously generate stimuli and insights without necessarily following a logical or linear sequence of actions. The imagination is the intelligence that integrates and guides the creative transformation of what some might perceive as an unlikely mix of participants. In 1804, Jean Paul Richter described the imagination as the "faculty of faculties" which he likened to the process of pollination: "In genius all faculties are in bloom at once, and imagination is not the flower, but the flower-goddess, who arranges the flower calyxes with their mingling pollens for new hybrids" (1973, p.35). Imagination is the conductor of creative action, a force that operates by making fresh links between previously separate entities, always open and receptive to new possibilities while forever seeking out opportunities.

The vitality of the imagination is frequently experienced within groups and communities that are given the freedom and support to create. The community of creation is an energizing force that acts upon the people within it. As the Romantic poets observed, the life of imagination is furthered by an environment where "flying sparks" pass amongst people and ignite new ideas. This interactive and participatory dynamic also occurs within the individual imagination. The community of creation that we discover in the company of other people exists within ourselves.

Today, the general sense of imagination may be defined as an ability to creatively engage the world. Where not too long ago imagination was primarily identified with "unreality" and fantasy, imagination is now increasingly being viewed as a primary creative intelligence. Although for some people imaginative activity might suggest mental images or ideas of things that are not physically present, the more pervasive sense of imagination is focused on its identity as a force that is capable of creating new life.

We speak often about the creative imagination as the basis of genius in the arts and science as well as happiness in daily life, but there is very little about this intelligence in psychological literature. What has been written is often far removed from the experience of imagining. Perhaps this is because psychology and imagination are based on very different languages and worldviews. The latter requires a constant flight outside the limits of what currently exists, and the former exemplifies the methodical rigors of operating "within the lines" of currently accepted inquiry. The linear patterns of conventional psychological thought simply do not correspond to the more circuitous and paradoxical ways of imagination. Conventional dichotomies such as the split between reason and intuition polarize the study of the creative act. Psychology imagines itself as an empirical and analytic science, and it is not surprising that it is reluctant to recognize and seriously investigate an intelligence located beyond its current sphere of activity. Imagination's identification with fantasy has no doubt contributed to its peripheral role as an object of psychological inquiry and as an accepted tool of inquiry.

Edith Cobb (1977) felt that when people enter into "reciprocal relations" with the natural world, they access creative energies that are generated by the ecology of forces moving within environments. In keeping with Richter's integrative vision, Cobb's ecological theory suggests that the intelligence of imagination operates through the "power of creative synthesis." She views imagination as interplay between the individual person and the "otherness" of the external world, all of which correspond to the movements of nature. This view of imagination concurs with the Chinese and East Asian idea of *ch'i*, the vital force permeating all of life, which acts most effectively when spontaneous like a force of nature (McNiff 2015).

Everything participates in an environment of creative integration. There is no need for dichotomy between the participants. Private reverie utilizes perceptions of the natural world as sources for creative play. Cobb perceives the space between the individual and the object of desire as the realm from which "imagined forms" are created by the instrument of "mind" (1977, p.56).

Imagination is an intermediary sphere where the interplay between inner and outer worlds takes place. It is an open and dynamic realm where narrow fixation is discouraged because it interrupts the ecology of creative relations and dulls a person's sensitivity to new influences. When we are immersed in reflection upon our mutual relations with nature, imagination acts as the integrating intelligence.

What can we do to cultivate imagination?

In keeping with Edith Cobb's vision, the creative imagination is an intermediate realm, existing in the space created between a person and an object of reflection. The identification of imagination as an intermediate realm suggests a place, or more accurately a state of consciousness, where the different perspectives and participants in a situation can meet, influence one another, and create new patterns of interaction. This condition can be likened to the Middle Way of Buddhism or the Taoist sense of nature that avoid the traps of polarization. The middle realm is not a static center of equilibrium and it is not to be confused with the term "middle of the road" or with compromise. Gathering the strongest possible elements and allowing them to interact freely within a safe environment, the imagination integrates and transforms ideas into new relationships. Paolo Knill's "intermodal" theory of expressive arts therapy is based upon the medial space of imagination (Knill, Barba and Fuchs 1995), as is Stephen Levine's "*poiesis*" that affirms suffering and fragmentation as inseparable from the depths of creative imagination (1992). All of life is vital to the process.

Imagination's middle realm is thoroughly immersed in the experience of the world but open to new perspectives, unfettered by fixed ideas, and always longing to create anew. It is a kinetic and dynamic area corresponding to the ancient Celtic conception of "thin places" where movements between matter and spirit occur with relative ease. Being in the intermediate realm of imagination can also be compared to what athletes experience when they are "in the zone." There is a relaxed but totally focused flow from one thing to another.

As with the aesthetic perception of beauty, the person is wholly engaged and detached at the time.

The middle realm operates according to what I call the "principle of simultaneity" (2015) that accepts many things happening at the same time. Different elements coexist, converge, and cooperate while staying completely true to themselves.

The possibilities for integration are endless, and kinesis is constant. As a new combination of elements is achieved, the movement continues. Creative types have a keen appreciation for how the pleasures of imagination involve continuous immersion in the process.

The imaginative realm is spacious and safe. The absence of an intermediate realm between polarized positions can create a tight squeeze that can be both restrictive and dangerous. When there is little room between opposing positions, they are apt to act out their needs for expression onto one another. When this happens, the "invaded" territory is likely to perceive the incursion as a threat, rather than as the stimulation of a partner in the larger interplay of creation.

As in the Buddhist tradition, the middle way accepts contradictory principles and enables them to interact with one another and to find a creative way of integrating their energies. While the middle of the road or centrist attitudes desire to eliminate tension, the intermediate realm of imagination encourages the individuation of the varied participants in a conflict. There is no attempt to take the edge off a strong position within the middle way. However, identification with one aspect of an oppositional relationship is discouraged. As soon as the mind becomes fixated on a singular position, it loses the ability to see the creative interplay and benefit from it.

The most polarized people probably cannot imagine life without their discontents. What will they become without self-defining antagonisms and fears? Letting go of the adversarial relationship becomes a primary threat to their existence and power. The middle realm is committed to stepping away from one-sided insistence. Rather than stifling conflict, it embraces William Blake's notion that progression requires a free exchange amongst contrary positions.

Creative leadership is based upon cultivating the intermediate realm. When meeting with colleagues, adversaries, and people in conflict with one another, the leader listens carefully and demonstrates how to accept varied and sometimes contradictory perspectives. In order to create an effective intermediate realm, the primary emphasis is placed on providing a safe environment that encourages people to express themselves authentically and honestly. Risk-takers, who act for the good of the whole, are affirmed. Participants are encouraged to de-personalize issues and positions, and to relativize their opinions and view themselves as participants in a broader discourse. When this aesthetic distance is established, people are better prepared to appreciate a situation "for itself" as contrasted with how they see it or how "it should be."

While welcoming this collective interplay, the leader maintains a vision of the total environment, keeps participants on task, and enables the process to carry everyone involved toward the most desirable outcome. Leaders in varied situations from the classroom, workshop group, workplace, or on the athletic field, are always respectful of the intelligence of the intermediate realm. They are committed to discovering what the creative and collective interplay can do to improve conditions. They help participants see the connection between what occurs within the creative discourse and what needs to be done to implement new ideas and goals.

How does healing occur?

My experience affirms that healing energies will always find their way to areas of need within a person or group. The essential attribute of the creative imagination is its ability to operate outside linear thought and operations. Discoveries, insights, and changes occur through the "complex" of imagination that integrates and sometimes makes use of unlikely sources. The first step in accessing the medicines of imagination involves the creation of spaces for practice. From artists and creative people, we learn that environmental structures are helpful in fostering expression and imagination. The productivity of the inner life benefits from external constraints, such as scheduled and regular activity, timelines for completion, and the needs of others. The intermediate realm of imagination is not without strict organization and expectations.

As we explore the creation of spaces to further the practice of imagination, I predict that clear, safe, and reliable structures will further expressive freedom. It is not enough to simply say to a person, or a group of people, "Take this time to imagine and create." Teachers and leaders are charged with establishing the overall context for creation and for inspiring actions according to a vision that is both tangible and open.

As people begin to work, the environment generates energies and outcomes which cross over from one realm of activity to another. Creations are contagious. Results achieved in one area spread to others. This contagion occurs within every aspect of artistic, scientific, spiritual, and commercial discovery. Atmospheric invasions are generated by new waves of excitement.

Creative imagination, as William Blake declared, is a very real energy of the body and spirit. This force passes from one place to another via inspiration that spreads in a way that can be likened to a contagious reaction that permeates a person or a group. The transmission of imagination has little to do with the planned outcomes of linear causes and effects. The life of imagination is based upon this flight of ideas and the creation of new relationships. Where a toxic infection weakens an operating system, the contagion of imagination quickens and animates experience. The intermediate realm of contemplation is a safe container that supports participants in making new integrations of previously separate materials. Once fashioned, the formative creation quickly passes from one area of life to another.

The creative imagination is propelled by the urge to cross over from one object of contemplation to another. Imagination's antithesis is the mechanistic containment of thought and expression within pre-existing lines of operation. The imagination flies beyond the parameters of what is presently given to create in response to images of desire. If these flights of imagining are to create in a productive way, they must be paired with the discipline and sensitivity that extend from imagination's greater purpose to fulfill its potential to serve life.

Crossing over assumes a movement from one aspect of life to another. The space that is crossed can be likened to the intermediary realm of imagination that transforms whatever passes through it. Participants in my studios repeatedly teach me that the creation of a safe environment is the most fundamental element in fostering imaginative expression in others. Most people need to feel secure and a sense of trust if they are to take risks and venture into unknown realms.

To the extent to which creativity requires a certain degree of tension and conflict in order to generate change and transformation, I find that these energies never need to be generated by leaders. There is plenty of tension and conflict within each of us and within our daily lives. Creative environments are safe places where these energies can be engaged directly without becoming entangled with the personalities and provocations of other people.

The practice of creative imagination is very much like the psychotherapeutic process in that both place the emphasis on personal discovery within a safe environment. The psychoanalyst D. W. Winnicott attempted to create a "holding environment" which supported the person in finding understanding. Winnicott had expressed dismay in reflecting upon "how much deep change" was "prevented or delayed" by his interventions. He concluded that the analyst's role is the creation of an environment which "holds" the person: "If only we can wait, the patient arrives at understanding creatively and with immense joy, and now I enjoy this more than I used to enjoy the sense of having been clever" (quoted in Davis and Wallbridge 1981, p.25).

It is the mature teacher, therapist, and leader who realizes that the most profound results are based upon creating an environment in which others can realize their creative potential. Insecure and inexperienced leaders are always placing themselves in the center of the activity where they feel the need to control, direct, and orchestrate outcomes. The most successful leaders get people wondering what the person "in charge" did in order to make things happen. Although the leader might establish a strong sense of presence and support, there is characteristically an ability to become invisible in order to allow others to act and create.

With the creative process, we want to help people to move in a relaxed way without thinking too much about what they are going to do next. The goal is to enable the movement to direct itself and to allow the leader to concentrate on caring for the overall environment that fosters expression. There has to be room for the movements to emerge on their own. If they come naturally, they are more genuine. The movements need freedom to be unique. There has to be a sense that the space will allow more expansive expression. Depth comes from a very simple orientation that is also spacious.

Summary

In conclusion, and in support of total expression (*Gesamtkunstwerk*) in expressive arts therapy, the use of different art media enriches the ecology of imagination. We cultivate imagination by feeding it the best possible resources, by deepening the mix of ingredients, and always trusting that this integrative intelligence will find its way to healing and creative transformation. Expressive arts therapy is uniquely based upon the healing and re-constructive powers of the creative imagination. Our therapeutic discipline enables the creative process to operate outside the parameters of linear thought and methods.

Expressive arts therapy has an immense potential to serve the world. The realization of this power depends upon:

- expanding psychological thought and methods to include the intelligence of the creative imagination that generally operates "outside the lines" of conventional analytic inquiry
- developing theoretical and operational skills within the expressive arts therapy discipline that will ultimately cross over and influence the larger discourse of human knowledge.

Expressive arts therapy needs to view itself as a vital part of the archetypal mainstream of creative expression, thought, and healing. As we increasingly move from the periphery and toward the center of the therapeutic discourse, we will be challenged to convey who we are and what we can do in ways that convince and inspire others.

The power of expressive arts therapy lies in the psychology and practice of imagination. Our discipline can look more deeply into itself and into the historical continuities of creative practice as a way of flourishing within the mainstream of therapeutic experience.

References

Cobb, E. (1977) *The Ecology of Imagination in Childhood.* New York: Columbia University Press.
Davis, M. and Wallbridge, D. (1981) *Boundary and Space: An Introduction to the Work of D. W. Winnicott.* New York: Bruner/Mazel.
Knill, P., Barba, H.N. and Fuchs, M. (1995) *Minstrels of Soul: Intermodal Expressive Therapy.* Toronto: Palmerston Press.
Levine, S. (1992) *Poiesis: The Language of Psychology and the Speech of the Soul.* Toronto: Palmerston Press.
McNiff, S. (1998) *Art-based Research.* London: Jessica Kingsley Publishers.
McNiff, S. (2015) *Imagination in Action: Secrets for Unleashing Creative Expression.* Boston: Shambhala Publications.
Richter, J.P. (1973) *Horn of Oberon: School for Aesthetics.* Detroit, MI: Wayne State University Press.

THE ESSENCE IN A THERAPEUTIC PROCESS, AN ALTERNATIVE EXPERIENCE OF WORLDING?

Paolo J. Knill

Introduction

At a time when schools of psychotherapy compete with each other to convince authorities of their effectiveness in order to get reimbursed, it might be interesting to find common "ingredients" that all of them apply and are found to have roots in what it means to be human. We might also raise the question: Shouldn't we consider such a universal "ingredient" to be a common research project and part of our educational basics, in order to lead an effective common campaign for recognition? The "ingredients" about which I am speaking should not be understood literally as substances that are added in cooking or chemical processes. The term "ingredient" is used metaphorically for therapeutic actions, interventions or settings that are consistently present in a therapeutic method and seem to be essential to the characteristic features of it.

I will begin with a study of the anthropological roots of a change agent's activity, the one who is the professional accompaniment to processes of change. Then I will continue with an examination of commonly shared necessities in the setting and relationship. Even though we will find great differences in the methods applied and their underlying beliefs or meta-theories, there is a commonality to be found in the conditions that lead into the process or that are applied in the main frame and form of a process of change. Following this discussion, I will share some specific "ingredients" that seem pertinent to the activity of change agents, including the necessity of what I call a "decentering into an alternative experience of worlding" and the necessity to increase the "range of play" (*Spielraum*).

The professional change agent as a universal phenomenon

Situations of change of individuals or communities usually have ritual containers within which they are framed in space and time. There are characteristics of these containers that depend on cultural traditions; there are, however, also characteristics that seem to be universal. One category of rituals of change is devoted to changes that concern life cycles from birth to death. Examples in our Western culture are the marriage, graduation, retirement, burial or birthday ceremonies. These ritual containers are called "rites of passage" and help in the societal bindings evoked by new role configurations. The universal characteristics of rites of passage are well studied in the context of expressive arts methods (Levine 1997). Another category of rituals of change concerns the loss of binding within the community and therefore a discomfort that usually brings conflict and crisis. The loss of binding can be evoked by illness, accident, loss or catastrophic events of a violent nature. The ritual container that is in place to restore the binding is usually called a "healing ritual." I prefer the phrase "rites of restoration," to give credit to the fact that we can see a restored binding without necessarily presupposing a "complete healing" of the individual's distress. Examples of rites of restoration in our Western culture are: religious healing rituals and all forms of psychotherapy, counseling, the hospital routine and the doctor's visit. Also today, one universal characteristic of all rites of restoration and many rites of passage has to do with the practice of leaving the everyday situation and entering into a devotional space for a period of time. There is a person or group responsible for that space or performance of rituals. I call this role "change agent" or "change agency." Change agents have to be ordained or graduated. This is a universal characteristic of the profession. Today they are called "professionals," and when we look at the root of the word in German, it still implies that you must have a calling ("profession" in German is "*Beruf*" and the German "*Ruf*" means "call" in English).

When we look at rites of restoration only, we note that the professional change agent is required to have certain commitments, skills and competencies. Today in psychotherapy for instance, these are defined by schools of psychotherapy in a manner similar to religious traditions. For example, the patient needs specifically to declare their helplessness or motivation as in the Native American tradition or in the Kyrie of the Catholic mass. As in the mass, they must find trust in the change agent (Gloria) and faith in the school of therapy (Credo) for the process to be effective. Consequently, change agents are asked to abide by the rule of their own purification as in the shamanistic tradition or in confessional practices; a characteristic tied to the demand of having worked through their own issues under ongoing supervision (Knill, Barba and Fuchs 1993).

What all rites of restoration have in common

Situations that call for a rite of restoration are always marked by an experience of distress or dis-ease—which could be described from a situational or individual aspect—that the person seeking help experiences.

Situational restrictions

- Unemployment as a result of a physical or psychological condition.
- One's own illness or the illness of a family member binds one to the home.
- There is no job suitable for the particular skills or traits of that person.
- There is not enough time or space, within an organization, for a team to look at their relationships, or deal with a conflict, etc.

Personal inability

There is a prevalent sense of not being able to do something about "it": "I tried enough," "I can't anymore," "I would if I could." Some clinical examples include:

- phobias
- obsessions and compulsions
- addictions
- hallucinations or amnesia.

It should be noted that phenomena, situational restrictions and personal inability are all interdependent.

We have noticed already that all rites of restoration have a spatial and temporal frame that distinguishes them from everyday reality. We have also considered, in these containers of change, the role of the professional change agent, who is ordained or professionally trained. When we look further for common characteristics, we need to examine the separation of realities that occur in the performance of rituals of restoration.

In the following, I will not use the term "reality" as synonymous with "world." All experiences are within world. I used the word "world" here without the definite article ("the") to make evident that world is not a thing or object. We are, so to speak, "within" or "part of" world. World is therefore also within our thinking and action in a way. Therefore, I used the word "Worlding" in the title (Fink 1960).

Personal inability and situational restrictions experienced in the everyday reality are part of the habitual experience of worlding of the suffering or troubled human. The predicament has characteristics of the literal reality (e.g., unemployment) or fantasy (e.g., paranoid thoughts). The experience of worlding of a person seeking help seems to be closed, having no exit and lacking an adequate "range of play" (*Spielraum*).

Even though the rites of restoration have a clear spatial and temporal separateness from everyday reality, there will always be sequences where that reality is concretely addressed in interactional practices connected to the habitual experience of worlding (e.g., conversational language and nonverbal cues). Today this is evident, for instance, in the opening and closing of a session, the "filling in" phase that the change agent uses to get familiar with an issue, problem or conflict, and the reflective phases that serve clarification or interpretation.

Of great interest, however, is that most rites of restoration initiate a phase or phases where an alternative experience of worlding is introduced through practices that engage imagination. Examples are:

- focusing on dreams, visions, etc.
- daydreaming, free association or guided imagery
- wish-oriented discourses such as, "What would happen if..."
- body language and its imaginary potential ("What is your shoulder saying...?", "What does that pose express...?")
- using art disciplines (drama, painting, masks, ritual dance or performance, etc.) or other methods of creative work
- using works of art (music, texts, photos, paintings, movies, etc.)
- using cognitive imaginary methods like a "change of perspective"
- desensitizing with pictures
- brainstorming...
- using metaphors.

In these phases the person seeking help is not in the habitual experience of worlding as in everyday life. With the help of the change agent and with the use of the imagination, without necessarily going to a trance state, being in this world is not habitual. The things emerging in this imaginary space are surprising or unexpected; it is truly an "other" or "alternative" experience of worlding. It is important that the events or things emerging from the imaginary space are unpredictable. In the dream, this phenomenon is fully experienced as not being in one's control. There is a similar sense of having little control in free association or guided imagery methods, while some control is exerted in the practice of artistic disciplines. However, only in the arts is there a "thingly" presence of the images, which all the people present can simultaneously witness. This is a phenomenon that we will have to examine later.

The alternative experience of worlding and the logic of imagination

In the emerging imaginary space, things are, in their surprising unpredictable unexpectedness, still logical and describable. These things, however, happen differently than in everyday life and its narratives. This difference expands the "range of play" in the restrictions, reflected in the story of the distress, in everyday life. Therefore, change agents apply methods of bridging the two experiences, in order to find inroads for a change, clarification or understanding that eases the distress. In psychotherapy, for instance, this bridging is usually called interpretation. The method of interpretation is rooted in a meta-theory that ranges from more or less explanatory to phenomenologically oriented methods of interpretation. Even though we can distinguish those methods of interpretation, there is little difference in the belief that an alternative experience of worlding has importance in this process. In other words, we could say that the practice of change agents shows that there is a common trust that the logic within the narratives of distress by the help seeker can be influenced by the narratives emerging in the imaginary space.

The connection between a story and imagination is presented by the Dutch writer, Mulisch. Although his understanding is built on the experience of a writer (storyteller may be exchanged with the word painter, musician, dancer, etc.), it also has validity for the dreamer or daydreamer.

Although the storyteller is telling the story, he is also not the essential storyteller. The story as such is the essential storyteller. The story itself is telling the story; from the first sentence on, the story is a surprise for the storyteller, and this is known to all storytellers (Mulisch 1999).

The logic of imagination in a work of art is stringent. This is not necessarily true for a delusion. A delusion as such is not a work of art, although a work of art may emerge in a delusion. Often when a patient is telling the delusion as a story, a novel-like logic may appear. If we follow this argument then, there must be something remarkable in the logic of an artistic work. This narrative logic is used in all the practices that attend to the symbolic richness of clients' works.

To guide the client from an alternative experience of worlding in the step back into everyday life is part of the rites of restoration.

Most change agents believe that it is possible to have a different relationship to everyday life if the logic of imagination, in its symbolism, has been understood and has found meaning in everyday life. The schools of psychotherapy, for instance, are distinguishable by their theories of interpretation (hermeneutics) for this process. It is essential, here, to understand that any guided step back is an interpretational act. Differences in theory exist in the epistemological assumptions about "who" (client and/or change agent) and "what" (meta-theory) is guiding us on that step. Even the so-called "phenomenological" approach, to be guided by the emerging "thing," is an interpretation. Bodenheimer distinguishes, therefore, between explanatory and answering interpretations (Bodenheimer 1997).

The alternative experience of worlding has two sources that may be anchored in everyday life. Once we have the symbolic content of imagination, there is also an affective sensory experience that is addressed especially in body-oriented practices and also, to an extent, in all other psychotherapies from art-oriented "focusing" and counseling to many psycho-dynamic and humanistic schools. Both resources of the alternative experience of worlding are usually used in the process of interpretation.

As a consequence, the phase of the alternative experience of worlding, within the rituals of restoration, is framed by an entrance and exit. In the entrance, the client leaves the troubled logic of daily life and enters the logic of imagination. At the exit, we are challenged with the difference as a confrontation. This "in and out" may be repeated several times or may be connected to a long phase in the center of a session. A characteristic of all the "ins and outs" of the alternative experience are aspects of "decentering" and "range of play."

With "decentering," we name the move away from the problem-bound narrow logic of thinking and acting that marks the helplessness around the "dead end" situation in question. This is a move into the opening of the surprising unpredictable unexpectedness, the experience within the logic of imagination. Finally, the decentering is followed by a centering again, guided by the change agent, relating the two, in an effort to find ease.

Providing a "range of play" contrasts with the situational restrictions experienced by the seeker of help. The phenomenon of play is the "doing as if," the open-endedness in the circularity of the here and now that results in a freeing up from the pressure to achieve results which we have, for example, in the attitude of games.

Decentering: An indispensable condition for alternative experiences of worlding

The positive effect of the decentering that we observe is manifested in many theories. Watzlawick (1983) demonstrates that the centering on the problematic matter has a tendency to produce more of the same and therefore worsens the situation. A decentering attitude, as induced by brainstorming, on the contrary, opens doors to unexpected solutions.

Creativity is sometimes explained as an ability that allows people to discover a new solution to an old problem or to see a new problem in an old solution. With a creative attitude, the ordinary way of looking at things is abandoned. Theories of imagination explain that imagination is not totally controllable; it is predictable only in its unpredictability.

We can distinguish three realms of imagination: first, the dream space as the least controllable; second, the daydream and trance space that allow some guidance; third, artistic activity that has characteristics of both dream and daydream. However, the latter is the only phenomenon of imagination that can be seen, heard or touched simultaneously by "artist" and "witness." The importance of these realms of imagination is recognized by psychoanalysis in its elaboration on the symbolism of the unconscious, by the humanistic schools in the validation of play and fantasy as a human potential and in the phenomenological schools where it is the existential that shapes meaning. C.G. Jung declared early on in his writings that the artistic act is of special value, because it is a "thingly" dream that can be witnessed. His understanding was that rather than painting a dream, in the act of painting, the dream continues on the canvas (Chodorow 1997).

Words we use in the context of decentering activities that open the door to the unexpected surprises are often captured with spontaneity or intuition. Although coming from another theoretical background, these words nevertheless point in the direction of an alternative experience of worlding through distancing.

The exit out of the narrow situational and personal restrictions of the help seeker, through entering a space of imagination, allows, in its decentering, also a distancing from the personal fate. This distancing happens in Jungian psychoanalysis within the container of archetypal mythology, in drama therapy through relating roles or stories of the world of theater, and in postmodern psychology through a distancing within the historic multiplicity of narratives.

In order to use the full potential of an alternative experience of worlding and its helpful distancing, we need to give our attention first to the analyses of the logic of imagination within that experience, before we go back to the issues of everyday life. A too-hasty return for fast results may result in a loss of important substance and information.

What does it mean to "exercise" the arts in decentering, and what is the difference between this and other decentering methods? All the methods of decentering that engage imagination, in one way or another, offer the kind of results we attempted to group into the phenomenon we called the "alternative experience of worlding." The use of the artistic process in this context, however, offers options that are specific only within the arts: direct witnessing of the artistic work as a materialization of imagination. The presence of a "thingly" act or object—for example, a painting, a sculpture, a poem, a scene, a music improvisation, a dance or a piece of performance art—is there to be witnessed directly by client and the professional change agent. We do not depend solely on the interpretation of clients, as it is the case when they talk about dreams, visions or daydreams. The story about a dream does not reveal the original image the client saw, but my image of that story that happens to be my client's account of the original imagery. Interpretations within the artistic mode of imagination, though, happen in the presence of a "third" thing, the emerged thingly work in process, and allow a confrontational field of acts and discourses, on the base of an embodied emergence. As Bodenheimer (1997) states, this confrontational field, handled more or less playfully and in an exploratory manner, can lead to "explanatory interpretations" (e.g., depth psychological, bioenergetic and spiritual schools) or "answering interpretations" (e.g., existential, humanistic and solution-focused schools).

The body–mind dimension

The relationship between the thingly aspect of media and its possible message, within the process of bringing forth an artistic work, is addressed in the research by Shalev (1999). The findings of this study elaborate on the effect the artistic work has within a therapeutic context.

Its effect permeates all functional realms of the "Brain/Mind," "Body/Psyche," in accordance with "Material/Meaning," along with the neurophysiological substrates. The composition, structure and dynamics of psychosomatic systems are similar to non-linear systems that have the potential of auto-poetic transformations. Therefore we can observe a resonance between the effect of artistic work in the context of therapy and the effect of a trauma (specifically post traumatic stress disorder). This phenomenon of resonance provides a therapeutic potential for an auto-poetic transformation that is more effective than traditional interventions which act exclusively in a cognitive, memory-oriented way (even though they may be based on fantasy or bodily experiences).

Intervention within the thingly process of shaping

The complexity of an imaginary reality on the basis of literal material shaping permits interventions that are concrete and placed "on the surface." These interventions can serve the purpose of grounding and testing reality. We may probe, for example, in a painting session by suggesting a bigger paper, or adding more water to the color, or closing the eyes for a while. Similarly, we may suggest to the "dancer" to use more space or to a "musician" to add the voice to the instrument.

Interventions with the "work of art" (oeuvre)

The "in and out," "to and fro" of the alternative experiences of worlding and the reality in it is discernible through the here and now of the artistic work, its initiation, process of becoming and completion as a "thing." In its graspable presence, it offers many options that can help to distinguish between the different realities. The distinction of the stage, canvas, studio space and audience space from the habitual experience of worlding is concrete and explicit in a sensori-motor way. In theater, for instance, an act of killing does not call for a literal ambulance or police officer, rather, these roles are carried out by an actress. Similarly, a painting of a fire will not literally raise the temperature in the room; however, it may evoke the fear of burning or the joy of a bonfire. In this way, fiction becomes a reality; to explore certain images with the full power of experience in perception or in the making, without, however, literal consequences within the "scene."

Personal enabling and situational coping with the achievement of the artistic work

As stated in the beginning of this essay, an experience of distress or dis-ease is marked by a situational restriction and/or individual inability. In the art-oriented work, within the rites of restoration, there is, however, the affective experience (literally, not symbolically) of enabling and achievement within a frame of limited resources. It belongs to the basic methodological skills of any art-oriented therapist to enable people who are not artists and who usually have a sense of "not being talented" to engage in art disciplines of some sort and to find satisfaction within them. Furthermore, these professional change agents are trained to understand one of the essential phenomena of arts: the role of limiting resources, within a restricting frame, in order to reach beauty. Consequently, the experience of an art-oriented decentering is literally a coping experience in a situation of restriction—an experience of discovering resources. While the help seeker may have said that she is not able to paint and she might have been resistant to painting in black and white only (a restriction that may have been suggested by the change agent), in the end, we may be in front of a painting that works artistically.

Diet and medicine

The concepts of "diet and medicine" reach far beyond the physical metabolism of the body. The word "diet" (in Greek, "*diaitá*") means originally a manner of living. Later it was used for a regulated manner of living to maintain health, and finally it made exclusive reference to eating habits. In a psychosomatic understanding, we could extend it to the regulated nourishment of psyche or soul. In such a concept, the term "diet" would also concern a corrective regulation of psychic nourishment and metabolism. We can apply similar reasoning to the concept of medicine. A substance must have two characteristics in order to qualify as a medicine. First, it must be composed so it can be metabolized by the system. Second, it must interact in a constructive way with the self-regulating forces in the system. The work of art, as phenomenon of the inter-structural relationship between the everyday and the imaginative reality, is a remarkable entity within rituals of restoration. Its special characteristics make it well suited for being metabolized in the psychic system in question. In fact, one could see the art work as that which arrived exclusively for that very system, even though it should not be confused, from a phenomenological perspective, with a mirror image or an appearance of the system's identity (Levine 1997). There are many traditional ways of relating to the art work that also satisfy the criteria of the second quality of a medicine. The transpersonal theory within intermodal expressive arts therapy gives clues as to how pictures mounted may have the characteristics of a totem or an altar, how poems read may have effects like prayers or mantras, how a song or music may console and how a mask may help to conjure fear when played. The exercise of the arts, in the decentering phase, gives the possibility to give "prescriptions," that may have an effect beyond the session time, as the following examples indicate (Knill *et al.* 1993):

- Paint daily! Go to your easel instead of to the TV monitor ("Diet").

- Read the poem that helped you in the session today every time your thoughts get stuck on that theme ("Medicine").

- Make a clearly visible place for this sculpture and look at it each time you get lost in these doubts again ("Medicine").

Experiences of worlding

The "doing as if" or the "we would now be..." of a play space will always have temporal, spatial or situational aspects. These "spells" create a distinction from the literal everyday space, time and situation and open up to an alternative experience of worlding that offers unforeseeable and unpredictable options.

The idea of widening the range of play by engaging imagination is a common concept in the practice of conflict resolution. Conflicts are seen, in these practices, as situations that lack choices, and give participants a sense of being locked into the matter of conflict (neurosis can be understood as a narrowness of that kind). Decentering therefore gives an opportunity to leave the zone of conflict with an opening to options for new actions and thoughts.

Therapeutic methods based on Systems Theory argue that a simultaneous intervention through perturbation and widening of the range of play may be effective for a surprising auto-poetic process of improvement. The impetus for discovery and fear are in balance in such play. Art disciplines can be seen as disciplines of play where the probing of the artist is a kind of perturbation and self-organization happening within the range of play defined by the frame's and the discipline's restrictions (material, space, time and means). The therapist is a player in the system that does not play the habitual game of the family. This is a popular saying about family therapy which is also true for many performance art-oriented therapies. Many music therapists play together with an individual client using this option.

We distinguish between play, game and the play disciplines of the arts (one still says "play music," "going to a play" and "playing a role"). It is interesting that only the play therapists were able to join in one association uniting all schools of psychotherapy. My assumption is that the strong belief in the method of non-directed play that is shared by most play therapists, regardless of the school they are coming from, makes this unity possible. In accordance with this argument, it should be possible for all the change agents practicing the disciplined play of the arts to find a common denominator and join together. Maybe the difficulty in doing this lies in the unanswered question: Why is it that play therapy with children is so successful and why is it not more explored with adults?

We need to look at the difference between child's play and adult's play. Children still have access to incantation and magic—they can cast a spell into a scene or role with one sentence, often without a stage and almost no props: "You be the dad now;" "I'll be drunk;" etc.

Non-directive play, involving difficult themes like sex, alcohol and death, is possible in naiveté and innocence—except for children who have been abused.

The experience and potential adults have in these realms brings the need for a discipline of play, a formal ritual, a container. The stage, the canvas, the dance floor, the distancing into fiction all allow us to approach these themes playfully; although they may affect us emotionally. Perhaps the ancient Death Dance or World Play (still performed in Einsiedeln, Switzerland) is a kind of archaic, adult play. What does it mean to "exercise" the arts in providing a "range of play," and what is the difference from other methods?

Arts disciplines as disciplines of play

The limits that define the frame of an art discipline, with respect to space, time, material and method of shaping, belong to the tradition of art-making. Therefore, interventions with respect to limits and frame are easily accepted and understood. These interventions and those occurring during the process of play may possibly restrict the range of play, but usually they do not restrict the act of playing and its content; on the contrary, they make the playing less threatening. Furthermore, those interventions help to distinguish between the different realities (literal, imaginal and effective).

The practice of the arts in therapy—a kind of play therapy for adults

Freedom and restriction—which make the frame of any play within the arts—allow for the distinction of realities through generally understood art traditions. There is, with some exceptions, a pretty good understanding of the "imaginary reality" in theater and movies, plays or musicals, even though the fantasy identification can sometimes become confusing. Still, the art frame of playful exploration allows us to shape themes that would be difficult to express or explore otherwise. The discipline of the arts is, so to speak, an anchor of hope which allows us to distance ourselves from the narrow ties of the one and only narrative or destiny.

Play as a kind of focusing

Trance-like presence, during the disciplined play in the art activity, is focused on the "surface," manifest in material, structure, form and shaping. The challenges inherent in the process of this shaping are in an existential relationship with the habitual worlding in the everyday reality and are symbolically and literally meaningful.

Play as experiential learning

The accomplishment in art-making is a literal enabling that has the merit of beauty and the "Aha!" of an aesthetic response. In consequence the disciplined play of art is also a learning experience that provides an individual enabling and a situational coping. The effect of this experience is cognitive and physical. We can observe it in the change of emotion, mood and tone of the participant. This coping process can also been seen as a training or "exercise" to practice coping with the situational restrictions and individual inability in the help-seeker's life. Within a cognitive frame of reference, the coping experience in the artistic process is confronting beliefs such as, "I am not able to accomplish anything," "I am not talented, have very few resources," etc. Art-oriented therapy, however, includes more levels than solely the level of cognitive argumentation.

- It is a rich exercise with repetitive experiences of accomplishment.

- It is a psycho-physical, concrete experience that allows for emotional and cognitive reasoning.

- It is a sensory aesthetic experience that touches, that is a "nourishment of soul." All the senses are engaged and, in its beauty, make sense.

- Beauty, as something that touches, can be motivating and convincing, bypassing the barriers built by cognitive reasoning and the logic of resistance and fear.

- With the repetitive experience of coping, beliefs in one's lack of competence and ability are challenged. In addition, the act of having created a work that gives satisfaction and pleasure to the eye of the beholder provides quite a confrontation to those convictions. There is a kind of contribution that adds beauty to the community, rewarding both to the maker and to the audience. Within the understanding of learning theory, one could see this experience as a kind of aesthetic reward or rewarding "soul food."

- It is also an experiential field of discovery that motivates curiosity. Discovery of this kind is one of the fundamental sensori-motor and cognitive learning experiences. The challenge, then, will be to bridge the discoveries of the experience in this field of play with the original question posed: What does it mean to "exercise" the arts in providing a "range of play," and what is the difference between this approach and other approaches and methods?

In the traditional understanding of coping, "exercise" has a fundamental position. In the practice of art-oriented decentering, however, the process is guided with an attentive supportive attitude that is open, and the dialogue is led with open questions. The openness in exercising the art is a necessary condition in gaining access to the symbolism and unconscious material emerging through the art work. This dimension in the practice of the arts is not restricted by the logic of the habitual experience of worlding and is not necessarily available in the usual coping methods. This openness gives the hidden a chance to be met and to be utilized as a resource. With this option come new perspectives, fantasies, ideas and imaginations for alternative ways to act or respond.

Final remarks

Even though we found great differences in the methods and underlying beliefs or meta-theories of rites of restoration, I have, I believe, shown a commonality in the conditions that lead into the process or that are applied in the main frame of a process of change. Two of the common "ingredients" that are pertinent to the activity of change agents, are what I call a "decentering into an alternative experience of worlding" and the necessity of increasing the "range of play" (*Spielraum*). We could recognize how these two aspects are closely related to the phenomenon of imagination, which, in the practice of change agents, usually is addressed within the realms of dream, daydream, trance space, play or artistic activities. Research usually focuses on the effect of the symbolic content of the particular imagination and the meaning of the experiential process. Research in expressive arts methods must start to recognize the difference that exists when we choose the arts as an alternative experience of worlding. There is not enough research done yet that includes the phenomenon of the thingly presence and physicality that dominates this realm of imagination. We have seen that this difference from the other methods of engaging imagination brings possibilities of intervention in the process and the work that are unique to all the art-oriented therapies. I have also pointed out the possibilities of addressing the coping effect and cognitive learning that are inherent in the art-oriented alternative experience of worlding.

Should not, then, all the arts-oriented therapies, in recognition of that special strength, have common research efforts and include the outcome of these efforts in their basic training?

References
Bodenheimer, A.R. (1997) *Verstehen heisst Antworten.* Stuttgart: Reclam UB 8777.
Chodorow, J. (1997) *Jung and Active Imagination.* Princeton, NJ: Princeton University Press.
Fink, E. (1960) *Spiel als Weltsymbol.* Stuttgart: Kohlhammert.
Knill, P., Barba, H.N. and Fuchs, M. (1993) *Minstrels of Soul: Intermodal Expressive Therapy.* Toronto: EGS Press.
Levine, S. (1997) *Poiesis: The Language of Psychology and the Speech of the Soul.* London: Jessica Kingsley Publishers.
Mulisch, H. (1999) D*ie Prozedur.* München: Hanser.
Shalev, A.J. (1999) "Psychotherapy for Traumatic Stress Disorders: Beyond Exploration and Exposure." Lecture presented at the Second Congress of Body, Soul and Trauma, March 11–14, Göttingen.
Watzlawick, P. (1983) *The Situation is Hopeless, But Not Serious: The Pursuit of Unhappiness.* New York: W.W. Norton.

3

LONGING FOR BEAUTY AND THE WORK

An Interview with Paolo Knill,
conducted by Stephen K. Levine

Stephen K. Levine: I'm interested in talking to you about the development of your work, to see how your ideas formed, the stages they went through and the contexts in which they've developed. How far back would you trace the beginnings of the development that led to your work in Expressive Arts?

Paolo Knill: That work has changed in the last few years of thinking about it. As it is, in the way we work, the work is so much in the foreground that I do not necessarily think about the first experiences that formed this passion about what we call Expressive Arts. In the moment, however, when you said that you'd like to do an interview with me about it, I suddenly realized: Wait a minute, this is an interesting question. What do I remember about the beginning of those experiences that I had when I'm engaged in any of my artistic ways of being in the world—with community art, when I improvise music or theatre, and when I paint or write? I notice that many images and stories come up when I focus on what was it exactly and when did that exactly happen. Certainly, when I look at those incidents, let's say about my art experiences as a child, I look from the experience of today, and it might sound sometimes far-fetched, but the fact that I can reflect on such experiences with today's theories or thoughts on Expressive Arts, means that it has a reality, and that is an interesting work. I can give you one example that blew my mind.

You have to imagine being in 1942 or 1943. I don't know exactly when. It was in the years when there was a danger that Nazi German troops would overrun Schaffhausen, where I lived, a kind of a half-island into Germany. The Swiss army had left the place—just given up this indefensible piece of land in order to concentrate on defending the strategically more interesting territory of Gotthard, the most important passage to Italy for the Germans. My father left, and many families were also without fathers. Also, you have to imagine that there were no cars, it was very rural and many houses were abandoned. In that situation, after some months, my mother said my father will come home for a two-day furlough. I waited and waited for him the whole evening and he didn't come, so we had to go to bed. My bedroom was adjacent to the room where my father's piano was, and I could usually hear anything that happened in that room. I fell asleep and woke up to an unbelievable music. I remember it sounded so full; it was the piano, but it sounded like ten pianos, and that fullness was something I had never heard before. I could not imagine how it was achieved; it was a miracle to me. You have to know that we had no gramophone at that time. Today I would call this "polyphonic music," and, as I found out later, the man who was playing was not my father. It was his friend who couldn't get home from our place to his home because it was further away, and it would be after the curfew. He slept in our house, and before he went to bed he played on the piano, not knowing that I was silently listening and had tears in a strange state of happiness. It is an experience I never forgot—it is often present when I listen to music, it was so powerful. In the morning I was told that this had not been Daddy—it was Mr Schwaninger. From that moment on, I wanted to play like that. So when nobody was in the house I went to the piano and found how to get to a full sound by using my elbows, and I discovered the distinctions between the black and white keys. It didn't sound the way I remembered from Mr Schwaninger, but after a while I found ways to create different timbres by using clusters of fingers that could sound simultaneously together and more like dialogues. What captivated me was the fullness that was rich in different timbres (created through the cluster-like chords). This was fascinatingly different from the melodies we sang—my father conducted choirs and my mother wrote poems and sang.

I started to develop techniques that brought me closer to a combination of melodies and fullness; I wonder what would have happened if I could have gone on like that. Much later at the conservatory of Winterthur and at Tufts University as a teacher, I adopted Jean Piaget's theory to a didactic method that led to complex musical skill patterns through exploratory play. Under guidance, as a 10-year-old, I might have found the counterpoint polyphony of J.S. Bach that Schwaninger played. However, once my father heard my explorations he scolded me: "That's not how you play the piano, now you go and take lessons." I was totally frustrated by the teacher who focused foremost on "Mary Had A Little Lamb," a simplistic melody pattern drill. After a change of teacher, I went on taking lessons. I notice today the new teacher followed what I now call the attitude of "low-skill/high-sensitivity." That is what motivated me again. He focused foremost on my listening and on sensori-motor awareness in his explorations with me, and, in the excitement, used my motivation to begin to teach manual skills and exercises for mastery. He took an aspect of musical material that was not primarily dependent on manual skill but on skills of sensory differentiation using improvisational exploration.

So, with this story I come back to your question about how ideas about the Expressive Arts were formed. One strong thread in my discourse considering art as an existential certainly must come from the experience that it is possible to bring non-artists into an artistic experience. The notion of "low-skill/high-sensitivity" certainly started here. Another guiding principle that I experienced was that it is the art that calls me into its power. In this story somehow the music called me. I was not expressing myself, it was that touching sound. It was an enormous challenge to get close to it. However, that knowing and that longing for something to meet me, something to grab me, something so strange, so other, like that night with Mr Schwaninger's music, that was what called me and helped me follow through.

SKL: Did you have some experiences in other arts as a child?

PK: Yes, through theater. The challenge was a little bit different, but I notice I talk also about a difficult time that came after a beautiful experience. For some reason, maybe it was the situation of war, we kids did a lot of theatrical play and enactments. There was also a "Folk Theater" movement that went on the stage in communities. Little primitive stages are still visible in rural communities with less than 1,000 residents. Our minister and a teacher got into it and asked my brother and me to play because we were apparently known as those who made bold enactments. I remember the nights in summer or ski camps, when we were asked to perform for the whole camp. Everybody had flashlights that they used as theatrical lights, and they made a stage and proposed scenes for us to play. And we just got very passionate about it, really. At midnight in the dormitory—the teacher wasn't supposed to hear—we had to whisper our scenes. When we got older, twelve or thirteen, we started to play erotic scenes; it was hilarious! A teacher noticed our passion for it and asked us to write and direct theater. I remember once I did a fairy tale with a whole group of children in the classroom. We had to construct the set and tailor the costumes, and we used a lot of old bed sheets and cardboard boxes. Probably it looked very crazy but the teacher liked it, even though nobody memorized the text and we had to improvise the lines. So I really got into improvisational theater without knowing it. I asked the other kids to do it with me. I told them, just start like this and do that and then we'll see where it goes. We had stage fright because we didn't know how the play would end; however, the fairy tale has an end. So when we got into it, it took its own path and found its own end. In this way we found our own favorite plays from stories that evolved improvisationally. This was an early learning for me about the work emerging rather than being a "fingerprint" of my ego.

My sister told my parents about my theater activities. She asked that we do a Christmas play. Finally, my father agreed: OK, for once, they can do that. He was totally into music, and theater was something strange for him. I don't know why he didn't like theater, maybe because one plays the ordinary and also the dark. We did a Christmas story with Mary, Joseph and the baby, but I didn't want to memorize the text. My brother and my sister were playing with me and I became the Prince—Mary was my lover, my princess (laughs), and it had quite, you know, an erotic touch. I remember how I went to my sister and said, "Oh, my princess, I love you!" In that moment, my father put all the lights on and said, "Christmas is over!" because I didn't do the true story—it was blasphemous. They stopped the Christmas celebration, because I made another ending, no, not only *another* ending, a totally different take on the story. When I look back, it was a very appropriate understanding for a child of thirteen. At that young age to notice that there is something in the arts that is not only self-expression, that artistic imagination is not in my control—even if I'm awake and I can tell what we do, it goes its way—I shouldn't be punished for what I play on stage, I was just serving the emergence of a story. Again, I went on doing it. I went on with this passion for theatrical play and community.

SKL: So you didn't come to the arts from a psychological experience or perspective?

PK: I certainly didn't have a psychological perspective, because there was no conversation about it in my childhood. My father was really not into any of it; he was a down-to-earth musician and carpenter. My mother was very intellectual, she came from an intellectual family and was a close friend of the sister of Ludwig Binswanger, the phenomenologist. Whenever she wanted us to understand something, she'd say, "Fräulein said..." She quoted her all the time. Apparently they had a Binswanger reading circle, reading a lot of Karl Jaspers, because she'd also say, "Jaspers wrote..." So if I had a perspective, it was a perspective that I didn't quite understand. Yet later in high school I started to read Jaspers and got interested in his thinking.

This reading comforted me in my experience of being thrown into and captured by the process of art-making without knowing its outcome or ending. At the same time, it gave me an anchor when the work arrived and forced me to meet what touched, grabbed, moved or shook me.

It was much later in graduate school that I got interested in psychology. I studied with Jung's successor, C.A. Meier, who held the Chair of Honorary Professor of Psychology at the Swiss Federal Institute of Technology. That was the first time I heard the words "Active Imagination." I was not aware how importantly that concept would later contribute to our theory building.

SKL: I know you came to Lesley College Graduate School (now Lesley University) in Cambridge, MA, in the early 70s, to a new program in Expressive Therapy. I'm wondering how that perspective affected you or how you were with it.

PK: When I came to Lesley, I was coming from New York as an artist; I need to explain what that means. When I returned to the USA in 1973 as a guest professor in the music department of Tufts University, I came from a career in avant-garde music, performance art and improvisation. This is while I was teaching the didactics of contemporary music (including electronic music and Renaissance instrumentation).

With our ensemble "New Consort" we were invited for experimental music performance art at festivals and on radio. First we worked with composers of American origin influenced by John Cage, then more intellectually oriented Europeans like A. Schnebel and M. Kagel (originally from Argentina). Playfulness was also a major factor. Later I got into Marxist conceptual music, where the programs included four pages of critical theory to translate the score. Paradoxically, when we were invited to Poland for performance experiments, we met with Grotowski's actors and trained with them in this extremely expressive body and voice work. Out of several invitations to Poland sprang a new improvisational group in Switzerland. We experimented with the new experience with its overwhelming effects that don't come primarily through the work, but through preparing the shaping techniques. These effects were disturbing and fascinating at the same time and certainly made us reflect along psychological theories—Reichian and Post-Reichian and those of Janov. However, we still were invested in the work of art, not only in its psychological impact. We heard about a theater director in New York, Alec Rubin, who was a trainer at La MaMa Theatre and at the Living Theater. We knew the New York scene very well from festivals in Zurich, so I decided to explore this way of going for the work of art. And when I came to Tufts University in 1973, I joined Alec Rubin's Theater of Encounter. While I explored the scene in New York and in the Boston Reality Theater, I was asked, together with Norma Canner, Mariagnese Cattaneo and Elisabeth McKim, to work on intermodal art education at Tufts University's Arts Institute, one could say in competition with Lesley College.

When Shaun McNiff asked me to join him at Lesley College in the new Expressive Therapies program, I was in the midst of navigating between three ways of working toward a performance. The first, which I came from originally, is motivated strongly by play; the second one is art-generated primarily through a concept; and the third one is through what I would call today "expressive techniques." This navigation created some confusion; in retrospect, I think the confusion was a necessary one. I am a person who tries to explore things thoroughly in order to find clarity.

SKL: The 70s was a very experimental time, there was a lot of emphasis on process. Was it mostly a process-orientation toward the use of media?

PK: I look at it today a little differently. I believe the distinction between process and art has to do with what you focus on. I cannot imagine an artistic process without the completed work that's there and wants to reveal itself, undisturbed by whatever the process was of the creator. On the other hand, the work is autonomous once it is out there; and the process can then become the encounter between the work and the viewer. Certainly when we are in a professional relationship as change agents, we are part of a process of change that includes experiences and reflections on all parts of the session, conversations on the original concern and the outcome, the experience of being in the art-making and the experience of encountering the work.

SKL: Was that the attitude at that time?

PK: No, we had many perspectives that came into our conversations. There were many teachers, including myself, who were influenced by the "expressive mode," as I described earlier, coming from experimental theater and movement work that paid primary attention to the process and had a tendency to self-expression. Psychodrama was part of the curriculum and in its cathartic version was on this side as well, even though it held to a theater-indigenous theory and language.

Shaun McNiff was a trailblazer in the method of dialoguing with painting, and in his publications developed it in the direction of what he called "Studio Art Therapy" in order to protect art from "clinification." I followed him with my intermodal drive toward "Performance Art" as the key competency for any change agent. We both adopted this concept and made it into a mandatory project at the introductory summer colloquium for expressive arts students at Lesley.

We paid more and more attention to the important fact that an art process includes an intention for the work, even though it might not arrive "on our terms." With this new challenge by the intentionality of the process of serving an emerging work, the attention changed from self-expression to the challenge of what arrives outside of us and asks for our resources in order to find its form. Reflection on this was difficult, however, because of a missing theoretical base; so the tendency was still there for many to guide and reflect in a way that leaned toward biographical conversations. In this situation the slogan "trust the process" (later the title of a book by Shaun) helped to get away from reflections outside of an "art-indigenous language," as we called it. In a way, we said, just let the art be in the center and teach or lead the art process.

SKL: Would it be fair to say that there was a shift from a more psychological to a more phenomenological perspective?

PK: Oh, yes, definitely. Even so, I had the impression that my phenomenological perspective—I say *mine*, because I am not so sure if everybody brought that into Lesley—my position was from the beginning not to make any psychological or psychoanalytic interpretations. I was not used to approach art from such a vantage point. At that time, I was used to my way of reflecting, especially in visual art, music and dance, I stuck to technique and form. And I thought it's my European way that when I listen to music, that I reflect about form, about melody and clusters of sounds, that I approach it from what I hear, for example, that something is rubbing, it's a dissonance, that I talk like that and not say that it's a conflict, or that we have here a contradiction. It felt foreign with my way of staying strictly with the making, and what I hear. The two words, structure and form, that I used were not so welcome—of greater interest was the expression of feelings.

This conflict drove me to study phenomenology seriously. In my sabbatical I went to Heidelberg University to study with Wolfgang Jacob, who I also brought to Lesley and who later was on the founding board of EGS. Unfortunately he died soon after. When I invited Wolfgang Schirmacher two years later to design the Program in Media and Communication and we built a scientific council including François Lyotard, the same thing happened. Although Wolfgang brought the best scholars in the field, we still miss Lyotard.

The major breakthrough came on that sabbatical. I was studying the field of *Daseinsanalysis* (Existential Analysis) and met its founder Medard Boss, the organizer of the Zollikon Seminars with Heidegger.

SKL: Does the term "expression" still make sense in your work?

PK: In French, "expression" is used in a different way—in an expressionistic way, one might say, not in expression as psychological self-expression. I painted for a long time in my life, so when I look at nature, I have the sense I need to paint. There are two things: there is the thing as it reveals itself and the thing as I respond to the revealing of it. I might respond very differently to that tree there, I might respond to that which looks to me white metallic because the sun is on it, and you might be much more fascinated by the shadow and its blueness besides the yellowness of the surrounding of what I'm talking about as metallic. And if I bring that in the painting then I express something of how the tree reveals itself to me.

SKL: But you're not expressing yourself.

PK: No, rather one could say your expression of color, form and matter brings the tree into presence.

SKL: I've read articles in which you criticize the concept of expression as self-expression but try to save the notion of expression for the expressive qualities of the work. Would that be a fair distinction?

PK: Yes. However, I notice this is still misunderstood by some expressive arts therapists. Even though the change agent is not making explanatory interpretations of the work or the artistic process, the main interest in the dialogue with the client for some therapists is about what feelings have been expressed, their meaning or what came up emotionally. This of course misses the whole point about art as the other, arriving, emerging, perturbing us and making it so that things might not be the same as before. Usually the whole processing seems to be on the work, but it's really about what is *self*-expressed.

SKL: And that's not your perspective.

PK: No, not at all. It is not interesting to me to be only looking at myself, getting more of the same instead of meeting the other.

SKL: When did you begin to formulate your understanding of the work, your theoretical framework?

PK: I am puzzled sometimes that I didn't have the urge to do it earlier than 1978. At Lesley it was Shaun who came out with the first books about our work. For years I used a manuscript I wrote in English as a handout in all my courses at Lesley. This manuscript was later used as a basis for my first English book, co-authored with Helen Barba and Margo Fuchs in 1993 (Knill *et al.* 2004). However two books did come out in German, in 1979 (Knill 1979) and 1983 (Knill 1983), the first one about principles and practice of the work, the second one about applications.

SKL: Is that the one about intermodality?

PK: Yes, *Ausdruckstherapie* (*Expressive Therapy*) in 1979 was the first book. I had written many articles before which covered part of the practice. Early on several were connected to intermodal improvisation, and in 1976 I had already contributed part of my intermodal perspective on special education to a German-language book (Knill 1976). There were also a number of newspaper reports and articles about my passionate engagement for music and art education based on the low-skill/high-sensitivity concept, mentioned earlier in this interview. I worked successfully with both kindergarten kids and composers at the conservatory using the same structures. I ended up becoming the Chair of the Swiss commission on early music education. Our saying was that we teach children to do serious contemporary music without staff notation and they love it. At the same time, I started to work using music in private practice with autistic children, together with a psychiatrist. It was my first step back into the clinical atmosphere.

You should know that I have a long positive relationship with psychiatric clinics. My father made it his mission to sing regularly with the patients in the closed wards and I was obliged to join him. I always loved to chat and play with the patients in the corridors. This was in the forties when no medications were known. Later in college I became friends with the son of the Director of the biggest psychiatric hospital of the region. His father and mother were psychiatrists and the family lived in the clinic. They also were artists. So we played often in the wards, knew the patients and felt at home in this big former baroque cloister. The parents urged us to do music with the patients and I got used to being with people who were in a florid psychotic condition (remember, this was beween1949 and 1953). The staff was very friendly and always at hand and the family had a respectful and authentic relationship with the staff and patients. So when I got back to the hospital where my father had sung with the patients, I asked to work with my new art-oriented method in 1969. I was welcomed with open arms and had experimental groups with half the staff participating, as well as a permanent art studio with an attending artist.

The work was presented in conferences by the staff. The psychologist and the head psychiatrists published something, which they called "Case Studies about the Knill Group," it wasn't called Expressive Arts Therapy. I myself used the material in my first English book, *Minstrels of Soul*, in 1993.

SKL: In this early perspective, you wrote on the theory of intermodality, how the arts go together and work with each other. Then there were further steps in your thinking. Can you say something about that, how your thinking developed?

PK: First I need to ventilate my irritation about the use of the term "intermodality." I feel misunderstood when I see how this term is used to make the argument that one has to mix art disciplines and that the change of one discipline to another one is the method. I don't know what happened, how the "intermodal transfer," as it was called, became a method itself. I don't understand it.

I mean that you don't need to do an intermodal transfer unless the work calls for it or the situation makes it necessary; nevertheless, we still work intermodally even when using one artistic discipline. This is because intermodal practice looks not only at the interface of art disciplines, but is also sensitive to the mode of expression or communication within the work. Is it the movement that comes through in a poem and could go in the dance or not? When we make a movie, what do I take up in the text or in the framing or in the music? Do I take up a movement or an image or the text or the context? Therefore, intermodal sensitivity is also the skill and understanding about what happens between the modes and disciplines, in a similar way as polyaesthetics pays attention to what happens between the senses.

I would say that the best intermodal practitioners can be found among moviemakers. We can learn from them about intermodal sensitivity in our work with clients in order to get them to the source of their own art in its fullest intermodal performative capacity.

Something about this distinction in the intermodal theory wasn't effective in my publications, and still it's not especially clear in German, where we use two words in this context, "intermedial" and "intermodal," which are not synonyms. Maybe I attempted to make a distinction that doesn't need to be there with such clarity, maybe it needs more confusion to be congruent to art. Then, suddenly something else will become important and will need our full attention.

This is exactly what happened in Switzerland. Our expressive arts psychotherapy training institute applied to enter the Swiss Charta of Psychotherapy schools and was accepted by them. One of the tasks all the schools had to do to gain acceptance was to explain what we do differently and how that works, and also what we do in a similar way.

Soon I noticed that it is helpful to find the commonalities first. Besides having "school cultural" variations on space, roles, setting and understanding of the process, we all work in essence with people who are in a "dire straits" situation, marked by a lack of play range to choose, find or create relief or solutions to their problems. We had ample opportunity to compare with the other schools and found that it is fair to say that, despite all their differences, all psychotherapies need to resort to imagination in one or the other way.

What suddenly called forth the fullest attention was the question: What in the different arts actually affects the change process and how is this different than other uses of imagination?

The difference of using art from other forms of play and imagination, such as free association, dream-work, role play, or circular questioning, is that art itself is a disciplined play with imagination. Bringing in the arts is a lived experience which is witnessed by others, while being awake and conscious. In a professional relationship of this kind, everyone has direct access to the work and process, as opposed, for example, to dream-work, in which only the dreamer has direct experience of the dream.

I soon recognized that this makes the way we intervene or reflect drastically different from other ways of using imagination in therapy. We make use of the extraordinary reality of the therapy setting, like all other methods; however, in EXA [Expressive Arts], we offer for a period of the session the atelier or studio and enter an alternative world of the imagination. It is still a world; however, it is differently lived and captured by a benign challenge—that of creating art. The skill to make this a fruitful artistic experience now became an essential goal of training. Therefore, we developed a renewed artistic perspective based on the competencies that are required by the change agent, competencies that connect to low-skill/high-sensitivity and also theoretically to our understanding of "active imagination," as it is called in Jungian literature. The phase of alternative world experience, in which we access the imagination through play and art, has come into the center of our work. We call this phase "intermodal decentering" (IDEC) because we do not place the problem at the center but rather "decenter" from it, putting it aside and giving free rein to the imagination.

Expressive Arts is different. It is resourceful in offering an alternative world experience in which the experience of consolation and the finding of solutions are lived experiences. I am very grateful to Herbert Eberhart who worked with me in elaborating this discourse on decentering. Herbert trained with me since the inception of Expressive Arts and started teaching from the beginning at EGS. He loved my saying that the arts are like "soul food" during the intense work involved in a change process. Though the work may be a challenge and bring up difficult feelings, it is also profoundly gratifying. In this sense, it corresponds to Rilke's words, "Only in the realm of praising should lament walk" (1985, p.33).

SKL: I have the impression that Herbert Eberhart wrote from a "solution-focused perspective."

PK: As we began to work on the book *Losungskunst* (Eberhart and Knill 2009), literally, "the art of solutions," but something more like "art: challenge and solution," he added to my notion of decentering a solution-focused perspective. I have to say that I was very grateful for his competence in the field of systems-oriented thinking and, related to that, the solution-focused school of Steve de Shazer, as well as the resource-oriented attitude and the narrative orientation of Michael White. We had week-long retreats twice a year in which we first worked through intense critical discourses in order to find an adequate philosophical base for the concept of decentering. In the book, we have a whole chapter describing this process as a sort of dialogue between Herbert, a psychologist and also a trained expressive therapist, and myself, representing the phenomenological foundation of our psychotherapeutic school, influenced by archetypal psychology and *Daseinsanalysis*, the art-based perspective on theory and practice and the salutogenetic or health-based perspective on illness. I was happy about this perturbation of my mindset and noticed that in a kind of deconstruction of these concepts a more adequate understanding could be arrived at. I wish this book would soon be translated, because it shows how we finally found the key in the well of the arts.

In our approach, we orient ourselves to the resources of the person, and we want to overcome being both "problem-tranced" and "solution-tranced"—both restrict the person's play range and create a secondary dire straits situation. Art itself is a beautiful resource in the experience of the world; within the arts we notice that we can reach beauty within restrictions that can be overcome. Moreover, looking at my art work with others, I can always perceive more than what I may see alone. So seeing *more* can be a positive experience in a suffering situation or when I have a "blind spot" toward possible resources.

This togetherness of client and change agent in the decentering phase, each awake, aware, and attentive to the arts, becomes a major learning experience. Even though it is an imaginative process, they are in it together through their relationship to the thing that is made. This is a witnessed experience that is interactive and "thingly" and that can be reflected on the concrete surface of the work and the process. It is a lived experience in the world and therefore relates to and affects the everyday world.

SKL: That's where the notion of "effective reality" comes in then—experience that works, that has an effect upon the person.

PK: Exactly. The person is awake, conscious and witnessing, and I'm there. I'm there as an artist, I help the person to have an experience. What I notice myself is that if I listen carefully to the person who comes to me, I'm aware that I will never completely understand her experience because I can't have the same experience; therefore, I won't make a decision like: "Now we have to go deeper with your suffering," or, "Now we have to focus on positive experiences." Instead, if I listen carefully to the phenomena of their talk, what is right on the surface, then it opens up to essential themes, as long as I am able to abstain from fishing for the problem or for the solution. It is so hard to say, "I don't know what that person really needs in the moment, except my being here to listen to them." When I am listening, I am listening for what the client is longing for, how the story reveals its future. My clarifying questions intend to tune in to the longing that has the impetus for change. Longing and yearning both can be concretized from experiences or visions, and can connect to resilience and resources without belittling the problem or the suffering, because in any suffering a longing is present.

Then I noticed that it's easier to decenter in the arts from this perspective. Instead of trying to make a decision about what clients should work on, I can find out what they *long* for. And doing art makes for an effective reality in which the longing for beauty and the work is experienced and which finds its resolution while always leaving a residual longing to go on with it!

SKL: Do you feel there has been a shift in your work and in your understanding of it since you left Lesley to found EGS?

PK: Yes. I have a more refined understanding of what we call the arts-based approach of Expressive Arts. In the decade before I retired as an Emeritus Professor from Lesley, the phenomenological tradition was in general accepted by the pioneering leadership there as the basis for our *Menschenbild* (concept of human nature) and for theory-building. I am aware that there was also a contrasting notion held by some faculty members, and supported by the professional associations' certification requirements, to hold on to diagnostic interpretation, which led to considering the process as self-expression. In addition, an increasing political influence had of course an influence in the understanding of the cultural aspects of healing and the arts.

In this particular period, before EGS started, Margo Fuchs Knill took over the intermodal core group and the supervision of all thesis seminars at Lesley. The role of the arts was emphasized and validated in her approach. In a faculty meeting, Margo and Shaun presented this as a new concept for the next accreditation process, calling it "Art-Based Thesis Project." This is when the term was initiated in Expressive Arts. Also you, Steve, had a strong influence in this period. Ever since you came to Lesley as an Academic Fellow, you influenced my thinking substantially. Your book, *Poiesis: The Language of Psychology and the Speech of the Soul* (Levine 1997), became the textbook for our classes. *Poiesis*, the knowing that takes place in the making or shaping of a work, as distinct from the knowing that reflects about it afterwards, became key in understanding what makes the open-ended intentionality of the art process toward the work so important. The reflection after the encounter with the surprising art itself cannot be premeditated; it is unique. This reflective thinking will be in the manner of *poiesis*, in which we give poietic exercises as ways of expressing feelings, convictions or beliefs.

During this period, we found the term "decentering" in Margo's handouts. It was used to describe the fact that working with the arts is forming, while at the same time the client's attention is being decentered from the deformed, from what is problematic in his or her life. This shows how in this time these faculty members were intensively engaged in the transformation of the field, even though the political climate in the program was difficult.

It was at the European Graduate School where we made the phenomenological perspective part of our mission and made the notion of art central to it. In addition, we had the opportunity to bring this discourse to Europe and into German, my mother tongue. Herbert Eberhart and Jürgen Kriz were especially important in bringing these ideas into the European discourse and in dialoguing with the research community.

This atmosphere at EGS brought a shift toward a multi-perspectival understanding of our field, keeping art in the center and attending to a language of reflection that is concrete, particular and on the surface of perception, instead of superficially reducing or generalizing about the richness of experience. I honor Margo here; she supported me in this process with her ever-present poetic writing and thinking, a well of wisdom to connect my poetic knowing with my reflective thought through the language of art. Yes, and you too, Steve, helped me to understand philosophy by listening to it as poetic.

SKL: When I look at the field I see a change in several ways. First of all, the extension of Expressive Arts beyond therapy into coaching, education and social change, that's one important aspect. And secondly the awareness that in some way art is at the center for what we call art-based work; psychology is not at the center. This seems to me a development that is very promising and offers a lot. I wonder what future directions you see the field taking or might take.

PK: Well, there are wishes and there are fantasies about that. Mine is that Expressive Arts claims its own philosophical and theoretical perspective congruent with its non-reductionist conversation about art, while fostering a mutual respect to other disciplines whose conversations focus on the psyche or, depending on their tradition, on "soul." When I sometimes hear people in our field saying, "We are not psychological," it makes me nervous. Does this mean we do not converse about psyche? It cannot be meant like that. Of course we have such a discourse, and it will increase with all the new fields Expressive Arts is expanding into—moving out into social change into peacemaking, coaching, consulting and supervision. Change agents in these fields may find conversations about the psychological process more philosophical and the psychological discourse much less clinical. Our method of Intermodal Decentering may lead a path into the future where the arts-based understanding of the work of art and the process of shaping become the stepping stone to a psychological conversation that helps the competency of the change agent to give responses, not explanations or answers.

I think it was Majken Jacoby who raised that issue in her dissertation at EGS. She posited that such a psychology should not marry the arts but should be in a better dialogue with the arts, a philosophical dialogue, not a political one. And today it is politicized, with the whole licensing formalities and guild formation in the field of therapy. As before in the history of professional organizations, we find the restrictive formalized guild power to secure work for its members if the market does not grow and money gets tight. In many countries, psychology and counseling become the basis for licensing, even though the European Association for Psychotherapy has declared that there are different scientific perspectives on a therapeutic process and not exclusively psychology. Meanwhile the guilds stay tight, accepting only psychology. It is not astonishing then that the market diversifies in non-licensed fields as has happened throughout history.

SKL: What I'm thinking right now is that in our desire not to engage in psychological reductionism of the work—to respect the integrity of the work, the way it comes to us, and is not us—in that desire we may have developed an aversion to psychological understanding at all, and that maybe what we need would be a new psychology that would be adequate to the experience of the work.

PK: Exactly. And I think it would be helpful to psychology in general, as Hillman posits with his notion of "re-visioning psychology."

SKL: I want to close the interview by asking you, what do you feel will be your greatest legacy?

PK (laughing): Since the work is not yet complete, I long for some more to emerge…

SKL: What you will leave for others is a difficult question, since you are not at the end by any means.

PK: When I look into history, the legacy the person thought would be in their work is rarely the legacy that later is the one that people talk about. I hope that my teaching, the way that I teach and lead, in courses but also in improvisation or community art, that will be my legacy.

SKL: Your teaching and the impact it's had on generations of students.

PK: Yes, that may be the most important legacy of all.

Note: This interview was conducted at the EGS campus in Saas Fee, Switzerland, in August 2011 and edited subsequently.

References

Eberhart, H. and Knill, P. (2009) *Lösungskunst: Lehrbuch der Kunst–und ressourcenorientierten Arbeit.* Göttingen: Vandenhoek & Ruprecht.

Knill, P. (1976) *Musik in der Ausdruckstherapie für Lernbehinderte in Musik und Bewegung.* Bern: Haupt Verlag.

Knill, P. (1979) *Ausdruckstherapie: Künstlerischer Ausdruck in Therapie und Erziehung als intermediale Methode.* Lilienthal/Bremen: Eres Verlag.

Knill, P. (1983) *Medien in Therapie und Ausbildung.* Lilienthal/Bremen: Eres Verlag.

Knill, P., Fuchs, M. and Barba, H. (2004) *Minstrels of Soul: Intermodal Expressive Therapy,* 2nd edition. Toronto: EGS Press.

Levine, S. K. (1997) *Poiesis: The Language of Psychology and the Speech of the Soul,* 2nd edition. London: Jessica Kingsley Publishers.

Rilke, R. M. (1985) *The Sonnets to Orpheus,* trans. S. Mitchell. New York: Simon & Schuster Inc.

4

MODALITY

A Phenomenological Concept for Expressive Arts

Jacques Stitelmann

Translated by Jackie Beaver

Some years ago, I commented on and developed Paolo Knill's concept of crystallization (Stitelmann 2003) and enhanced it with the concept of composting. Since it is one of Knill's essential contributions to art therapy, I would like to look further into the often misunderstood concept of modality. Knill's concepts of modality and inter-modality are central to expressive arts therapy, along with his concept of the work, which is closely linked to modality.

Unfortunately, modality is often used as a synonym for mediality, which refers to particular media used for expression. Sometimes the term is taken for art, in which expression is given form, or confused with sensations used to make connections with art works.

Modality is a phenomenological concept that helps us think about the way we engage our attention when we encounter an art work, rather than telling us about the art work itself, or the psychological experience of its maker.

Working through, work and working

Traditional art therapy movements, anchored in psychology, consider the products of creative processes, or art works, as products of a creator, and, more specifically, of his/her psyche. The idea that unresolved aspects of psychological problems unconsciously find a way to be expressed and even resolved through the artistic process, has been ardently put forward and verified time and time again.

For some therapists, such productions benefit from verbal interpretation; links are made with psychological problems and explained in order to undo the psychical knot. It follows then that productions can be seen as expressions of illness, while health is associated with the development of talk, generally explanatory talk. The art work is linked with aspects of its creator's psychological suffering, which is considered to have caused the art work. Thus the creator, freed of his/her blockages, is better able to give shape to his/her existence. In this kind of therapy, art and different media are used with the intention of bringing out the impalpable and psychological unknown.

For some, artistic productions reveal the psyche, allowing us to understand and analyze it and so make diagnoses. For others, artistic expression is a transformational act through psychological growth, brought about by the art-making process, which is itself symbolization, such that verbal explanations are unnecessary.

In this orientation of art therapy, the right medium is one that will convey the psychological aspects that are thought to be most in need of expression. The internal world of the client and the therapeutic relationship established by a therapist and client partnership are the principal points of departure; the means of expression are merely tools, they mediate between the therapeutic partners and between the creator and his/her unconscious. Sensory issues are carefully considered; particular physical/bodily channels of communication with the world are favored by one or other type of medium—which of these channels of communication are necessary for stimulating one or other psychological aspect that is lacking expressivity? In this kind of art therapy, particular art forms and media can, much like medicines, be prescribed or advised against because of their purported effects, as if we knew their psychological effects in every kind of situation. For example, it would be deemed inappropriate to use liquids when working with autism, as they could stimulate anxieties of liquefaction that are associated with this pathology; it would be inappropriate to use drama with schizophrenic patients or those with borderline disorders as it would stimulate depersonalization; on the other hand, painting and drawing would be prescribed for psychotic patients as these afford possibilities to express a whole range of emotions and fantasies using color and shape. In this orientation, materials and sensations are thought of as things, means, ways of knowing more about the person's internal world, itself considered a thing, whose equilibrium is necessary for health. The level of reality worked upon during therapy is the internal world. In this instance we talk about *working through*, the elaboration of psychological problems and life experiences through a human relationship, mediated by creations and interpretations.

In another traditional strain of art therapy, the therapeutic partnership is interested in art as a level of reality. The beauty and expressivity of the art work, its aesthetic success and its effect on the onlooker are important elements. Here, there is no analysis of psychological causes and life experiences that could be linked to productions, even if it is accepted that the artistic process sometimes has indirect, secondary psychological benefits, for example, in terms of self-esteem, making sense of life or stabilizing relationships. The medium used and artistic thinking are essential elements: the plasticity of clay, the space and lighting of a stage, the type of character to be acted out, the color tones of paint, the appropriateness and expressivity of a drawn shape, feelings evoked by poetry. Clearly, this is all about art and the medium used: the creator gives him/herself over to using the medium in an art work; putting something of him/herself into the work is a bonus that could engender secondary and indirect benefits. In this instance, we talk about *work*.

The phenomenological art therapy movement, developed in Lesley College, among other places, and then within the European Graduate School (EGS) network by Paolo Knill, together with other practitioners and researchers, proposes a third perspective. This is where neither the psyche nor the material used is the essential level of reality, but the meeting of multiple material, immaterial and human elements in a creative experience that is happening.

From this perspective, the art work is not a thing, no more so than the psychological experience. Rather, it is a process of unfolding, extending, opening and spreading, of encounter, a formation of forms, a process of *Gestaltung* (Prinzhorn 1922). The word *work* allows us to conceptualize the art work as well as the process of work. It also allows us to consider how the art work works on us. Even so, we should be talking about *working*, the working out of forms which unfold and spread out.

Forms appearing in this *working* are entities that develop in space, in a place that is here, a place of co-presence, where art works, materials, people and the environment intermingle. They develop in time, in the present moment, not determined by minutes and seconds, but a phenomenological perception of existing in lived time, as

David Stern so eloquently tells us in his book, *Le moment présent en psychothérapie* (2003). Forms develop in terms of modalities, in terms of the kind of attention human beings develop, through which they can be in touch with the world.

It's a complicated kind of system of environments, each endowed with different modes, ways of being—a bit like the parallel universe of science fiction—through which experience unfolds, leaving participants more or less free to go from one to another.

We are not interested in thinking about the art work, the medium or the psychological material in isolation, but as a complex whole relating to a situation; the process and its becoming, the fact that it becomes and the manner in which it does become; giving rise to reflection upon meaningful elements of the form, making sense of the experience and feeding a desire for more experiences to come.

Modality and mediality

Paolo Knill's main ideas about modality were developed in his book *Minstrels of Soul* (Knill, Barba and Fuchs 1995), where he puts forward five modalities for consideration: image, sound, act (play-acting, staging, and fiction), word, and movement.

For Knill, music is about the modality of sound, as it wouldn't exist without some way of producing sound and a sense of hearing. John Cage's composition 4'33, consisting of four minutes and 33 seconds of silence, confirms this idea. Hearing and not hearing sound: silence is an essential dimension of music. 4'33 draws our attention to the use of sound and time in music composition.

Knill uses the idea of imagination to explain modality. For him, modalities are ways of imagining. Imagination is the stuff of dreams, musings and reverie, reflected in the human being like trees in still water. In Knill's words, "Imagination is the visiting place of soul" (Knill *et al.* 1995, p.25). Milner wrote about this in *On Not Being Able to Paint* (1957), where she differentiates rational thinking from a thinking in images that is active during periods of pictorial creation, a thinking which supports the most archaic processes of the unconscious and preconscious psyche.

Anthropologists also frequently differentiate between mythical thinking, which produces works of art, ritual and mythology, and rational thinking. Wilfred Bion (1965), a celebrated psychoanalyst, proposes that we see reverie as dynamic thinking in dream, musing, artistic creation, and free association. For Bion, this kind of thinking offers human beings a sense of existing and meaning, allowing them to change and evolve throughout their lives. At the Atelier in Geneva, Switzerland, we differentiate three kinds of thinking, each having its own particular logic: everyday, scientific, and dream thinking.

For Knill, the soul speaks through dreams and reverie. In dreams, the imagination is experienced passively, while in reverie it is more actively lived.

In traditional arts and rituals, Knill observes that the imagination is primarily a way of thinking in action. He notices that, in general, art works are intermodal — that is, they unfold themselves through several modalities at the same time or in succession. We only have to think back to the medieval tradition of mystery plays, when whole communities acted out the lives of mythical figures, with specific songs, costumes and accessories, in particular places, usually in the church square or in the city streets.

For Knill, modality is a modality of imagination, a dimension in which the imagination develops. He maintains: "It is important to understand the sensory aspects of imagination" (1999, p.40). He associates modalities with the sensory capacities of creator and spectator, as well as with the different arts.

Arts such as painting and sculpture are, above all, concerned with *image*, poetry and fiction with *word*, music with *sound*, dance and mime with *movement*, and drama with *act*. He emphasizes that the arts can be experienced through several modalities. We can "hear" a painting by the sound of the paintbrush on paper, we can "feel" a piece of music through the musician's gestures and movements.

No art can exist without a primary or dominant modality. By this, he underlines the existential and phenomenological dimension of any contact with an artistic occurrence.

My exchanges with other art therapy professionals, even expressive arts therapists who refer to phenomenological thinking, have led me to realize that the concepts of modality and mediality are regularly taken one for the other. But, in fact, an essential aspect of expressive arts therapy rests in their differentiation.

Mediality refers to the medium, to the materials used to create the art work. Photography uses images, painting uses colored pastes, sculpture uses stone… These materials are completely other, they are not-me, and it is this, in large part, that is their force. Their otherness raises questions for us; they bring the potential and limitations of their materiality to the art work, with and through which the creator must develop his/her creativity.

In fact, making the art work, the *working*, has two outside influences: the creator's internal world and the materials used. These outside influences, as well as the phenomenon of their encounter within the *working* are the origins of the creative process, which can be considered like a reverie that happens in their in-between.

The core idea of modality has not to do with description, so we can know and define otherness or things, but with feeling and understanding our encounter with the world. Materials and art works express aspects of this encounter, in order to understand the reality of our existence better without hindering the unfolding of that existence. As such, modality is a phenomenological concept.

By confounding modality and mediality we lose the essential specificities of each. This mistake is partially due to a materialist and naturalist way of seeing things within current society and contemporary art therapy that says a creation is a thing that exists because it can be perceived and measured, and is therefore by nature, separate from the self. Accordingly, a creation can only be known by what we can objectively perceive of it, which, in its turn, can be subjected to explanatory mental activity originating outside the said creation. We struggle with the notions of subjectivity and intersubjectivity.

It seems to me that the error of using modality and mediality as synonyms of each other in expressive arts therapy is also linked to a deviation from the phenomenological position by Knill himself. In effect, Knill has wanted to deliver the artistic happening from the clutches of psychology, which, in itself, is an extremely interesting idea; in doing so, he has come to emphasize the art work and the process of creation, in other words, the key elements of artistic work, rather than the psychological experience of the creator preceding creative action. Sometimes, he can attach more importance to the art work, direction, and choreography than to workshop participants!

There is however, an element of contradiction in his intentions: Knill proposes that modality is a *modality of imagination*, which is, despite everything, a psychological perspective, since he defines imagination as dream thinking, reverie, and art.

Distancing oneself from psychology in favor of the art work runs several risks and disadvantages:

- Loss of a phenomenological perspective which demands the sensory encounter of phenomena as distinct from professions of admiration or confidence relating to creations.

- Fewer chances of benefitting from psychological thinking and research, even though some psychological movements such as Gestalt, systemic and some post-Bionian and Winnicottian psychoanalytic movements offer interesting reflections on the art work, which could enrich our way of thinking.

- Loss of a critical attitude towards the art work, which is essential for a scientific perspective. Clinical experience shows that sometimes the expressive content of an art work and the manner in which it is presented can be due to psychological defense mechanisms or resistance to the therapeutic process, an artistic trick, an act of non-living. If we do not know how to recognize it, we are at risk of encouraging this kind of non-living, when the goal should be to encourage an unfolding of life.

The concept of modality is complex and intersubjective, and is probably misunderstood because it is not yet sufficiently defined. At this point I would like to make some clarifications of the concept, with a few complementary reflections. Nevertheless, much work still remains to be done to develop Knill's intuition of modality into a full concept.

Modality

The term is used in several scientific domains: linguistics, logic, psychology, philosophy, music, law, and statistics where it takes on different meanings. However, it seems to me that it expresses three important ideas:

- Different situations have essential particularities that the term "modality" seeks to express. Modality, then, is that which differentiates one situation from another. For example, "This painting is blue," or, "This sonata is played in a minor key," or even, "Ice is a modality of water."

- Different actions take place according to the particular way in which they are each executed. For example: "To lead a workshop you must suggest a warm-up activity, followed by the workshop itself and finally a period of reflection, often verbal," or, "To validate the contract you must answer questions one to six, then date and sign it."

- Suggestions can be implied and not necessarily articulated explicitly. Qualitative aspects are expressed in this idea of modality. For example: "This apple is nice." Or, "Would you like to do this?" or, "Could you do this?" or, "Are you allowed to do it?" Or, "Unfortunately I'm experiencing a paralyzing sense of stage fright."

These ideas all concern art therapy but the last of them is of direct interest as it allows us to consider how the speaker, the creator, experiences their "production," how they approach the situation, action or suggestion. This is a phenomenological perspective. The object being apprehended is considered as a kind of opposite, towards which we are turned and towards which we direct our intentionality. Modalities can then be considered as aspects of Husserlian intentionality.

An intentional encounter takes shape within a modality and gives rise to both object and subject together. As such, modality is neither the subject's sensoriality nor the object's materiality, nor even art and the cultural norms within which transitional creations develop: modality is the dimension in which an encounter between the subject and the world takes place. Modality is a dimension of poietics.

I suggest we look at modality in so much as it is the way in which a happening unfolds, the way we turn towards it and the way we experience it.

Although it is possible to live each moment of our lives in several modalities, in reality it is impossible to experience them all at the same time. We can only be aware of one or maybe two of them in any one lived moment. The others are relegated to the back of consciousness. We experience this impossibility in *complex arts* such as opera and cinema, where it is difficult to focus on every aspect at once, which can also make for a better appreciation of their aesthetic power.

Looking at a painting I see colors, a large spectrum of color dominated by bluey greens, rhythmic brush strokes and an assortment of short, energetic strokes around the edges of the canvas. I can make out longer, wider, vertical shapes in the middle, a man, a child, a cloud. Memories, imaginings, emotions resonating within me unfold and spread out from this visual contact. At that very moment I am living in a modality of image, for seconds, minutes, maybe longer. There is the world and there is me, existing as image. I no longer feel my body, standing before the painting, I no longer hear the wooden parquet creaking when other visitors walk past me, nor catch the whiff of floor wax or the blooming chestnut trees in the gardens outside, I cannot taste the thyme-fragranced fish that I ate for lunch, nor am I aware of the uniformed security guard who is calmly pacing up and down the room, while the stream of visitors flows from room to room. I can only see in colors and lines, in spatial rhythms bound up with the painting. Memories emerge from the depths of my mind, landscapes from my childhood or my youth and the feelings they evoke, with me now in the painting.

But I can leave this modality and experience the same painting through the musical instrument held by the child in the painting. In my imagination I can hear the strings of a lyre being plucked, birdsong emanates from the wood in the background and from the park next to the gallery. The creaking parquet annoys me, a small girl is crying, she reminds me of my own daughter, when she was little, quite some years ago… I no longer see the painting's colors, nor the rhythmic organization of its lines and dots, I see the inside and outside worlds in sounds.

Switching from one modality to the next, I enter another parallel world, interior and exterior environments change, they are the same, but not quite; they are other realities. I realize that when I am in a particular modality, I distance myself or am distanced from the possibilities of other modalities for a certain length of time. I can control this intermodal movement and more or less pass from one world to the next, as I wish. Just as it is difficult for non-musicians to hear several lines of melody played concurrently, in a symphony for example, it is difficult to perceive a smell, color, movement, and a word at the same time.

Sometimes doors open between worlds, and new attractors, as Knill calls them, beckon: another visitor's colorful outfit pulls me out of a world of sounds and throws me back into color, the rhythmic sobs of the little girl recall the rhythmic spacing of tree trunks in the background of the painting, and a door reopens onto the world of images. The undulating step of a woman passing close by opens a door to the world of movement. At each doorway I can choose to enter a different world or stay where I am.

Although every human being is able to journey to each of these worlds, I think we have favorites or ones where we feel more comfortable. I am sensitive to the world of images, particularly colors, rhythms and lines, the use of space. I am sensitive to the world of sound; loud noises upset me, a chance sound can seem musical; a speaker's voice comes to me as a range (*tessiture*) of tones, as much as a string of meaningful words. And I am sensitive to tastes and smells. Each of us can encounter the world in six ways, six modalities, and in such a way that we become specialized, develop a greater capacity for enjoyment and pleasure in some of them more than others.

Week after week, clinical experience confirms the possibility that existential suffering can also largely reside in one of these modalities, leaving the others available for the enjoyment of life. We will pick up this idea again, later on.

Classical therapies essentially develop through the modality of word; expressive and poietic therapy unfurls and unfolds within all modalities of existence.

Knill, Barba and Fuchs (1995) propose five modalities: image, sound, act, word, and movement, I would suggest the addition of a sixth one that opens towards the world of taste and smell. Although their close sensory association in the arts points to a single combined modality, I could imagine them as two separate modalities, but further research would be able to clarify this point.

Personally I am quite sensitive to this modality, such that my creativity and that of some of my patients find it to be fertile ground. The world of taste-smell gives rise to a certain number of therapeutic openings. For example, ten years ago we developed a workshop at the university hospital in Geneva for patients with neurological disorders resulting from accidents. One of our tools in this workshop was a range of smells. We realized that it was an extremely dynamic way of forming a relationship with these patients, and for them to use their creativity, despite major injuries and handicaps. I have often performed and led culinary arts workshops, which allow participants to engage with the world of tastes and smells and to accomplish some interesting therapeutic work that would not be as possible in other modalities. One thing which drew me to oil painting was the smell of linseed oil.

Every art work can be experienced in different modalities. Every modality has its own particular vocabulary and grammar.

Image modality manifests itself as space, color, light, rhythms of lines and dots, representations of shapes, relationships between content and the formal support or container. In order to "feel" an actual image you need to be in its presence, in a visual face to face. States of depression have sometimes been linked to low levels of light, whereby visual contact with the image is compromised.

Sound modality is about the vibration of air and space. The notion of time is involved; sound requires a certain amount of time to manifest itself as rhythms, tempos, tones, long and short waves, melodies, and harmonies. Feeling sounds is related to where you are and where the sound travels from or through. It's impossible not to hear a sound if it occurs where you are; you cannot close your ears as you can your eyes. Inspiration for many a torturer!

Word modality has to do with the existence of words and language. Words can indicate metaphoric sounds, material things, human facts, relationships between things or events, actions, feelings, imaginings. Sentences make it possible to assemble them in more and more complex ways, to make abstractions, speculations. The spoken word requires a human presence, actual, written, recorded. Words can be used for everyday thinking, useful and functional. They can be the vector for rational thought, approaching the status of mathematical symbols, or they make speculative and philosophical reflection on the human condition possible. Words can recount events, invent and narrate stories, they can be forged into poetry. Meaning, breath and sonority, culturally defined or emanations from within. Sentences can be pulled apart to recover the roots of language and thought. Words and language hold cultural sway. Much human conflict can be attached to misunderstood and miscommunicated words.

Movement modality is equally multidimensional. It can manifest itself through body posture, when we can experience vertical, horizontal, and diagonal positions, through movements within the body, rhythm, contraction, and relaxation. It is a modality that opens up the field of touch, contact with the world via the skin. It is the moving about in space, adapting different parts of the body, torso, limbs, in front, behind, above, below… Movement puts the body in space, in relation to other human beings. In the 1960s, studies of proxemics highlighted the cultural dimension of physical communication and accepted physical distances between humans during their interactions.

Act modality is about staging fictional identities. We are ourselves and someone else at the same time; we inhabit stories and invented realities. It is a world of "as ifs" where the limits of imagination are the limits of possibility. Play time-space is defined; players encounter each other and act as if they were characters who live an imaginary life. Made-up, invented, fictive, even if they are meant to tell us something about reality, they are neo-realities. Imagination, emotion, physical presence, stage setting are major ingredients. In this world, identities are set against each other. Some actors cling to a role and graft their own lives onto it. Everyone can explore hidden or shriveled dimensions of their identity through fictional role play and staged life stories.

More than any other, taste-smell modality lets us experience what it is to consume the world, where salty, sweet, bitter, acidic, spicy, smooth, and fruity tastes and smells circulate on the edges of our being, in the undergrowth of a world that infuses us. Have you ever eaten your own or someone else's art work? What happened next?

Each sense facilitates particular modalities, but is not the modality. Each art form affords an enjoyable, aesthetic, and playful experience of modalities, relying on underlying cultural norms, but is not the modality. Each kind of worldly material sets modalities in motion, but is not the modality. Modalities are different ways in which we encounter and are oriented towards the world, the way the world opens itself up to us and questions us. Modality is the way transitionality unfolds and manifests itself.

The therapeutic use of modality

Getting to know a patient, like any other person, takes place in the different modalities available to us. Modalities are dimensions of the relationship we weave together. What capacity for transitional encounters do we have in common? We each have our preferences, our particularities, facilities, and difficulties; we have each explored and liked exploring some worlds more than others. Some of these are useful to our daily lives, others are filled with desire and creative impulses, and some with monsters, anguish, and suffering. Some seem like gardens, others are deserts or wild virgin forests.

In which ones will we meet?

Experience has led me to understand that for the most part, the lack of living expressed by patients at the beginning of therapy, which has motivated their request for therapy, is stored in one or two modalities, leaving other modalities available for them to manifest themselves in a dynamic and creative way.

There was a schizophrenic patient who, despite possessing sensory capacities, lived his body without feeling either hot or cold, hardness or softness. He stood upright in the middle of corridors, rigid, like a plank of wood, his head raised towards the sky. He heard voices speaking to him, chastising him. It was futile to venture into the worlds of word or body; he was unable to form a relationship there. So we did drawings, mostly without talking, and sometimes when he quietly hummed a tune to himself, I did the same. It wasn't until much later that words were reinvested; initially there were words we could use to describe the drawings and objects in the world, and then gradually we began to talk about movements linked to drawings and relationships between people.

And then there was a young boy who told me long stories, not really with words, but with noises, actions, action figures, things he could bang or rub together, things he could push around, pierce and poke. He couldn't draw; his body jigged about as though it didn't belong to him, his limbs flung about in all directions as if torn by indecision. But his stories were densely peopled; he changed his tone of voice and the noises he made for each character and revisited them week after week in a complicated story where two groups confronted each other ferociously, until the bad guys died, but always came back to life. In each session, he organized the room so that he had space to reconstruct the battle scene; the whole room became a play-set.

At the beginning of a therapeutic intervention, the therapist's job is to sort out the frightening and upsetting modalities from those that quiver with life and where creativity is possible. It is not only a major poietic diagnostic tool, but a way for therapists to get a feeling for the direction in which to orient themselves with the person. Once these modalities are identified, it is generally useful to start work from a place where creativity is still possible. The therapeutic alliance is built where encounters can happen.

Intermodal decentering, much favored by expressive arts therapists, invites us to move away from repetitive suffering experienced in everyday life, towards artistic spaces that are available for experiencing other feelings, sensations, and ideas. It is also about moving away from suffering modalities in order to reconnect with life through those that offer more favorable conditions for transition.

Inter-modality is about the coexistence of several modalities. Clinical experience leads me to consider two kinds of inter-modality: *alternating inter-modality* and *simultaneous inter-modality*.

Alternating inter-modality supposes a more or less rapid oscillation between two or more modalities over a period of time. For example, doodling on a page, changing it graphically, and giving it a title can take a couple of minutes and uses two modalities—image and word.

It is useful for the therapist to locate the doorways between worlds and to go through them to whichever world is more favorable for the transformation of forms and human relationships, to further the person's artistic exploration and unfolding. This kind of inter-modality can be even more rapid, taking seconds or fractions of seconds, or it can be much slower, as in a whole day workshop when the morning is given over to sound and the afternoon to image.

Simultaneous inter-modality uses several modalities at a time. For example: the same doodle could evoke the smell and the movements of someone picking a flower. Two modalities are present at the same time—smell and corporeal movement, such that the modalities of image and word have faded into the background of existence; writing and drawing would then represent the mediality of this creative action. Simultaneity of several modalities can set up echoes between different forms. It is probable that these forms have less expressive and transformational power when experienced through only one modality.

Notions such as rhythm are trans-modal, meaning that they facilitate the simultaneous coexistence of several modalities in an appropriate manner, holding them together as a bundle. An example of this would be dance (movement), which generally relies on music (sound); both modalities of sound and movement are inhabited by rhythm, which brings them together.

The coexistence of modalities provokes unsteadiness, surprise, a disturbance in the established order of things in the world. But this makes it possible to see things differently, to have a new outlook on the world, a new perception and experience of ourselves.

It can be useful to explore more difficult modalities during the course of therapy, when the therapeutic alliance is sufficiently developed for such a companionship to be possible. It can sometimes happen that abandoned modalities are re-inhabited, so the patient can mobilize more modalities in which to feel themselves alive. Eventually, the possibilities and resources experienced in living modalities can be reintroduced into the more difficult ones.

The evaluation of modal and intermodal progression during therapy is a fascinating aspect of art therapy, and probably one of its main particularities. Generally, the changes that we talk about in terms of modality are well received by institutions, as we are the only professionals in the institutional team that can talk about and document such things with sensitivity, in any depth or precision. A phenomenological attitude respects the patient, their lived experience, their point of view and their resources. In this respect, Knill has opened the way for us, for which we are profoundly grateful.

On the one hand, we could say that it is not the work, the art work, that is important, but the working, the formation of forms, the *Gestaltung*, which happens in different modalities. On the other hand, we can say that the art therapist's skill is the ability to accompany the patient's working with their own working. Ideally, the two will crisscross each other and weave together a therapeutic relationship that is full of life, in which living passes from one to the other.

Let the poet in me have the last word.

> One day
> my gaze went from me
> left its mooring
>
> Then
> the crackling of leaves in the breeze
> bells in the distance
> a ray of sunshine on the green meadow
> grasses yellow dancing
> conifers exhaling
> arm flesh in cool shade
> leaf sap on my tongue
>
> The elsewhere of tides

References

Bion, W. (1965) *Transformations*. Paris: PUF.
Cage, J. (n.d.) 4'33. Available at www.youtube.com/watch?v=HypmW4Yd7SY, accessed on 01/16/17.
Knill, P. (1999) "Soul Nourishment or the Intermodal Language of Imagination." In S. K. Levine and E. G. Levine (eds) (1999) *Foundations of Expressive Arts Therapy*. London: Jessica Kingsley Publishers.
Knill, P., Barba, H.N. and Fuchs, M. (1995) *Minstrels of Soul: Intermodal Expressive Therapy*. Toronto: Palmerston Press.
Milner, M. (1957) *On Not Being Able to Paint*. London: Heinemann Educational Books.
Prinzhorn, H. (1922) *Bildnerei der Geisteskranken*. Berlin: Springer.
Stern, D. (2003) *Le moment présent en psychothérapie*. Paris: Odile Jacob.
Stitelmann, J. (2003) "Between crystal and compost: A gardening interrogation of Paolo Knill's theory of crystallisation." *POIESIS: A Journal of the Arts and Communication 5*, 48–59.
Stitelmann, J. (2009) "Le phénomène Poïétique." *Art et Thérapie 102–103*, 34–40.
Stitelmann J. (2015) *Formes et Modalités*. Genève: Edition du rebond.
Stitelmann, J. (n.d.) www.poietique.ch, accessed on 02/21/17.

5

THE POIETIC BASIS OF BEING

Thoughts on Expression and the Other Person Based on the Work of Merleau-Ponty

Majken Jacoby

Expression's condition and the field of the human being

One of the basic perspectives and challenges of the thinking of Merleau-Ponty is that the elements of his thoughts are interdependently connected and constituting one another. One conception or element cannot be captured without considering the others. To lay out a "first" and a "second," i.e., first we may consider an expressing, sensing "I" and second, there is "the other person" is bracketing the fact that they come together. The other person is there from the beginning, or always already there, as phenomenologists say in order to avoid the dubious idea of "beginning," of constituting who we are and how we may understand our situation by giving something the status of "first." In the thinking of Merleau-Ponty everything conditions everything else simultaneously, as if in a "now," and yet we are historical beings with a past and a future, with changing hearts and viewpoints that include and exclude each other.

All the same, there is a point of departure to any narrative, and to Merleau-Ponty it is the sensing of the living body. Sensing is the axis of his thinking as it expressively occurs to the bodily, "incarnated" human being. Because sensing happens the way it does, the world, my life, relations and the work of art appear as formed expression.

By sketching Merleau-Ponty's notion of sensing I will first describe the "situational field" of the human being in the world, his expressive condition. Then I will focus on "the other person" as his partner-in-expression, this fellow shaper who helps me, stands in my way, ignores or falls in love with me, or is absent when I need him, and last I return to the notion of form that appears in the work of Merleau-Ponty.

The living body is, as already said, a key notion to Merleau-Ponty. It is not the physiological body, and neither is it the body as a vehicle of ideas and thoughts. The living body (*le corps vécu*), inextricably bound to the world through sensing, is the shaping condition of human life's multiple and ambiguous expressions. To the living body, the world appears as a shaped and shaping habitat of views, landscapes and things, taking up their position in a space with a changing horizon. The living body sees, hears, moves, gestures. It is touching the things of the world with hands, ears or eyes; it is sounding forth a space that reciprocally shapes the sound. The living body of the human being inhabits a world that, all things considered, makes sense: today the sun is out, yesterday it rained, and the guest I am expecting can walk from the train station without getting wet. This primary sense-making is what determines the specific and changing situation of our daily lives, this is what conditions expression, the ongoing forming. The living body in the world is the living of a formative principle, so to speak: except living is never a principle.

It happens through sensing. Sensing is not a passive reproduction of images, neurophysiologically occurring "inside" the human being and projected "out" upon the world. This is the classical empirical approach, but to a phenomenologist like Merleau-Ponty sensing is not passive; it is actively taking part, even when the sensing person seems to "do" nothing actively apart from opening the eyes. Seeing, Merleau-Ponty's preferred sense modality, together with all sense modalities, happens to a living body in the world, and the constellation of body-in-world is the "making" of form.

"The Intertwining – the Chiasm" is the title of a chapter from a book Merleau-Ponty never got a chance to finish before his death. The title contains the principles of the act of sensing, as they appeared to him at the end of his life. The act of sensing, primary sense-making, manifests itself according to two disparate "modes," one characterized by its quality of intertwining and binding together, the other by its chiasmic, crossing-breaking quality. The appearance of the formed world, the "expressed" world, is thus the result of the act of a paradoxical principle, the continuous-discontinuous acting of sensing: sensing tears apart and binds together.

Reading Merleau-Ponty, one is struck by the two clusters of words that throughout his work characterize the qualities of the intertwining and the chiasm. Words like fabric, veil, weaving, tissue, folding, enfolding, confusing, overlapping, intermingling, simultaneity describe the notion of intertwining. They are images, or conjure up images, of a world of togetherness. They seem to indicate that more than anything we are together, interdependently and organically evolving from what was to what will be. They give a sense of continuity and coherence, of connection and cohesion, and in that sense they speak of a world where change happens as an evolutionary and causally traceable process.

The other chiasmic word-cluster consists of words like fissure, hole, cavity, separation, rupture, rupturing, tear, edge, splitting, breaking, punctuation, crisscrossing. These are words that ring into an uneven world of instability and discontinuation, of displacement and disjoining, where incidents and accidents suddenly emerge, and changes take place unforeseeably. This is gathered in the notion of the chiasm. As the chiasm does not necessarily carry a sense of "falling to pieces" as an expression of despair, so "the intertwining" of the other word-cluster does not necessarily point to an evenness and cohesion that is essentially hopeful. Despair and hope emerge in the double determination of intertwining and chiasm: in their contradiction, so to speak. One cannot imagine the one without the other. They are complementary, point to differences and "same-nesses," even make them possible in so far as any differentiation needs differences—and these are, one could say, being's basic differentiation principles upon which all expression stands—but they do not form an opposition, an either-or, like a team of cohesion-players playing to win against a team fighting for no cohesion. Hope and despair, and with them all states of being, are connected to the twin-existence of sameness and difference, as founding principles of expression, of formation's possibility. Neither is more founding than the other; we are founded on paradox. That there is a ring or an atmosphere of apprehension around words like "breaking" and "rupturing" has doubtlessly to do with their association to destruction. Destruction, however, need not come as a rupture or a break; there is equally the destruction that has a character of dissolution, or the destructive character of the meaning-net being held too tightly around us as in all the variations of fundamentalism, or the destructive effects of petrification, or the destruction that follows when no distance is possible. It is a sneaking, silent destruction that comes not as a volcano but as a gradual poisoning of the air; the breathing becomes laborious, reflection stops, and we go blind and deaf.

In a porous world of weaving and fracturing, of joining and disjoining, it is senseless to imagine a world where everything makes sense, where everything, in one way or another, fits in wholes without fractures or fissures, without doubts and questions. Fracturing, weaving, fissures and wholes are equally foundational, not each other's denial or eradication. Dislocation and displacement are as inherent to the human world-field as are cohesion and continuity; sense and senselessness make each other. Together they guarantee the openness of the field. Together they are the precondition of poiesis. And the synthesis, the inventing of a conceptual principle that folds the one into the other, will, instead of bringing more understanding, reduce and obscure the changing view of the open space. It will deaden the flesh's passion of becoming, necessary for any impregnation or formation, any speaking, and, accordingly, fall into inconsequence, one version of ruin, and one more condition of destruction. What makes sense is forever married to what does not make sense.

The propensity to close the holes of incomprehensibility and ignore contradictions is not difficult to understand; apart from the fact, however, that it is an experiential impossibility to reach total comprehension, any thing or idea would dissolve in familiarity and predictability, as would we, if we imagined away incomprehensibility. We live as much from what makes sense as from what does not. We become alive in the tension of what we do and do not grasp and know.

This is the field of the human being, a characterization of his or her expressive situation. Here the subject, one could say, "takes up his position in the world of meaning." Here the subject stands as the reflecting, imagining, shaping and speaking member of a world of coherence and rupture, alternately making sense and no sense of his life; the human field of the poietic, erotic tension of value and sense making.

The attraction of expression

The tension shifts and intensifies the moment another person enters my field; indeed, my field remains mine, and yet it becomes my field-with-another-person-and-his-field. Our gazes catch each other. This reciprocity of the gaze, which becomes almost threatening "if each of us feels his actions to be not taken up and understood, but observed as if they were an insect's" (Merleau-Ponty 1962, 2001, p.361) and which makes a loop without beginning and end, arrests momentarily my acting and disturbs. Who is there? I become eminently aware of my own bodily—and to myself partially visible—shape as well as his. He is like me. We are different. We take part in the same world and share a twin-life, and yet we are different to a degree that communication beyond the initial glance may be a task too demanding. I do not know what he will do and say. His presence is like a question, what does he want? There is a pull, an attraction to this other body that is not a thing but a person, and by turns I feel comfortable and uncomfortable, like a stranger not only to him but also to myself, when he is there. For a while, perhaps just for an instant, my "position in the world of meaning" is less self-evident, it is being scrutinized, looked upon by other eyes, and, by that simple fact, it is under questioning. What has changed? When I place myself close to him our gazes are almost parallel, we see roughly the same; surely the children I have been watching playing on the sidewalk have not changed. Yet, now they have become children-playing-while-we-look. It is a different experience. Together with the other person comes his "position in the world of meaning," and our reciprocally overlapping field-net has gained in complexity. Meaning opens to its other possibilities. The presence of the other person, even his mere existence in my imagination, has an impact on my situation; it crystallizes the complexity of being-together-being-apart. It brings to the foreground the multiplicity and contradictions of our common ground. Does he, do I, do we know our position in the world of meaning? Maybe he would like to join the children in their ball game, the rules of which I do not know. Maybe he hates kids.

"My" field is thus never just mine. It is composite, a field-web of overlapping other fields, the impure common ground of bits and pieces, of stories and images that shape meaning and position us. On the one hand my field-web secures for me a certain hold on the world, a bodily sense-making that goes without saying like an erotic primacy, and on the other hand I am exposed to the demand of making sense of things and events myself. The backwards, reflective look understands the past on the condition of one perspective or another. My history becomes history seen through the light of change. It "requires one more moment, bounded by the horizon of its future, and requiring in its turn further developments to be understood" (Merleau-Ponty 1962, 2001, p.135). Understanding is partial, even when we really seem to "get it," and the memory that sweeps over my past binds together events, places and times that may or may not take me by surprise, as if, nevertheless, it were in the grip of an infatuation. The ground is uncertain.

This other person—fellow human being, *Mit-Mensch*, potential friend, traitor, lover, neighbor, thief, child—possesses himself in the same certain-uncertain way as I do and as sensing and thinking possess him. To "have" sensibility, sensibility must have had him. His seeing is a variation in Seeing, and he is a self by virtue of his ability to exchange his vision with another, to position himself differently in a world of Visibility and Mobility, elements of the element of flesh that lies in-around him and between us as latent possibility-traces of shaping. He is a self I cannot quite localize: where is this self, that is him, is he "in" his voice, "in" his facial features, "in" his body's mass, this thing that is not a thing, but speaking and looking at me, like me? If I approach him "frontally" he eludes me. He is, rather, "by my side;" and he is different. He is what would be lacking, if he did not exist.

"…there is a myself who is other, which dwells elsewhere and deprives me of my central location…" (Merleau-Ponty 1962, 2001, p.39). I am not at the hub of the world, not even of my own. The other person embodies an otherness that opens my field, so much so that I become other. I am thrown off my center, decentered. Centrum moves off toward the periphery, it holds not forever: who is subject and who is object? There is always another, and although his space was always already prefigured in my space, I am stirred up by his elusive yet bodily being-there. Not that "his space" is prefigured as a manifestation of the Structuring World Spirit behind the material world, but prefigured as the living body"s necessary bond to the living body of the other, complementing one another as of one system of call and response, the one attracting the other. He is another that is my other, taking part in the same world and looking at me, seeing with eyes as eye-like as mine, holding my gaze, or shading for the sun that is also my sun, buttoning his coat against the strong wind that makes me shiver.

The presence of the other almost forces reflection on me. Is there an eros of reflection? Certainly there is a joy when the words come out right, their message adding to what can be grasped, and there is a strong pull-push in that which disturbs and disrupts and questions the hold I seemingly have on the world. Does it turn into disgust? I want to "get it." I want to understand not only as a way of asserting my will upon an unruly situation, to order it into meaning-positions that so far made sense, but as much to stay in touch with the other person and the pleasure-pain-disgust-anger-surprise that comes with it, the eros of living with or without rather than living carelessly, inconsequentially. I want to be disturbed. I want to reflect.

My bodily, silent world-knowledge and self-awareness is jerked loose from its habitual position, it is pushed out of equilibrium and that calls for an act of expression: Words? Gestures? Something wants to be shaped. A distancing has occurred, the necessary distance of reflection.

Living and looking bodies are pulled toward each other. Their moving-seeing-and-seeing-further attracts and distracts them, and time and space add more dimensions to their changing relationship. It is a partnership of proximity and distance, and it appears as acts of expression of gesturing, reflecting, thinking, imagining.

The existence of the other person in my life is forever. I cannot possibly think him away. I can call him back any moment, if not in the flesh then in imagination. I can forget or ignore him, I can turn my back on him but our reciprocal bodily awareness has from now on (and this "now" has always already happened) thrown me into a place where not only the "otherness" of the world, but also the otherness of the other person echoes forth my own otherness, and reflection emerges. Is this I? I am an object to myself. I look for my face. I search for my face in his face. The categories blur. He is like-me-unlike-me. We are subject-object to our selves and to each other, and we speak, including one another in the loop of speaker-and-listener. A loop of shaping.

The pull of shaping is erotic. I long to speak and act. Speaking and acting force themselves on me when there is someone to speak to and act with. There is a desire of the flesh that condenses and concentrates when the other becomes a reality to me that makes mine real. I must speak. I must act. Indeed I can refuse to respond, I can ignore the desire to shape, and whatever is between or in front of us will retreat and its possible value will be denied or lost. But not forever; next time, with another other perhaps, it is there again, offering me the possibility of shaping. Expression unfolds in a realm where the other person exists; he may be ever so far away.

Thus, the existence of the other person and my relation to him secures my thinking and my speaking, my words and my thoughts, my bodily acting. The desire of the flesh tends to crystallize between us, and we-of-the-world are caught in language: "Hello" acquires a sense. If speech and reflection specifically characterize human beings, then the other person and I become humans to each other by speech; speaking is essentially a speaking to, a being spoken to. In the attraction of bodies to bodies, and with their oscillation between proximity and distance, are born the twins of language and reflection, the in- and ex-carnation of the flesh.

There he is, this witness to my existence and its expression in all senses of the word. He is my co-seer, whose seeing makes mine real, whose eyes on me turns me into somebody "to be seen," a some-body of self-seeing and world-seeing, a partner in Visibility. His witnessing turns me into "expression" that ultimately only makes sense if it is conceived as a call to be responded to. By being more than alone, literally or imaginatively, the not-yet-maybe-never-possibility of the flesh becomes an actual possibility. Now I can. I can, because something else and somebody else can. There is an "act-ability" in the fissuring and intertwining of the sensible that breeds action, and because I am not alone it becomes actual. I speak to him and because of him. The other becomes a witness to the silent and audible voices of reflection, acting and speech. The other that is also myself.

He is "with" me, this other person, he is a *Mit-Mensch*, a fellow human being, also when he stands as my adversary, also when he ignores me or is absent. He figures in my landscape. If he did not, my field of meaning would collapse. In what shape he will appear is impossible to say exactly, and of what kind our relationship will be is equally open. However, there is a relation between us, if only for a moment, if only until one of us turns away, ignoring or refusing the other. An aborted relation is a relation nevertheless. "The refusal to communicate, however, is still a form of communication" (Merleau-Ponty 1962, 2001, p.363).

There is an attraction between the same and the different. There is eros between the world and me and between me and the other person.

Exactly the otherness, "the alien presence" (Merleau-Ponty 1962, 2001, p.363), the tension that comes with that thing, person or event, which positions itself by making small or big waves in my world; its very strangeness pushes me toward articulation, be it in lamentation or praise, in artistic expression or the expressions of everyday life. The attractive and repulsive otherness, in the world, in the other person and in me myself, is foundational to my sense-making: the poietic basis of my life rests upon and is bound to a co-habitation with aliens as well as non-aliens.

To sum it up: there is an unending circuit between the human being, the other and the world. It is, in principle, never cut off, we are always caught in "the tissue of being," even though we forget it or deny it, even when we feel cut off and isolated. Despite this unbreakable tie, we are handed over to, or exposed to, our own sense-making. As I take up my position in the world, the other person takes up his, and as much as I am unique and singular, my singularity presupposes the other and his strangeness to my world. Our relation is equally one of joining and disjoining. He embodies exemplarily the cluster of paradoxes and contradictions that shapes me and pushes me into articulation. By his sensing living body he demonstrates our togetherness and separateness as in one instant. We are same-and-different. There is another myself that is another himself. In everything he does, the tension of sense and non-sense between his actions and mine is constellated; his looking at me turns me into something seen, as my look upon him does it to him. I become a member of the visible world, one of very many "members" yet superbly singular, and I begin to see myself, literally and metaphorically: I search for a face. Through the other person I am drawn into the world of reflection and language, of expression in all media, transcending the matter of my corporeality. Our communication and relation rests on the "fundamental contradiction" (Merleau-Ponty 1962, 2001, p.365) between twins who are also strange to each other.

The existence of the other makes shaping possible; it is the eros of the relationship that pushes us to strive for form. The differentiation and precision of speaking depends on careful listening, as well as listening is dependent on being spoken to. The precision of any forming or shaping depends on the shaping I meet. The other person throws me off balance, in doubt, cracking the situation open by his mere presence and thus forcing me to think and act. He is with me, closely and at a distance. He is my co-actor and my witness. Articulation happens in our joint situation. I speak as a response to a call from the otherness of the person who witnesses me as other.

Is it a love affair? Sometimes. The joy when something works is indisputable. It is this longed-for side effect that is only obtainable when whatever is there-to-be-shaped finds its "right shape"—the shaping medium not withstanding, whether it be a relation between me and the other person, thing, idea, thought, work of art, even if it be ever so ephemeral. There is a pleasure, when the words come out right, and relief, surprise and satisfaction when they also are understood, "caught in the other end," as Merleau-Ponty (1993) says in the essay "Cézanne's Doubt." It makes sense to more-than-me, and it shatters the loneliness and isolation that, at times, accompany me and indeed follow in the wake of expression not caught in the other end or misunderstood.

The desire of the flesh, this invisible realm of possibility in which both I and the other person are steeped, guarantees nothing specifically, just opens to the possibility of "something." My relation to the other person is indispensable in order for me to be not only one of many but also one of a kind, for my finding my face. It is indispensable for my ability to reflect and speak, imagine and materially shape. Sensing itself depends on the other person; his sensing opens to more and different aspects in mine. He is forever built into my life, and the particular relationship follows all kinds of courses. Our ambiguous selves (abyss, node, cross field, act-ability?) take up their positions in the middle of the contradictions of things.

If it is an affair of love, it is what can happen when the uncertain space of multiple interpretations and shaping possibilities is more-than-usually-open, and, accordingly, when the contradictions are allowed their paradoxical presence. It is a space we can only stay in for a limited span of time. The space of love is the space of possibility, as a fleeting concretization of the ephemeral sphere of the flesh. It is the space where Victor Turner's communitas happens, the sense of unity and care among human beings equally exposed to the uncertainty of the folds and fissures of being. And, according to Turner (1969), it will always pass. If we try to hold on to it in its spontaneous shape and demand or command it beyond its manifestation, or rid it of its paradoxical base, it petrifies.

If there were no other and otherness, if everything made sense from finite and definable points of view, the world would forever stay flat, stretching from here to there. Similarly, if my relation to the other person would be rid of its ambiguity, the relationship would lose its attraction to an all-pervading familiarity. I would dissolve into a desert of known-ness. I would be without distinction, have no voice, no individual style, because there would be no otherness to make the life-giving crack in the familiar. There would be only an engulfing eternity of the same; no thought, no reflection, no future, no past. The poietic basis of being would be replaced by prosaic functioning.

The experience of otherness is vital to my survival. I cannot survive only alone or only together. And, certainly, I cannot survive only different or only same. By literally being born by another human being and being different and strange even to her—"She has your eyes, but look at that nose, where does that come from?"—I am immediately also a stranger. I am immediately set apart.

Can our likenesses be found, if we are not allowed our strangeness? The other as exactly other, and the other as another myself, this fundamental contradiction is vital to the poetic act of finding form on all levels of expression.

Finding form: The aesthetic condition

The notion of form that emerges from the above has, so to speak, "otherness" as a built-in quality. Firstly, it is form-as-participation. It is equally in and out of the eyes of somebody, it even gives eyes to this living body of somebody: form is not an acquisition of her or him, but "captured at the other end."

The body in the world, a partnership between two separate entities, is the point of departure of the shaping of difference and sameness. Form is body shaped by another body, being's desire of linking body to another body, world, thing or human being. We take part and we act our part in a pulsating and porous field, the circumference or horizon of which is open, uncertain, incomplete, always up for questioning, always situated upon other fields, yet never completely identical with any other but slightly askew. Expression in its infinite variations is the incessant attempts at shaping the relation to the world, with ourselves and each other; it is the continuous formulation of the shaping of the inhabitant among other inhabitants; to expect its completion or full formulation is a contradiction in terms, and to see it as a progress towards an imagined perfection blurs vision to the fact, that falling away, dying out and fragmenting is as much part of formation's foundation as is coming into being and into form. Expression is steps taken in a fog, with no guarantee of a stepping stone somewhere, or somebody to go to, yet *Wechselgesang*,[1] *Weltmöglichkeit*[2]...

Second, it lies in the paradoxical otherness of the dynamics of sensing. Sensing itself makes a mark, without which there is no sensing, shaping by virtue of the double acting of the intertwining and the chiasm. The coming-into-form carries the double paradox, on the one hand of otherness as that which-is-not-the-same and, on the other hand, as fragmentation, breakdown and dissolution. Following these contrary principles of manifestation, Merleau-Ponty unites an always incomplete form-realization of experience with a certain stability and coherence. Form keeps, and it also breaks down, appears anew or appears differently, sometimes almost at the same time. Stability is carrying instability as a founding condition. The experience that something changes is only possible because not all changes simultaneously.

Merleau-Ponty links the notion of form, expression, to the world without placing it either as an ideal formality in matter itself or "in" an otherworldly realm of formative "ideas," or, on the other hand, as a subjective and relative manifestation that is only culturally determined: the fact that the world appears as form links us to it, and vice versa. The linking goes two ways. The appearance of form does not happen "according to a norm;" it is the "beginning of a norm," a beginning that takes place all the time, one might say. There is always an element of incompletion to any view. The formative condition of sensing sets the stage on ambiguous ground and the formed world appears as simultaneously changing and stable. However, it secures a shaped "something" that allows us to shape further in innumerable ways and in "all" media, in thought, language and artistic expression. Because of the openness of the notion of form, the expressive range is principally endless. Even though the singular formative act closes in upon itself, the formative horizon is always open.

Artistic expression is connected to the same notion of form. Otherness is inherent to artistic expression as to other kinds of

---

[1] This loosely translates as antiphony, an old music form of call-and-response; literally it means "antiphonic world-possibility."
[2] The possibility for something to become real, actualized and out in the world; call-and-response leading to a possibility in the world.

expression. Moreover, artistic expression positions itself as other in relation to everyday expression. Everyday life is, one might say, constituted by qualities of recognition and cohesion. It is determined by familiarity. The power of daily life derives from being-as-usual. It stands on the necessary illusion that "things" stand on and "acts" happen on stable ground, allowing us to comprehend and function rather unhindered by thoughts of the contrary. Its worries and pains are "comprehended" and comprehendable. It rests, so to speak, on an exaggeration and maintenance of the intertwining aspect of sense-making. It "forgets" the disruptive side of the world.

The artistic expression and process have a less restricted relation to "things as they usually are." Since the artwork cannot help us catch the bus or go to the grocery store, it does not need to stabilize habits and the conditions of everyday life. That is taken care of by everyday living itself. On the contrary: it de-familiarizes. One might even say that artistic expression "lives" from standing next to life-as-usual and watching its "strange" unfolding, strange itself. It becomes an embodiment of what is other to everyday life. By its mere existence it creates a fissure between the usual and the un-usual, and in that sense it "remembers" what everyday life must forget in order to be everyday life.

Of course, everyday life is not a continuous flow of "the same," but if "the same" were not the dominant quality, everyday life would cease to be. Artistic expression opens to the otherness inherent not only to itself, but also to daily living. It questions the self-evidence of everyday categorizations. It reminds us of the chiasmic and disruptive and strange side of the world.

Expression in art plays with the limits of the supposed and real necessity of categorizations as such. The artwork becomes a concretization of the categorical confusion we tend to overlook and want to order in place. Otherness becomes otherness in the encounter with the same; the expression of everyday life and the artistic expression test reciprocally the validity of each other, ask of each other disturbing and unanswerable questions. They give a contour to each other; they allow each to evaluate what is.

That is what partners do. They "intertwine" and they "chiasm." The otherness of form secures the possibility of form, secures that "sameness" will never "win" over what is "other," as otherness will never eradicate the same. The existence of all that is also there, and particularly the other person, the fact that we are not only alone, activates the formative possibilities toward realization as well as annihilation.

We are given a world and given to a world that appears on the basis of a paradox. The paradoxical and ambiguous ground of sensing is what we are exposed to, stand on, and a sense of the beauty that comes with the twilight and the possible as well as the bright colors and the decisive statement is the challenging gift of being alive. That is the expressive condition of the human being. It binds together and pulls apart, it appears as finite form and it breaks and frays at the edges.

The human being is the living of an open formative principle, bound to a unique and concretely shaped position in the midst of multiple formative possibilities. The possibility of the singular and precise expression—"this is what I think"—is preconditioned by what is already said or thought, what is not thought and what is unthinkable, and it prefigures more thought, more saying. It is the acting "now" of the intertwining and the chiasm. It is *eros* acting on contrary ground, pushing "I" and "other" into a shape of expression and meaning among multiple shaping possibilities.

We cannot elevate our shaping, our stand, our position in the world of meaning, above the contrary tendencies and the ensuing tensions of intertwining and chiasm that make it. We cannot command the world according to our position. We can, however, act, make a mark while being marked, and thus stay in touch with the poietic basis of Being.

References

Merleau-Ponty, M. (1962, 2001) *Phenomenology of Perception*. London: Routledge.
Merleau-Ponty, M. (1973) "Dialogue and the Perception of the Other." In *The Prose of the World*. Evanston, IL: Northwestern University Press.
Merleau-Ponty, M. (1993) "Cézanne's Doubt." In *The Merleau-Ponty Aesthetic Reader: Philosophy and Painting*. Evanston, IL: Northwestern University Press.
Turner, Victor (1969) *The Ritual Process*. Boston, MA: Aldine De Gruyter.

Part II

THERAPY

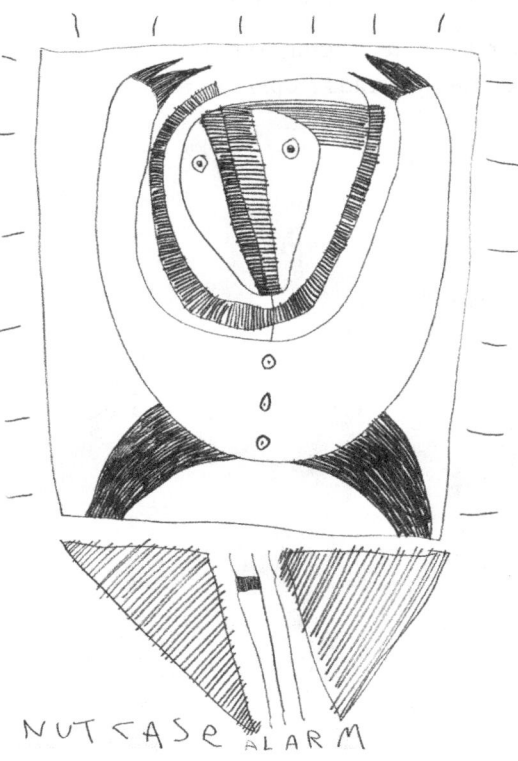

Nutcase Alarm   Rowesa Gordon

Practicum on the Eating Disorders Ward: Sonnet 1
Shara Claire

Bone-etched, your surface is a kind of gray:
its quality of light turned dark, like fear.
(The elevator opens to my day.)
My wish: a mountain stream to rinse us clear

of heavy lines that mark off *this* or *that*,
or *do*, or *don't*—these rules, they weigh more now
than you. I touched your sweatered, narrow back
and felt the knot of what you won't allow.

And what I won't. Sweet bird, I'm not so far
from land you call your own. Your stories stir
the vinegar of longing—*more bone, more*—
within my own confines. Still a concern.

(Eleventh floor. I'm here, hoping to pin
a little sign to you that reads *I win*.)

6

THE ARTS WORK

The Process of Intermodal Decentering in Professional Conversations

Herbert Eberhart

Relationship is Alpha and Omega

Relationship is an important dimension of any form of psychotherapy, counseling or coaching. A professional relationship in a process that includes art-making needs the professional to hold an attentive and open presence. Additionally, the relationship should have a containing or "holding" quality so that the client or patient feels safe enough to explore and try out new artistic expressions, new thoughts and even new feelings.

We like to speak of the need for an "appreciative curiosity" (Eberhart 2002, p.2). This expression emphasizes both an appreciative, caring, respectful, non-judgmental attitude and an invitational, animating, playful curiosity that wants to know more, explore deeper and go one step further.

The quality of an encounter shows itself partially in both the verbal and non verbal behavior of the participants. Carl Rogers and others have pointed out that the congruency and authenticity of the professional plays an important role. Not all dimensions of a professional relationship can be externally monitored or videotaped. Some of the most important ones are only recognizable in the encounter itself. For example, false curiosity from the counselor has no worth, and may even have negative effects. It has to be authentic, to mirror a real interest in the other person and the way he is trying to manage his life.

My own professional experiences show that in a first meeting it helps to find out what is important for a client. "What is your favorite thing to do in such a situation?" is a question that leads in this direction.

This is one of the successful ways "to develop the fit," as one would say in systems therapy. For me, as an old, experienced psychologist, it is also favorable when there is a situation where clients are able to help me. For example, I could ask them to repeat a sentence very slowly, in order to help me make a verbal note of it.

The result of such a professional relationship is, metaphorically, a sort of dance where the evolving melody leads both partners' movements. Sometimes one of the two initiates a new sequence of steps and the other follows.

An adequate language

During the last decades, expressive arts work (EXA) has carefully developed different ways to enable clients to approach the arts and find adequate forms of expression in all modalities. The same attentiveness and carefulness is needed for the language portion of a session. In a coaching session, for example, the time allotted for conversation normally is much longer than the time for art-making.

In this phase of our methodological development, we have to give more attentiveness to the verbal part of our work. I am pleading for an "artistic language" within art-oriented professional work. It is neither poetry nor prose. It is an elaborated form of everyday language that is sensitized toward expression and wording.

This language is not yet worked out in detail. It will need the collaboration of other professionals in the field. Some aspects from my own perspective may be formulated here.

An artistic language moves near the senses. That means it is concrete and specific and avoids all sort of generalizations and abstractions. Instead of nouns—a preference of German speakers—we try to use verbs and adjectives. An artistic language is rich and open to varied and new perspectives. This leads to a preference for the subjunctive mood and attentiveness to all sorts of metaphoric expressions, especially the ones that are spontaneously used by clients. Overall, sensitivity to wording seems to be the main point. This sensitivity is as much about listening as it is about the formulation of words and sentences.

The resource-oriented foundation

Art-making in an EXA way is always resource-oriented. A client without education in any of the different art modalities will never reach a "work" without having, or being led by, a resource-oriented attitude. The client needs to trust themselves, to trust the process, the evolving something, the pleasure of the unexpected. And this needs the professional companionship of a witness and facilitator.

I personally have learned a lot from the founders of the solution-focused approach: Steve de Shazer (e.g., de Shazer 1985), Insoo Kim Berg (e.g., de Jong and Berg 1998) and Michael White (e.g., White and Epston 1989). However, when working with the arts, something more is needed. First, an understanding of the possibilities of art materials and some experience with forms of low-skill artistic expressions are necessary. This results in clear instruction. We also need playful, inventive, curious trust in the art process, and a sort of courageous modesty. This means letting the artwork find its way and having the courage to intervene in a clear and friendly way. There is no doubt for me that there is also a spiritual aspect to the work, although we don't like to speak so much about it in our field, lest we be placed on an esoteric fringe.

Resource-orientation leads therapeutic conversations and also directs the observations and focus. This doesn't mean that the concerns, problems or suffering of a person are neglected or overseen, but that the focus is on resources: their appreciation, activation and cultivation. This includes a careful exploring of goals and visions that describe a "good future" in the realm of the concerns.

In my experience, it has been helpful to explore not only actual concerns, but also positive former situations that had some similarities to the present one, and to make a sort of inventory of "all" (behavior, attitudes, characteristics, people, circumstances and so on) that had helped and furthered good steps. Doing this, hope, that powerful catalyst of motivation, rises, and it rises without speaking about it. It is not as much a hope in the process, or in the capacity of the professional, but a hope in possibilities and capacities. I always do this before working with the arts so we can start the artwork in a sphere of hope.

Challenge and playfulness
(or: "doing something else")

In my clinical practice, the episode of art-making is normally presented as an episode of "doing something else." I ask my clients if they are ready for it or if something more needs to be said. If they give consent, and they regularly do, I add, "Then we have to stand up." And we both do it. This simple movement changes the situation totally. At this moment there is no doubt that "something else" will happen. If it is the client's first session, he has no idea what will happen. If it is the third or fourth time, he is eager to hear or see what sort of material or task I will present this time.

I like to work with everyday materials: a pot of water, some empty glasses and a small stick to compose "a little serenade" in a series of takes, a big sheet of thick white paper to do "anything you want" with, or some sandwich bags that can be easily formed into a set of figures for an exhibition. If there is enough time, I ask the client to enrich the created work in an intermodal transfer—perhaps a short poem, which normally ends in a little performance.

These instructions animate exploration and sensual discovery, leading sometimes more toward sensitivity, and sometimes more toward challenge. In any case, there has to be time for a tuning in. It includes a sensitive and sensual first contact with the art material, a trying out, and, depending on the situation, a selection of objects and colors. In his detailed comments, Paolo Knill explains the importance and the different ways of doing this in different art disciplines (Knill 2005).

The arts live in their own realm. It is the task of the professional to support his client, but also to let him be carried off in this realm. It leads to another reality and type of perceiving, and opens to beauty. Some things are required for this to happen: the space provided has to be safe and open—this means clear frames of time and space, and an attitude that is ready to welcome any surprises that may arrive. This is possible when the professional decenters himself. He is a servant to the emerging work. This often means to be an attentive, interested and curious witness. But sometimes it includes leading or animating, or breaking a rule, or adding another material, or expanding the available time.

My personal experiences show that with my clientele, who are often professionals themselves, one has to find a mixture of playfulness and challenge. With a client who is a manager, this "mixture" might be more on the side of challenge, along with something that obviously cannot be foreseen within the artistic process. This is also true for clients with a perfectionist side. A short time limit is a good way to reinforce the challenge. A short time frame is helpful as well for those who tend to hesitate or make a lot of plans before they begin something new. What I try to avoid is giving a person the impression that he has to do something childish or that it is possible to do the artwork in a casual way. Mostly it is helpful when a playful or curious side of a person is triggered by the artistic task.

All these remarks do not mean that I would try to invent a tailored task for each of my clients. I do it more by intuition. What matters first is that each client becomes very engrossed in the art work, even if it is only a ten- or fifteen-minute task, and second, that at the end there is a work that at least is OK. Often the reaction is more positive. Clients are surprised and pleased by the emerging work, sometimes at the moment of its arrival, sometimes not until we begin to speak about it.

The bridge to everyday life

Art-making itself may have a soul-lifting, nourishing or even healing effect, if there is enough time to stay with it. In a coaching situation where the artistic episode is short, it needs adequate processing to guarantee a sustainable effect.

Back to language, or recognizing work and process

When the work is finished, I ask the client for a description of the work and the process that led to it. If the work is something tangible, we first choose the "best" perspective for observers.

The "aesthetic analysis" (which is a bit of a misleading name) is a description of work and process and is a part of the decentering episode itself. It can be seen as a continuation of the decentering via other means. For me it is, above all, a bridge from doing and experiencing to speaking. And it stays clearly within the alternative world experience. That means that we try to stay on a descriptive level, to "stay on the surface," as we call it, and to avoid any sort of interpretation, whether referring to psychological theories or to the client's own experiences and concerns from their daily world. Some of my clients require quite an effort to remain in a descriptive mode, and not to tell me all the interesting interpretations and associations that come up. It helps when I tell them that in a later stage of our work ("harvesting") there will be a possibility of returning to these connections.

The aesthetic analysis is an important stage. It opens the eyes to the richness of the work, to details and surprising perspectives and it makes clients aware of their creative potentiality and their capability to prove themselves in a challenging situation. And at the same time it is the first distancing from the clients' own experience.

Harvesting

When we leave the art studio and sit again on the chairs where the conversation began, the time has come to build the bridge to the situation of the client. The formulation of the initial question for this stage of the work is intentionally very open.

We ask for possible connections between the decentering phase and the previous situation. That means we ask for free associations. We are not looking to special symbolic structures or categories of meaning. None of the ideas that come up have to be justified or explained, and we don't stop our questioning before having written down at least six different possibilities.

I like the term "harvesting." It shows something of the essence of this stage. The formulations that come up are not logical derivations or summaries of things that happened during the decentering. They are "fruits" falling from the "tree of self-healing" (or self-organization). Sometimes a formulation may sound quite reasonable and logical. Sometimes neither coach nor coachee has the slightest idea what an association could mean.

I make a verbal note of all that is said in this period, then read all the associations again and let the client choose the one that seems, for the moment, most attractive. My personal guess is that one could work with every one of these associations. But no doubt it is more effective to work with the one most compelling in the moment.

The formulations that come up in the harvest mostly are general, abstract and sometimes even obscure. "The rhythm," "playfulness," "to sense the power in the body," "to construct," "I am the driver," "passion," "spontaneity." These are concrete formulations that some of my clients have liked to work with. Very seldom does a formulation from the harvesting stage include something like an instruction on how to act. Mostly they are hints or "second degree solutions." We have to work to shape them into a form that we are able to directly deal with. This leads us to the last stage of this work.

Integrating

Let us begin with an example.

> In our initial session, Mrs Inewsky, a young counselor, chooses from her list of eight associations the formulation "I am the driver" as most interesting. I ask her what that could mean concretely, and she answers, "I lead. If I don't do what all the other counselors do, it is OK." And then she adds, laughing, "The melody will come out in any case." In the decentering phase she has worked with two "rain-sticks" (see below). She is currently on vacation from work.
>
> "When will you be back at work in your office, and what would this signify?" I ask.
>
> "On January 24th, when I will have new clients again, I will look at what melody will come out," she answers.
>
> "What could I observe?" I ask.
>
> "I will be more cheerful, more relaxed, not as hectic as usual."
>
> Since these formulations are not really concrete, I reply, "You see, I've only known you about an hour. If I were there in your office on January 24th, invisible, but a careful observer, what could I concretely see?"
>
> "You would see me smiling. I would move quietly, at a moderate pace. I would greet new clients cheerfully. And maybe I would even make a joke."
>
> "And if I could possibly see inside of you," I add, "what could I observe?"
>
> "I am relaxed, excited, joyful and curious, interested in what sort of melody would show up." The conversation goes on a little more. Mrs Inewsky thinks that she will begin to improvise more in her work—looking at a conversation with a new client more as an experiment and maybe even as fun.

As this example shows, the conversation phase of integration serves to concretize the associations arising in the harvest and to deduce consequences for the situations in question. At this moment nobody knows if the chosen associations point to a "real" connection between the decentering work and the initial concerns. We work on a totally hypothetical basis. Only the outcome will show if the connection was real and important. And it nearly always works!

The arts work! (Three examples)

To illustrate the effects of this work, here are three short examples from my private practice.

Zara Inewsky

Zara Inewsky, the counselor in the above section on integration, has been working in a vocational guidance center for a year. She is not native Swiss, but she worked in a similar profession in her home country for a few years, then finished her postgraduate education in vocational guidance in Switzerland. She comes to me for supervision. She works exclusively with jobless clients. Her main concern is the pressure she feels as a newcomer to "produce" a solution for each of her clients. She is also aware that she puts pressure on herself, and says that she wishes "to treat myself in a more tender and loving way."

In one session, we have a long conversation where I ask her to report things that work well in her professional life, and to describe a future without pressure. I also ask her to describe three occasions where she was tender toward herself. Following this, she agrees to move into an art-making phase.

I give her two rain-sticks with the task of working on a sequence of sounds that pleases her. After the fourth take, she has found a rhythmic melody with some variations—a tapping on the floor that "would inspire me to walk through the room." The aesthetic analysis brings a detailed description, and the harvesting brings the following associations: the simple rhythm, the courage to variegate and take space, to accept beauty, to follow beauty, to feel the strength in the body; I am the driver; I am permitted to.

In the next months, the chosen association "I am the driver" turns out to be one of the actual life-themes of Mrs Inewsky. In the second session, she refers to another association ("the courage to vary") and wants to know how to do this more in her daily work. In an interim evaluation two months later, she reports that "the experience with the rain-sticks is an unforgettable one, but the results from it still stand on shaky legs." Then she tells me about her mother, with whom only peak performances were noteworthy.

In the next sessions it becomes clear that "things are on the way." And it turns out that changes in her behavior toward clients and colleagues are easier than changes in her self-image. When we close our collaboration about seven months after beginning, the melody of the rain-sticks is still present. It was with her through all these weeks and months as a concrete experience, a sort of vision and an anchor for her developmental goals.

Mrs Reinold

Mrs Reinold is a lady in her seventies who lives alone and deeply misses her string quartet that hasn't met for about a year. She writes poems, but has never had the courage to present them in public or make an effort to publish them. She has two sons and stays in loose contact with the elder and is in an enmeshed relationship with the younger. Since his divorce, her younger son has lived in Mrs Reinold's town with his eight-year-old daughter who is often with her grandmother during the week. Mrs Reinold wants "to have a goal in her life and to reach this goal" or—more concretely—to stay authentic and also open to the possibility of "coming out" as a poet or something else.

After our first session, she presents two poems at an event—but following this success, our work is more or less stuck. Mrs Reinold speaks about herself in quite a harsh way and is ashamed that so many people were, and still are, able to manipulate her throughout her life.

In our third session she shows herself totally horrified by the atomic disaster of Fukushima and begins to speak about the "black world views" of some well-known Swiss poets and philosophers. To bring her back to herself, I propose a decentering episode and she agrees. I give her the same task with the rain-sticks as Zara Inewsky.

Mrs Reinold likes the steady, quiet flowing and is fascinated by the "massive sound" that results when all the grains fall at once and by the total silence that follows. She gives a detailed description of the work and process, and has no difficulties with associations during the harvesting: "interruption of the usual," "terrible silence, then normality," "avalanche without any track," "unexpected," "relationship: it isn't the same without listeners," "Japanese wood-carver: a wave of threat and demonic spirit," "the usual, without relation to the excessive."

As the most interesting one, she chooses the Japanese wood-carver and especially "the demonic spirit." When asked what this could mean, she comes back to the atomic disaster and speaks about the dynamics starting with a small fault and growing into the immense. "What could this mean for you personally?" is my next question. She sees three significant aspects:

- it is not me that has to intervene
- I want to have open eyes
- it has to do with fatefulness.

And she adds, "It tells me to be a calm observer. If I knew that it would be a process, I could breathe with more calmness. This requires humility."

Listening to her, I am not sure if she will speak about Fukushima, herself, or both. So, I leave it open and close the session by telling her that the next weeks will reveal which of these aspects would be meaningful, or if something else would show up. When she returns to the next session, after three weeks of holiday at the sea, she tells that she was able to forget everything and be totally present in each moment. For the first time she presents me with some of her poems.

She plans to group them all in order to publish a small anthology at her own expense.

In the case of Mrs Reinold, the relation between the decentering episode and the active pursuing of self-elicited goal is obscure. However, after the decentering work, Mrs Reinold began for the first time in years to make concrete and reasonable steps toward something important to her.

Claire

Claire is a therapist working with mentally disturbed individuals. She is in postgraduate education for supervisors and coaches, and she wants coaching sessions to support her in the work she is beginning to do with groups and teams. An agency has given her a mandate to work with a group of about 20 people from different professions and workplaces. The group meets once a month for three hours "to further teamwork."

During the first three coaching sessions we work on concrete proceedings of group work and teamwork, including a piece of community work. I see that Claire is a serious worker, well-prepared, able to structure time, but with almost no experience in handling groups. Therefore, she is eager to learn tools and procedures.

In the fourth session, Claire wants to work on a new and unfamiliar feeling of "pressure to perform" (*Leistungsstress*). She describes it as a mixed feeling of pressure, anxiety and being gripped. It is the first time that Claire has mentioned something personal, so I decide to do a decentering work with her.

I give Claire a big sheet of thick white paper, instructing her to explore its size, solidity and surface quality. As she looks at me inquiringly, I tell her, "I am giving you six minutes to shape this piece of paper into whatever you want. You will receive no other materials." This instruction is extremely short and challenging. My experiences show that efficient, productive and ambitious clients like short instructions and challenging tasks where they cannot be absolutely sure of success.

Claire, startled and momentarily hesitant, puts the paper on the floor and begins to fold it. This isn't working, so she crumbles the whole sheet and stamps her feet on it to make it softer and more pliable. Then she begins to tear off pieces of different sizes, and with the larger part of the sheet, builds a tower-like ruin with a roof and attached wall. The smaller pieces of paper arranged in a half-circle form a sort of town wall.

Claire gives a detailed aesthetic analysis. During her work, she was especially fascinated by the small crack that evolved when stamping on the paper. This crack seemed to influence everything that followed. Out of a long list of associations in the harvest, she chooses "movement" and "to let it evolve" as most interesting.

In the few minutes that are left in this session, Claire expresses that she feels it will be most effective to move physically with the whole team if her familiar feeling of being pressured rises up again. Later sessions show that this turns out to be effective. It is not only the physical movement that helped, but also the freedom she was granted in our session to do unusual things and to trust the process.

Why does it work so beautifully?
"Overfilling" or "multiplicity of perspectives"

Coming from systems theory thinking (e.g., Bateson 1972), the synergetic theory of self-organization describes circumstances under which highly complex, open systems are able to change from an initial form of stability to a new one (order-order-transitions; see Eberhart 2007). I find this theoretical framework a fascinating one because it fits into more situations within disciplines such as physics, chemistry, neurobiology, sociology and psychology. The self-organizing processes in physics, chemistry and other fields are supported by imports of energy. Kriz (2007) has shown that in psychical systems and human environments, energy is replaced by complexity.

According to these considerations, the decentering procedure would provide the psyche with various and "adequate" information that is logical, self-discovered, surprising, and non-threatening, and which animates a largely self-organized change. The procedure fits also with Honermann (2001) who outlines "1) a context in which there is permission to trust, 2) a holding, sustaining relationship between therapist and patient, and 3) a mistake-friendly atmosphere that supports experiments" (my translation) as the necessary presuppositions for professional procedures furthering self-organization. Kriz (2007, p.26) writes about an "overfilling (*Überfütterung*) with information valuable on multiple levels" (my translation). Knill and the author (Eberhart and Knill 2010) have written about "enlarging play space" and "multiplying perspectives."

The encounter with poietic potentiality

The broad conceptualization of the poietic act by Stephen K. Levine (1997, 2009) as the basic human experience, being able to let something new emerge from a not-knowing starting point, describes, from a philosophical viewpoint, how the effects of the decentering work can be understood.

In a similar direction, but on a different theoretical basis, comes the following argument: art-making in an EXA way, as I understand it, is near to play. This sort of play is—as Knill (Knill, Levine and Levine 2005) emphasizes, experiential learning, and the evolving work is a confirmation of one's own coping skills—which is, for many clients, a surprise. It seems obvious that the client connects this coping experience with the coping demands in their everyday life.

Confirming and revealing resources, and the significance of surprises

The above-mentioned experience of successful coping challenges all the familiar ideas of a client's insufficiency. Usually this experience follows a stage of conversation where it has been impossible for the client not to become aware of some of his resources and at least a few partial successes besides his concerns, difficulties, troubles and insufficiencies.

As mentioned before, the confrontation with the work and the joy of discovering its beauty is almost always a surprise for the client. Neurobiological findings of the last decades show that some experiences have a neuroplastic effect, which means a change in behavior and/or experience, where motivated individuals act concretely or imaginatively with emotional involvement. When the activity is also tied to a surprise reward, the neuroplastic effect (that is, the probability of a change) is at its highest (Mentha 2011).

Psychological theories have until now disregarded the importance of positive surprises for intended changes. Artists and art therapists seem to be more open to this. We need to let go of old supposed securities, to trust the process and to open ourselves to what we call "the alternative world experience," or in the words of Paolo Knill, "a truly non-possessive attitude within… (an) erotic engagement" (Knill *et al.* 2005, p.139).

The arts work in different ways. If a professional wants to see them influence the daily life of a client, they need to both "prepare the field," as described above, and to "build a careful bridge" from the art-process and the emerging work to the client's ordinary life experiences.

References

Bateson, G. (1972) *Steps to an Ecology of Mind. Collected Essays in Anthropology, Psychiatry, Evolution and Epistemology*. Nashville, TN: Chandler Publishing Company.
De Jong, P. and Berg, I.K. (1998) *Interviewing for Solutions*. Pacific Grove, CA: Brooks/Cole Publisher.
De Shazer, S. (1985) *Keys to Solution in Brief Therapy*. New York: W.W. Norton.
Eberhart, H. (2002) "Decentering with the Arts: A New Strategy in a New Professional Field." In S.K. Levine (ed.) *Crossing Boundaries, Explorations in Therapy and the Arts: A Festschrift for Paolo Knill*. Toronto: EGS Press.
Eberhart, H. (2007) "To say 'Yes'—A basis for individual change. Experiences in settings of therapy, counseling and coaching." *POIESIS: A Journal of the Arts and Communication 9*.
Eberhart, H. and Knill, P.J. (2010) *Lösungskunst. Lehrbuch der kunst—und ressourcenorientierten Arbeit*, 2nd edition. Göttingen: Vandenhoeck & Ruprecht.
Honermann, H. (2001) "Selbstorganisation in psychotherapeutischen Veränderungsprozessen." Dissertation Otto-Friedrich Universität Bamberg.
Knill, P.J., Levine, E.G. and Levine S.K. (2005) *Principles and Practices of Expressive Arts Therapy: Toward a Therapeutic Aesthetics*. London: Jessica Kingsley Publishers.
Kriz, J. (2007) "Zur Wirkungsweise der Kunst—und Ressourcenorientierten Arbeit." In H. Eberhart (ed.) *Kunst wirkt. Kunstorientierte Lösungsfindung in Beratung, Therapie und Bildung*. Zürich: Egis-Verlag.
Levine, S.K. (1997) *Poiesis: The Language of Psychology and the Speech of the Soul*, 2nd edition. London: Jessica Kingsley Publishers.
Levine, S.K. (2009) *Trauma, Tragedy, Therapy: The Arts and Human Suffering*. London: Jessica Kingsley Publishers.
Mentha, D. (2011) *Die Neurobiologie der Ressourcenorientierung*. (To be published.)
White, M. and Epston, D. (1989) *Literate Means to Therapeutic Ends*. Adelaide (South Australia): Dulwich Centre Publications.

THE QUESTION OF QUALITY ART IN EXPRESSIVE ARTS THERAPY

Shaun McNiff

The egalitarian and inclusive spirit of expressive arts therapy is guided by an assumption that every person can participate in making art. This is what defines and differentiates us from other approaches to artistic expression. I have made my contributions to this line of thinking. However, I believe the position can be enriched by a critical discussion of the idea that artistic expression can be as elemental as physical processes like breath and the body's movement, and that these gestures may have what we describe as *quality*.

Expressive arts therapy has even used the challenges presented by different skill levels as the basis for showing how facility with particular media can sometimes interfere with authentic and new expressions. And if a person shows an inability or lack of interest in working with a certain material of expression, our unique orientation to using all of the arts provides another medium for them. Through the totality of the process of selecting and engaging media, talent or skill are never considered to be preconditions for meaningful participation. This inclusive vision of artistic possibility in expressive arts therapy is more empirical than romantic; it challenges all of us who witness the work to perceive aesthetic significance in endlessly variable human gestures in various media. And of course there is a history within art therapy where spontaneous expression is valued as revealing unconscious content and where any concern with aesthetic features is viewed as an obstruction or cover-up.

Approaching art made in expressive arts therapy from the perspective of quality is provocative and in my experience, the issues generate lively discourse and a broad exchange of ideas. Some say,

"How can you even raise this subject?" feeling that quality and skill do not matter in using the arts in therapy, that our discipline exists within a framework that does not introduce any discussion of these matters which they feel impede free expression. These attitudes are guided by both psychoanalytic and process-art values. Other people, often motivated by negative experiences and judgments in the past, may choose the arts and therapy as a career because they want to get as far as possible from determinations of artistic quality in their own expressions and what they do with others. And finally, where there is a pervasive attitude in therapy that artistic expression is inseparable from the person making it, many of us affirm these intimate ties while also emphasizing the necessary autonomy of the artwork as a partner and guide which can be viewed in relation to its quality—and qualities.

Discussion of quality art in expressive arts therapy was a fitting theme for the special issue of the *POIESIS* journal celebrating the 80th birthday of Paolo Knill. His teachings and writings have made important contributions to the subject. This is the kind of philosophical and thoroughly practical conversation about the nature of things and their details, characteristics, nuances, relationships, complexities, contradictions, and incitements which has always ignited the sparkle in his thought and expression.

The primary question posed here concerns the definition of artistic quality in therapy and whether or not it influences overall value and satisfaction. Other questions spin off from this core issue:

- Is it possible or desirable to engage in value-free aesthetic activity?

- Is aesthetic quality different from psychological quality in relation to art made in therapy?

- Is quality determined solely by the particular therapeutic context?

- Can what the artist and others consider unattractive, disgusting, difficult-to-observe expression have a positive, even transformative role in expressive arts therapy?

- Is quality related to these provocations and activating effects?

- Is it possible or in any way productive to separate the process and products/outcomes of artistic expression?

- Does sensitive and supportive witnessing and observing neutralize the potentially damaging effects of quality assessments?
- Is there a place for perfecting artistic expression in therapy?
- How might virtuosity as well as unschooled expressions both further and limit discovery?
- Is authenticity of expression the gold standard of expressive arts therapy no matter what a person's skill level?
- What degree of skill quality does a therapist need with a medium to use it effectively in therapy with others?

Hopefully, the following reflections and discussion offer a framework and starting point for an ongoing critical examination of artistic quality in relation to far-ranging and endlessly variable conditions of practice and personal style. I envision Paolo Knill inviting us to dig into the questions, play with them imaginatively, and appreciate their role in describing expressive arts therapy.

Defining quality

We might consider two different and complementary aspects of quality as a basis for our discussion:

- *a standard* (according to which things are assessed and compared and to which people aspire)
- *an essential characteristic.*

These two features may support one another in making determinations of quality in expressive therapy practice, and often there is creative tension between them.

There are generally two kinds of *standards* of artistic quality that people use: categorical and situational. The former tends to be unqualified, unequivocal, and absolute, whereas the latter is more qualified and influenced by varying conditions. A situational standard is not necessarily a manifestation of what is currently called a relativistic judgment. Rather it is defined by the empirical conditions of distinct moments in time.

Although the general orientation to the interpretation of artistic quality in person-centered therapeutic practice is highly situational, traces of categorical standards permeate everything we do. These positions may include: every person can create quality art or, the reverse, only talented and skilled artists can make quality art. Other categorical judgments embedded in therapeutic values may be: artistic quality does not matter in therapy, artistic quality *does* matter in therapy; the value of an art experience is assessed exclusively in relation to process, or conversely only according to an objective assessment of the product or outcome, or, value always involves both process and product.

Situational standards might consider that quality art is determined by an individual person's unique ways of expression. Within a particular set of circumstances, process might be the primary focus; another set of circumstances might address the product, or a combination of both. The conditions of therapy might at times call for a quality focus on disintegration and/or integration.

All of us are prone to making categorical statements about issues of quality in arts therapy practice. As I stated above, I have my own beliefs and convictions that guide practice with a philosophy and sense of purpose. However, I have learned how helpful it can be to keep a soft and flexible hold on the controls of these inclinations, often driven by a need to eliminate uncertainty, so that I can more effectively model the critical and open approach to practice that I encourage.

Professional artistic standards for arts therapists offer an illustration of the contradictions that exist when the creative tension and partnership between categorical and situational assessments is lost. There are major variations in relation to the artistic competencies of creative arts therapists. Interestingly enough, certain sectors of specialized disciplines prone to categorical judgment argue against multi-disciplinary expressive arts therapy as a "jack of all trades" discipline which cannot have a depth of media expertise. These categorical judgments are clearly projections, since vastly different skill levels exist in all of the creative arts therapies, including the most specialized.

On the basis of four decades of international observation in both art therapy and expressive arts therapy, I do not see a lower level of quality artistic expression in the latter. Both disciplines are apt to show a similar spectrum of artistic skills on the part of therapists and ranges of artistic expressions made by participants in therapeutic sessions.

The nature of the art produced in therapeutic sessions is more apt to be influenced by the aesthetic values of the context, the backgrounds and expressive styles of participants, materials, time factors, and the ways in which individual therapists and group leaders operate—all thoroughly situational.

Regarding the second kind of quality listed above, even the most traditional assessments of artistic standards determine quality in relation to the work's expression of *essential characteristics* that it uniquely conveys. These features in turn shape the more comprehensive character and aesthetic perception of the whole.

An artistic expression, like a human being, can be viewed in relation to qualities that are unique to it. Thus, the determination of essential characteristics or qualities of art involves both highly personal perceptions of individual things together with more universal, transpersonal, and archetypal features shared with others. Although I like to think that the things we make carry traces of artistic DNA, fingerprints, psychological concerns, and other indelible marks, they also change. There is a plasticity that keeps immutable connections to a particular person but also seeks inherent refinement and relationship to things beyond itself.

These issues of quality relate to the substance of therapeutic experience. James Hillman (1999) feels that the definition and affirmation of character, the unique aesthetic and thoroughly individuated style of a person, one's image and form, is a driving force of life. When the often peculiar, unusual, and perverse qualities of persons run contrary to more categorical standards of society, we are apt to have conflict. Artistic expression gives us the opportunity to play with these forces, make something with them, and initiate small acts of potentially contagious change.

A context

Much of the confusion attached to the issue of quality in the arts therapies and the fervor of those who feel that it is off-limits results from mixing frameworks and bringing "art world," "art school," and hierarchical standards of artistic quality to therapy. In addition to making distinctions between categorical and situational standards, we need to locate our discussion in this essay with the values of a particular context, in this case expressive arts therapy. However, I also agree with Paolo Knill's assertion (2005) that the expressions made in therapy do not have to be limited to a notion of art therapy art, dance therapy dance, and other forms of "therapy art" (Knill 2005, p.97)—even though the majority of expressions may fit this genre. While images and expressive gestures made in therapeutic situations primarily serve the purpose of the professional discipline as it is practiced in a particular form and place, they can also share qualities with more universal features of art that transcend the therapy context. The expressions and our attitudes toward them are able to move between realms of experience; there is no need to label them as belonging to just one. In this respect they are like persons who play different roles and experience complexities that cannot be exclusively tied to fixed categories, superficial identities, or how they act in a particular setting.

Another fundamental distinction regarding this discussion is that assessments of quality in expressive arts therapy are generally being made by the people who make the art, the participants in the therapeutic process, and not by therapists or other people external to the immediate experience. The matter of quality in this respect does not involve judgments made by so-called authorities, as we are accustomed to thinking in the broader artistic context of society. When working with artists outside of a therapeutic context, I have found it equally helpful for me to avoid making judgments about quality. This is best done by the person making art with my assistance, usually guided by the same principles I use in therapy, for the most part directed toward widening perceptions and ideas about value, seeing new possibilities, relaxing judgment and the often-harsh critics that we carry with us, and realizing that we sometimes cannot see and overlook quality in things that are different or outside of our established schemes of value. Our inner judges and critics are plentiful and people do not need me contributing more of this. I see my role as helping the person refine, improve, and expand their capabilities to assess and achieve quality expression (McNiff 2015). Inside and outside therapy this might involve seeing how the things that disturb or offend us may be bringing something new that dislodges habitual perceptions or zones of acceptance and comfort. Quality is thus not necessarily nice and comforting, and may in this respect be attached to creating chaos, fragmentation, and the breaking of established patterns in order to change and shape something new (Levine 2009).

I believe that if we therapists disallow or forbid any discussion of quality in relation to another person's experience in therapy, we are not only going against the nature of the artistic process, but the primary elements of change as discussed later. When he visited Lesley University during the 1980s and early 1990s when Paolo Knill was with us, James Hillman liked to talk about how the hand in painting wants to "get it right," and the same applies to the body moving, the voice singing, or the words taking shape on a page. He felt that there is an innate critic living within the expression which attempts to manifest itself and its unique character as well as it can. He spoke of how this instinctive aspect of the process of expression was different from the "super-ego judgments" and dismissals that we know so well and want to keep outside the therapeutic studio, unless of course we decide to engage and confront them in our therapeutic dramas and play, revisiting past experiences that live on inside us, creating new ways of being with difficulties that liberate us from fixation, victimization, fear, and giving power to what we need to change; all of which is reinforced, I believe, when we do not permit considerations of artistic quality in expressive arts therapy.

When asked to give a succinct sense of artistic quality in therapy, I mention features such as authenticity, expressive energy and impact, individuation and uniqueness of style and subject matter, degree of risk and challenge, and lasting power, all of which apply to art in general. There is also merit to the colloquial response—it is hard to describe but we know it when we see it. If pushed for one overriding aspect of artistic quality, I would say it is the ability to transform difficult material into something new and life-affirming, again in keeping with the depths and significance of art throughout history. The following descriptions of actual experiences relate to these attempts at conceptual definition and perhaps transcend them as life always does, especially when expanded to include the work of others who add to this discussion.

The role of artistic quality in establishing expressive arts therapy

Issues of artistic quality have had a consistent place within my practice of expressive arts therapy, beginning with the event that first attracted public attention to the work. This event gave me the opportunity to start graduate programs at Lesley University, which led to the establishment of expressive arts therapy (McNiff 2009). In 1972, the Addison Gallery of American Art organized an exhibition, which I directed, of studio art made by people at Danvers State Hospital. The purpose of the show was to present the expressions in a context where they were viewed as art, and not just through the lens of mental illness. Most of the participants in the exhibit suffered from chronic and serious afflictions; and of course the general public was interested in their life conditions, and how they may or may not influence the artistic expressions presented in the show. The studio in the mental hospital was the daily social context for these artists and the place where their work was made, but when viewed in the gallery, the works were shown and experienced alongside the luminaries of art in the surrounding galleries.

The art made by the hospital residents spoke for itself independently of individual and group identities and the tendency to place the artists into particular mental health "populations." Viewers looked at the exhibit in relation to what they generally experience in museum environments, and they appreciated the aesthetic quality and features of what they saw. The show received considerable attention from local newspapers, which led to a grant, enabling it to travel to museums and university galleries throughout the Northeastern United States. There were many positive effects upon the hospital artists who had the opportunity to view their work in galleries. They observed how the expressions could move between worlds, which perhaps suggested that the hospital artists could do this too. The art led the way in proposing different roles to be played in life together with new ways to be perceived by others and themselves.

Of course much of the art made in expressive arts therapy, and within my own practice, will not be shown in a museum, and this underscores how there are always various aspects to the therapeutic experience in keeping with the needs of the particular person and context of practice. The field is also open to a diverse range of philosophies and practices which benefits all. This multiplicity goes together with being an art-based discipline where there are endlessly variable methods and ways of seeking change and meaning. However, within this spectrum there is an important and necessary place for values of quality in artistic expression as applied to the needs of particular situations. The Danvers artists all had severe challenges in relation to confidence and a positive sense of themselves, their relationships to others, and their capacity to contribute to the world. The Addison Gallery exhibit offered an artistic medicine. As is always the case in trying to serve others, it may have ultimately done more for me, and for expressive arts therapy, in sustaining and advancing what we try to bring to the world.

The dean of the Lesley Graduate School saw the show during exhibition at the nearby Carpenter Center for the Visual Arts at Harvard University and expressed interest in getting something started at the school, giving me the chance to establish the first expressive arts therapy masters program. Soon after this came the opportunity to meet Paolo Knill and work closely with him. The inception of our relationship and the establishment of expressive arts therapy thus had direct connections to the aesthetic aspects of art made in therapy.

Sustained experimentation

At that time (the mid-1970s), Knill was working primarily with music. His approach was permeated by a commitment to enabling people to express themselves authentically, originally, and confidently with voice and instruments. He encouraged exploration of sounds, improvisation, and developing the ability to listen, respond, and build upon natural expressions.

Approaches to artistic quality were always accompanied by an acknowledgment of skills in relation to what a person could and could not do with the musical materials. In music, perhaps more than all other artistic media, skill differences are distinct and accompanied by the inevitable comparisons between abilities to use instruments and the voice—immediately apparent on a sensory level through sounds permeating the space. Knill's core practice has thus always been challenged by questions of skill and quality. His philosophical orientation to involving all participants in meaningful musical experience and his reluctance to simply approach what people did as "music therapy music" presented opportunities as well as challenges.

Group expression was used as a primary way of involving people with varying abilities. If a clear and simple instrumental rhythm is established and sustained, usually by leaders and others with an ear for the beat and the manual ability to repeat it, others are carried by the strong and clear pulse. In this way, the group experiences a collective sense of quality achievement in relation to expressive release, the contagion of creative energy, and togetherness, which has a corresponding influence on individual participants. The same applies to vocal improvisation with others. Music in expressive arts therapy is often done in groups. Those of us with backgrounds in more individual art forms, like visual art and writing, were drawn to music for its ability to merge different people within varying skills into a single communal expression. Dance and drama combined both individual and group expressions, but their collective expressions, as significant as they are within their own right, could not compare to how many people became one with a vibrational and aural poignancy that gathered every sound into an immediate and relatively constant presence.

There was no question that the primary objective of these group sessions was the creation of quality sound experiences. Disharmony, confusion, dissonance, and jarring sounds often played their part in the improvisations which did not exclusively define quality as harmonious and orderly. But when trying to express discomfort through music, we always did this as well as we could, searching for the sounds that most completely conveyed the emotion. As Rudolf Arnheim (1974) demonstrated through his Gestalt theory of expression, certain structural configurations in a painting, dance, or musical composition will convey a particular emotion better than others. Expression is embedded in the formal qualities of art works, and the resulting emotional effects directly correspond to these features (Arnheim 1974). When we wish to express anger, sadness, or joy in art, we experience how certain forms will do this more effectively than others and we always make every effort to fully express ourselves since therapeutic satisfaction and outcomes are connected to our ability to do this. As group leaders we do not strive for low quality art; we always try to introduce structures that further the most complete expression of feelings.

Much of music in expressive arts therapy happens in partnership: the more skilled players often help to motivate, carry, and accommodate the abilities and needs of the others. The questions of skill and quality became more apparent with individual musical expression or music-making in small groups. Also in expressive arts therapy, we encouraged therapists in training, who might have personal backgrounds in different art forms and minimal musical training, to use music in their work. As contrasted to the merging of sounds that can happen in groups, these situations made it necessary to deal with the issues of musical competence.

In his characteristic way, Knill offsets the absence of technical abilities with an emphasis on complementary perceptual qualities, thus expanding the field of aesthetic quality to potentially include any person willing to make the commitment. He later formulated (2005) the "low skill/high sensitivity" principle to encourage inclusiveness in the work while not side-stepping a careful examination of quality, skill, the infinity of personal differences, and the challenges we face in dealing with these factors while engaging people in the process of artistic expression.

"Low skill" can be complemented by "high sensitivity" (Knill 2005) in helping to motivate participants in expressive arts therapy and in selecting media of expression. However, in addition to "low skill/high sensitivity" we can also have "high skill/low sensitivity," "low skill/low sensitivity," and "high skill/high sensitivity." All of these variations, and more, characterize the landscape and challenges of expressive arts therapy.

I was one of the early participants in this process of investigating music with Knill and he reciprocated by working with me in the visual arts. My personal history as a maker of music was flooded with quality demons—failures, negative judgments, active discouragement, and the consequent feelings of not being good enough, particularly with the voice. In my family, with its share of accomplished vocalists, if you didn't sing like Luciano Pavarotti, you did not sing at all. I often wonder what would have happened if I had had Mick Jagger or James Brown as models, suggesting yet again the influence of judgments according to an external standard rather than consideration of what the person is uniquely capable of doing and not doing. My family was affirming, especially in relation to my visual art, and of course it is possible that they may have been right about my voice. But I had rhythm, and perhaps some low skills and high sensitivity, and this could have been an opening to music.

Norma Canner, another member of our original team, helped define artistic quality in expressive arts therapy as emanating from authentic and uniquely personal movements and gestures. Rather than judging quality according to an external standard distant from our experience, what is it about our expression that is unique, special, and not comparable to what other people do? I describe this as the authority of experience, the particular and sometimes even idiosyncratic things that we might know better than anyone else. We all have these resources and can use them as a basis for building the most individuated artistic expressions. I did this with my painting at a time when it was stiff and stuck. I observed the distinctly spontaneous nature of my handwriting and said: why can't I access these qualities in my paintings and drawings?

Canner's dance and movement sessions reinforced the directions I was taking in the visual arts and helped me see how movement is the basis of expression in all media (McNiff 2015). Movements emerge naturally from one another if we commit ourselves to the process and allow the emergence to happen. Canner welcomed people who had no formal training, believing that they could make more direct and immediate contact with natural expressions, as opposed to trained dancers who she felt needed to unlearn their schooled patterns of moving. This was not simply an effort to advance inclusion by avoiding or dismissing standards of quality. We were deeply committed to the best movement we could make in both art and therapy. In my training groups I furthered this aesthetic by using Shunryu Suzuki's *Zen Mind, Beginner's Mind* (1989) as a core text and encouraged appreciation, practice, and enhancement of innate ways of expression, dreaming with what we already have and do not see. Since I had very positive past experiences with dance, perhaps even more than visual art, this approach was tested through musical experimentation.

The work with Knill was all about expanding my ideas about quality and my perception of it in relation to music and sound. Before anything could happen I had to risk showing myself and feel that there was a purpose. In order to do this I needed a guide who furthered motivation, offered a safe and stimulating environment for exploration, and who was able to respond in ways that sustain participation and confidence. Knill does these things naturally as a co-participant in every phase of the process that he is leading.

For example, rather than verbally analyzing and talking about his impressions of what I was doing, he would respond musically, picking up on a rhythm or providing a counter element. The expanse of sound was amplified and affirmed, channeling yet more energy and engagement back to me. These shared improvisations stimulated me to try different things, expand the sounds in new and not-yet-experienced directions, and to perfect expressions. Process alone was not enough. The experience of making music was inseparable from the sounds or outcomes which not only influenced me and others but had a considerable impact on the ongoing process, either feeding it with their qualities and moving it forward to new places or arresting confidence.

When we finished with the music, Knill might speak about particular things I did that contributed to the improvisation. These conversations helped me understand the music more completely, and to recall and internalize the qualities that seemed effective in their influence on others. We also discussed areas of difficulty and discomfort. Sometimes I discovered that the things that I felt might not be working were not seen the same way by others. But often these sensibilities about what was not quite right were accurate, and the perception of them, combined with clear articulation and discussion, typically helped me to find new ways of engaging the situation. All the conversations after our improvisations, even when tied to my fears and vulnerabilities, were about how to more fully realize the expression of the music, how to relax my judgments and inhibitions, and let the process of art take the lead in shaping outcomes and bringing me to a different place.

In the late 1970s, Paolo Knill and I initiated an experimental group called the Healing Lab where we could experiment with the expressive arts therapy process. It continued well into the 1980s. In addition to the two of us, group members included students and graduates of the expressive arts therapy program. Since expressive arts therapy was new, the lab offered opportunities to experiment with areas of expression that were unfamiliar. I was able to explore deficits in my background where I had bad histories, especially the voice, as well as new interests like drumming, free dance, and contact improvisation. Through almost a decade of experimentation I was able to build confidence, understanding and a more complete practice of expressive arts therapy. I realize now that in these sessions I always worked on furthering expression and quality in new areas of the arts.

I can report major shifts in my life and work emanating from these experiments. Music-making, especially rhythm and percussion, gradually became a core element of my work. I also became increasingly sensitive to how the pursuit of overall depth and quality involved an immersion in what might be considered the shadow domains of artistic expression, areas where we are more vulnerable and perhaps insecure. This work reinforced and solidified my commitment to multidisciplinary arts practice and the whole spectrum of human expression. I similarly encouraged students with MFAs and high levels of skill in a particular medium to become engaged with less-developed expressions.

In establishing expressive arts therapy, we turned the prerequisite skill values of the other creative arts therapy disciplines inside out. Yet we were always focused on developing quality expression, doing the best we could, experiencing concrete changes, and this corresponded then and now to the experience of people who participate in the therapeutic sessions we led. In addition to actually augmenting skills with new areas of expression, we learned about their therapeutic and psychological effects. These were the first concentrated experiments with art-based research (McNiff 1998), which emerged as a formal discipline through parallel experiments in our thesis program. Concerns with quality and understanding permeated everything we did.

The dynamics of artistic experimentation, especially with media where we feel unskilled and incompetent, correspond to the dynamics of change in therapy. I learned to love and forgive my history of failed musical expression, the terrible memories and art traumas, the missed opportunities to go in different directions, embracing them all as part of the complex of a life's formation, which now makes a stage for playing it all out differently, as well as I can. Changes occurring within the structure of the music according to sensibilities and assessments of what is working and not working become a basis for understanding the corresponding shifts in other aspects of our lives. In my experience, the micro effects of changes in artistic expression are the most reliable ways of furthering transformation in the macro spheres beyond our immediate actions and control. In art, we establish a basis for transforming our soul wounds into new beginnings. The pursuit of artistic quality as described above is arguably the major motivating force in making adjustments which generate palpable feelings of change, potentially inciting a creative contagion in us and others.

Quality and change

In conclusion, I would like to return to the relationship between artistic quality and change and the possibility that small and humble shifts can generate larger effects in our lives. In response to Stephen K. Levine's invitation to participate in the special issue of *POIESIS* honoring Paolo Knill, I said that I needed to write something about quality and how I constantly reference Knill's "low skill/high sensitivity" principle in my efforts to encourage critical discussion of the subtleties of the issue.

Levine replied, "Sounds good—I remember *Zen and the Art of Motorcycle Maintenance*—the main character was searching for quality."

I revisited the book, by Robert Pirsig (2006), and was impressed with two core points that resonate closely with the arts in therapy—that world improvement is an amplification of the most elemental things that we do as well as we can, and that fanatic positions are always tied to doubt and the absence of self-confidence.

The notion that personal and social change can extend from modest physical acts and emotional states, as described above, has informed my work from the start. It offered a concrete way to commit myself to what otherwise appeared to be hopeless situations in the lives of chronic mental patients in a state hospital. I observed and documented how artistic actions and patterns, especially when characterized by quality, can stimulate corresponding effects on persons, families, and groups.

And maybe even more importantly, we might remember Pirsig's second point and see how fundamentalisms, in us, our professions, and larger social spheres, can be linked to doubt and a lack of self-confidence. Welcoming our many shadows and vulnerabilities, as I have tried to demonstrate here, goes against the grain of the certainty that professions are hardwired to promote. Artistic quality with its attendant fluidity offers another and perhaps more realistic standard for how we can grow and change, thus becoming and modeling what we strive to do for others.

References

Arnheim, R. (1974) *Art and Visual Perception*. Berkeley and Los Angeles, CA: University of California Press.
Hillman, J. (1999) *The Force of Character and the Lasting Life*. New York: Random House.
Knill, P. (2005) "Foundation for a Theory of Practice." In P. Knill, E. Levine and S. Levine (eds) *Principles and Practice of Expressive Arts Therapy: Toward a Therapeutic Aesthetics*. London: Jessica Kingsley Publishers.
Levine, S. (2009) *Trauma, Tragedy, Therapy: The Arts and Human Suffering*. London: Jessica Kingsley Publishers.
McNiff, S. (1998) *Art-based Research*. London: Jessica Kingsley Publishers.
McNiff, S. (2009) *Integrating the Arts in Therapy: History, Theory, and Practice*. Springfield, IL: Charles C. Thomas.
McNiff, S. (2015) *Imagination in Action: Secrets for Unleashing Creative Expression*. Boston, MA: Shambhala Publications.
Pirsig, R. (2006) *Zen and the Art of Motorcycle Maintenance: An Inquiry into Values*. New York: Harper Collins
Suzuki, S. (1989) *Zen Mind, Beginner's Mind*. New York: Weatherhill.

8

A TANGO IN THE RUINS

Encounters with Beauty in a Harm Reduction Environment

Sabine Silberberg

It is 9am. A staff member opens the door to the lobby. Several people rush in; the line-up forms at the coffee dispensers. Others approach staff immediately. Urgently. "Have you heard that G. is in the hospital? They made him wait for hours in Emerge!" or, "I didn't sleep all night, couldn't go back to my hotel because a guy I bought drugs from threatened me; I owe him money."

During breakfast, I notice a client's eyelids droop, his head slowly lowering, his body slumping forward. Not an unusual sight. I slowly approach his table, gently touch his shoulder, and try to get his attention—a brief risk assessment—but also to let him know that I will need to remove his tray, and keep it for him until later. He is at risk of aspiration should he nod off while chewing on his toast, or lower his face into the porridge. It often takes time for clients to understand that this approach is not a penalty for using drugs, but that there is a health concern. The client for the after-breakfast appointment doesn't show up. It's the third week in a row. He is struggling with crystal meth use and finds it difficult to keep track of days and time. Most likely he'll drop by this afternoon, having just woken up.

The next client makes it to the appointment. She is interested in the video program I am offering and takes a look at the waiver, which is extensive. A disclosure of HIV+ status, or the tape in the wrong hands, can unfortunately have negative repercussions for clients. While she is in my office, I hear two male voices shouting elsewhere in the Centre. I run down the hallway toward the voices, hear the words "faggot, fucking junkie, wagon-burner," and threats being made toward each other. One of them is raising his fist. Another staff member appears at the same time, and we manage to calm the situation down, each walking with one person in different directions. Eventually both of them will leave for the day. I return to my office. Just another morning.

And so goes the introduction to my master's thesis, written in 2005. Upon rereading, it still holds up to my experience of the average day. Writing gave me the opportunity to focus on what it actually is I am trying to offer in this environment—a day health program for people living with HIV/AIDS in Vancouver, BC, on the West Coast of Canada. The clients are considered most at risk of deteriorating health due to multiple factors: the majority of them are living with active addiction, mental health concerns, and cumulative effects of marginalization, such as poverty and grossly inadequate housing. All of them have histories marked by abuse and/or violence. Many of them have experiences with the prison system and in the sex trade. They are of multiple gender expressions and sexual orientations, largely isolated without any personal support system and often also disenfranchised from health care. The chaos deriving from living within destabilizing circumstances makes it difficult to follow up on appointments, adhere to a medication regimen, or even to wait in the Emergency room for their turn.

My work takes place as part of a clinical team consisting of five to seven staff, including nurses, recreation therapists, a music therapist, a nutritionist, and two counselors. With a background in art therapy, hired as a counselor, I have now been trained as an expressive arts therapist over the past three years, and I have integrated this approach into my work as much as opportunity allows. My role is not to offer expressive arts; it is very much based in crisis intervention, addiction counseling, some advocacy, and diffusing challenging behaviors.

Most clients have not had positive previous experiences with counseling. They may have been court mandated to it in the past, mandated by their methadone-prescribing physician, or they plainly associate it with insurmountable challenges and pain. Because there are few clients who are interested and able to work within an appointment-based structure, the clinical team has developed a way of connecting with clients that we call "hallway counseling." This idea of a "floating intervention" is based on valuing even the casual conversations anywhere in the Centre, because they may serve as a seed for a more involved therapeutic relationship in the future.

Signing out a towel becomes an opportunity for engagement. Filling in an application for an annual disability bus pass may open the door to discussing a safer way of smoking crack. Crack. The opening.

So, this is what is different about this place from a few others: the fact that the Centre works with a harm reduction philosophy in its pragmatic application. Currently it is one of two agencies in North America that officially provide supervised injection services under a health research trial. Supervised injection, as part of the still controversial harm reduction approach, is nothing new to several European countries or Australia. Clients bring their street drugs into our Centre and have access to a clean, hygienic injection site and equipment, as well as harm reduction counseling and supervision by a registered nurse to prevent infection and overdose. HIV in the Western world, in particular Vancouver, has largely shifted to an addiction-related epidemic; the sharing of needles has become the main cause of new infections (Kerr 2000; Wood, Tyndall and Spittal 2001). This can be viewed as one outcome of the IV-drug use related stigma, the resulting repercussions, and in consequence the caution of users around disclosure.

Particularly, the practice of injection-based addiction has to be kept in the dark, to the back alleys and hotel rooms. An additional crucial factor is the lack of access to enough clean needles, which was exacerbated by the flooding of the local drug scene with cocaine. To give an impression of the significance of this change: an "average heroin user" injects maybe three times per day, an "average cocaine user" up to twenty or thirty times per day (Tyndall *et al.* 2003), hence the infection risk became exponentially higher. A public health crisis due to the high HIV-infection rate demanded action in Vancouver in the 1990s, and fortunately activism and a fertile political landscape produced tangible results, with an eye on the success of European supervised injection sites. Harm reduction is therefore the "new kid on the block" in approaches to addiction in North America, and—in a nutshell—is characterized by accepting drug use as a choice, respecting the dignity and rights of drug users, and seeking pragmatic solutions through non-coercive service provision (for more information see Canadian Harm Reduction Network 2007; Denning 2000; International Harm Reduction Association 2007).

"Meeting people where they are" is a central premise, and at this interpersonal core is where harm reduction meets expressive arts therapies in an environment that strives to foster engagement and relationships with people who consider themselves "rejects" and undeserving (Wood, Zettel and Stewart 2003). "Meeting people where they are" makes sense on first encounter. The challenge lies in its application over time—and the focus then may not be as much on the user as on the sometimes elusive internalized judgment of the service providers. After all, come on, we all know that addiction is bad, right?

Within this often chaotic context, with clients who are often intoxicated, high, in chemically altered states (whether they used the drugs on site or not), my approach has been to use the expressive arts as a way of building relationships. An attempt to "seduce" them out of numbness or an-aesthesia into…and this I had to find out…into what, exactly? What did I have to offer; what do the arts have to offer? Would they be interested at all; would they accept the invitation? My expectations were low. My personal critical perspective of societal dynamics mixed with the professional experience of supporting people living with multiple diagnoses and stigma—how could I not see them as vulnerable symptom-carriers of a social order with a much larger problem?

A certain cynicism had grabbed hold of me long before—it's the "making-do" attitude that works like a coping mechanism, sometimes, when social activism mixes with health care provision. It's the "knowing" about certain states of suffering as being produced and reproduced by social circumstances that need a much larger scope of intervention than only the remedial support of an individual who is suffering without many available resources. The questions remain— what could possibly make a difference here? How can the arts permeate the thick underbrush of challenges?

What I found were moments. Beads. Eventually these beads reappeared. They felt strung together. With gaps. The moment of surprise when addiction counseling resulted in being taught how to play the harmonica, and a musical dialogue began that by now has carried into its second year. These sessions follow an open format— sometimes the client makes it, sometimes I find him nodding off elsewhere in the Centre. Sometimes he gets so drowsy during our time together that his speech slurs and it becomes hard to detect what he tries to communicate. And at times it seems best to let him nod off, to attend to other matters of my work during this time we planned to have together, only to suddenly hear harmonica sounds and I turn around to a big smile and the knowing that addiction has just become part of our relationship, not something he had to leave at the office door. For him, the harmonica has been fun to wake up to. Relating has become about play—not only about an outsider's agenda for his drug use—about joining, about shared experience. In his own words, "It broke down the walls."

I have had spontaneous moments in the art studio, encouraging the painting process of someone who had just used a powerful and very toxic stimulant, methamphetamine, or crystal meth, and found herself with an intense urge to create. Many of the resulting "splash paintings" were exhibited later during the Centre's Open House and found a positive and encouraging reception by the community. And the client's identity shifted a little bit toward "artist."

Aiming at sensitivity to clients' (sub)culture, as well as an understanding of the often contrasting culture of the service provider, is an important part of inclusive service provision here, especially since community building is what we understand to be a crucial therapeutic factor. Some Centre clients, who make regular appearances as drag queens in local gay bars and clubs, have also performed in the Centre's occasional drag show. The play with gender, the celebration of "outsiderhood" and sexual desirability through campy femininity, had always stirred my own longing to experiment. As a self-labeled butch lesbian who considers herself part of the larger transgendered community, I joined a drag performance in female drag with a colleague, providing a background choir to the star drag queen at a Halloween show in the Centre. Playing with gender expression and sexualization by joining in the community ritual, which had the distinct flavor of initiation to me, has made a difference in dissolving the more traditional segregation of "us and them" that easily emerges in health care settings.

Expressive arts therapies emerged to show adaptability to circumstance, and to join in the opportunity to—just as harm reduction philosophy proposes—meet people where they are. This meeting requires an understanding of the conditions of structural outsiderhood or life within a "permanently liminal state," as described by anthropologist Victor Turner (1995, p.145). Many clients express feeling stripped of all privileges, including access to care, support, and ultimately meaning. It would be challenging to assume this state to be a great opportunity for creativity. The expressive arts have been a flexible tool to reach and join, to make an offer of play and to begin to manifest what Turner (1995) calls the "powers of the weak" (p.108), symbolizing the sentiment for humanity, a call for innovation and change.

Conveying acceptance may be a long-term process here, as well as reassigning power to the clients as the experts of their own lives. Relationship, at the core of both harm reduction and expressive arts therapy, asks then for a self-reflecting therapist. The internalized bias toward addiction that most of us grew up with is abstinence-based. Disapproval of active use can then be blatant or subtle, and drug users will pick up on cues to reinforce their own shame and withdraw from connection. We live in the throes of these morals, and we live with our difficulties of witnessing clients' long-term suffering. We are asked to learn to be with what is flawed or broken without the power or tools to fix it. The personal and professional intersects once again. What then may be helpful? What will get us out of the ruins of traditional approaches in society, culture, therapy?

What pulled me out of my own ruins many times were the unexpected encounters with what I experienced as beautiful. Here we are in this environment, surrounded by chaos, suffering, loss of sensuality or escape from sensory receptivity, and certain degrees of "sense-lessness." We are witnessing the "anesthesia" of chemical dependence, dissociative coping patterns, or even prescription medications that combat a virus while producing life-sapping side effects. Suddenly harmonica notes penetrate the soundscape of restlessness, a paragraph read out loud in the writing group makes everyone go quiet, and next to the food line, the place where most fights occur in the Centre, some vibrant paintings juxtapose the tension. Or I receive what I take as a "connective" compliment from the star drag queen after she finished my makeup for the show: "You look like a hooker in training!" Many times these moments gave me not only shivers, but a sense of privilege at witnessing something startlingly beautiful, and an intense love of my work and these people. "Beauty is the skin that truth wears when art holds it up for us… to an unflinching and unflattering light…unsettles, or frightens, even horrifies" (Hawkins 2004, p.88).

Out of disorder and chaos, within an environment fraught with stigma, loneliness, grief, and anger, or what is often considered ugliness, emerges the raw beauty of connection, joy, resilience, mutuality, and lightness. "Beauty arises out of that which is alive," writes Knill (Knill, Levine and Levine 2005, p.253). And Hawkins (2004), as an advocate for witnessing/honoring the women who went missing from Vancouver's Downtown Eastside, as someone who seems to understand the commonly defined "ugly"—the prostitute, the junkie—speaks to the power and impact of beauty in this context:

> But whether beauty delights or disturbs, it can also [...] reach in and touch some essential part of you—and therein lies its power—to open spaces into which the world can be written, and you into that world. With its core of truth [...] beauty's power to command focus, to startle us back into wakefulness, to reinvigorate us, to destabilize us, also imbues us with a sense that something else is possible, even hope, and therein lies its promise. (p.88)

This speaks to what I have been witnessing—the seduction into life and aliveness, called by beauty, for moments, hours, days. The dance of tension between sensitivity and an-aesthesia is what commits me to this creative process. My experience resonates with the metaphor of tango, the "dance of the underdog." This relational challenge, with its sudden changes, drama, and intensity of relating and distancing, demands intense presence to the moment, and it is informed by an aesthetic attitude that aims to draw a whole community toward "coming to our senses." In my role of therapist, increased sensitivity to opportunities, openness to that which wants to emerge, and offering of impulses without expectation or control are essential in the negotiation of forces in this particular dance. Letting go of preconceived ideas of practice may therefore help re-institute dignity for clients who know "choicelessness" as their only option.

And maybe we will want to be careful—this approach is not for the faint of heart. Expressive arts therapy within an environment like this can give voice to people who are experts in walking the fine line between hope and despair and, most often, life and death. They are often reduced to being the recipients of services, but I have learned that their resources and resilience have much to teach. Although many of us do not choose to be aware of this reality at all times, it is a human condition with which we are confronted.

Witnessing moments, acts, and creations with the flavor of beauty here had a profound impact on me. Beauty can be raw, it can be rough, and its delivery can be difficult to digest. Beauty can take you hostage. Or as Majken Jacoby writes, "Beauty tends to come unexpectedly. It sneaks up on us and takes us by surprise" (1999, p.53). Encouraging or witnessing the emergence of beauty in the lives of those living with multiple challenges then calls on us to be with what we often dismiss and keep at a safe distance—life in the ruins, too much to bear—that which is reduced to suffering only. Beauty brings us face to face with both pain and promise. The arts offer a reconnection with aspects of soul we might have lost sight of, and beauty may act as a catalyst for this, opening us to what *is*, in a different, more hopeful way.

The arts are available when the clients are. These clients have shown themselves to be able, on their own time and within their own structure, to engage in creativity, art-making, and play—despite the chaos and instability in their lives. Harm reduction therapy cautions us not to expect change in drug use if we don't have anything to offer. The expressive arts can make a contribution here, and both clients and therapists are called into the process. Through continuous offer and invitation, the life- and hope-affirming impulses of art may help move people toward the will to survive, or even beyond survival into a different way of aliveness. As a therapist working in this context, I cannot predict or plan the when, what, and where of connection and meaning. But I do hope to connect clients with the arts as an additional relationship to provide another focal point with enough incentive to reorganize their lives differently, and not only around drug use.

My relationship with the work is itself a creative act. While the dance of contradictions will remain, our ability to stay with the experience of nothingness and fragmentation without imposing a new structure can help shape lives to be lived more creatively—while developing through the arts a "harm reduction for the soul"—with beauty as a powerful ally.

References

Canadian Harm Reduction Network (2007) Available at www.canadianharmreduction.com, accessed on 01/17/17.
Denning, P. (2000) *Practicing Harm Reduction Psychotherapy: An Alternative Approach to Addictions.* New York: Guilford Press.
Hawkins, K. (2004) "Let their names be spoken: An exploration of beauty and the art of witness: Honoring the women who went missing from Vancouver's Downtown Eastside." *POIESIS: A Journal of the Arts and Communication 6*, 88–101.
International Harm Reduction Association (2007) Available at www.ihra.net, accessed on 01/17/17.

Jacoby, M. (1999) "The Necessity of Form: Expressive Arts Therapy in the Light of the Work of K. E. Logstrup." In S. K. Levine and E. G. Levine (eds) *Foundations of Expressive Arts Therapy*. London: Jessica Kingsley Publishers.

Kerr, T. (2000) S*afe Injection Facilities: Proposal for a Vancouver Pilot Project*. Proposal prepared for the Harm Reduction Action Society, Vancouver, BC.

Knill. P.J., Levine E.G. and Levine S.K. (2005) *Principles and Practice of Expressive Arts Therapy: Toward a Therapeutic Aesthetics*. London: Jessica Kingsley Publishers.

Turner, V.W. (1995) *The Ritual Process: Structure and Anti-structure*. Hawthorne, NY: De Gruyter.

Tyndall, M.W., Currie, S., Spittal, P., Li, K., *et al.* (2003) "Intensive injection cocaine use as the primary risk factor in the HIV-1 epidemic." *AIDS 17*, 6, 887–893.

Wood, A., Zettel, P. and Stewart, W. (2003) "The Dr. Peter Centre Supervised Injection Project." *The Canadian Nurse 43*, 1, 43–48.

Wood, E., Tyndall, M.W. and Spittal, P.M. (2001) "Unsafe injection practices in a cohort of injection drug users in Vancouver: Could safer injection rooms help?" *Canadian Medical Association Journal 165*, 4, 405–410.

9

STEPPING INTO LOCKED SPACE

An Algorithmic Dialogue between Choreography and In-Patient Work

Rebekah Windmiller

Through 20 years of making dances, one simple notion has kept me going: the belief that the dances I choreograph have something to do with my life. Since I do not work in narrative or concepts, the work of letting an abstract and formal choreography seep into my everyday life requires a step into imagination. By allowing new images and ideas to surface, I am offered glimpses of how the work has become an inquiry into the particular idiomatic expression of my life.

Eleven months ago, I began working in an in-patient psychiatric unit at Interfaith Medical Center in the Bedford-Stuyvesant neighborhood of Brooklyn, New York. Most patients experience acute mental distress and have been diagnosed with schizophrenia, depression, schizoaffective or bipolar disorder. I have been committed to an "oeuvre orientation" (Knill 2001) in my work with patients, and it has been challenging to facilitate the art-making with methods that will allow the creative process to flourish. The particular needs of my patients have challenged me to find fresh ways of thinking about expressive arts therapy in this setting.

In this article, I will look at a choreographic structure for a recent solo dance and its relatedness to the expressive arts work done at Interfaith. First, a description of the dance itself will provide a sense of its progressive action. This is followed by a glimpse into an in-patient environment, giving a context for the work and the challenges presented there. Next, I offer an example of mural-making as a particularly effective application of expressive arts therapy that arose out of the studio work, and finally, I will close with some thoughts on how the studio and clinical work have informed each other.

Moving summer space: A step in the studio

Last fall I decided to introduce my six-year-old daughter, Kalliope, to the work of the Merce Cunningham Dance Company. (*Summerspace* is the title of a Merce Cunningham dance first performed in 1958.) I took her to see the world premiere of *Split Sides* (2003) at the Brooklyn Academy of Music. As a working mother, it had been too long since I'd been to the theater, and my desire to see live dance was strong. I have always loved Cunningham's innovative choreography, so I did expect to be moved by the onstage occurrences and the sound score by Radiohead and Sigur Rós, but initially I kept my focus on Kalliope's experience of the evening. However, as I sat in the audience, my mother-self melted away and my artist-self emerged, transforming me like winter into spring. I watched the dancers move through tilts, twists, curves and arches, precarious balances and complex rhythms as the music and backdrops mingled with the steps. As I left the theater, feelings of desperation to dance and an immense longing to create my own steps propelled me forward, yet also stopped me cold. It was as though the dance had warmed me into the beauty of an early spring day, and then too soon the heavy heat of a humid summer rushed in, making it difficult to move.

The following week, I returned to the studio to begin rehearsals for an upcoming show. For several weeks I struggled with creating steps that made sense to me. While I felt inspired by seeing Cunningham, I also felt an oppressive demand to create something outside of my usual movement patterns. Frustration remained at a peak. I often found myself lying on the floor, nearly falling asleep. The relief came when I decided to simply explore steps for their own sake. I began by going back to basics and repeating pedestrian steps, keeping the upper body quiet. I wanted to hold my goal clearly in mind: to understand why I make a step.

I began with a simple step to the side and called it step one. I repeated the side step and added a forward step, calling it step two. The steps began to accumulate[1], moving sideways, then forward,

---

1 Choreographer Trisha Brown first used an algorithmic structure in her 1971 dance titled *Accumulation*.

and adding step three: a backward step with a directional shift. The repetitions grew familiar. Then the new move, step four, brought me straight ahead, this time from a profile view. As I worked that day, I felt as though a spring wind had come rushing through the window and set my feet in motion. The dance flowed with ease as step after step moved me around the studio, ending with 37 accumulated steps, each one becoming more directionally and rhythmically complex. I began to understand that making steps is simply about being in space and moving through it.

As I worked over the weeks, my upper body wanted to respond. As the accumulation progressed, my arms and torso began to further shape the space, define the energy and inform the steps. I began to feel a sense of freedom from psychological or narrative meanings in the movement as the repetitious, structured steps directed me through the space. The feeling was similar to watching the Cunningham dancers work their way through movement sequences derived from predetermined "chance" forms.

I later discovered that the dance structure I used could be called an algorithm. An algorithm is a step-by-step procedure designed to solve a problem or guide the execution of a finite task. Algorithms are primarily associated with computer programming and are generally quite complex. But simple algorithms are all around us: following a recipe, for example, or a map. The idea is that step one must be completed before step two, and so on.

I first became aware that this dance was connected to Interfaith when I began rehearsing it during my lunch hour in nearby parks in Bedford-Stuyvesant. Some of the local people passing by were curious; others seemed not to notice. No matter what the response, I felt as though the dance was being exposed in invigorating and risky ways, and that this exposure breathed new life into it. It was as though the predictability of the choreographic form touched the chaotic and uncertain nature of life: The Long Island Rail Road roaring past, teenagers playing basketball nearby, the drunken man watching from a distance, mothers passing with babies in tow. Somehow, this "accumulation" dance was becoming a sort of tentacle, reaching from my life into the community where I work. I had to question further: If the dance has arrived in the community, has it also crept into the 9th floor locked unit where I spent most of my time?

Breathing sky space: A step into a locked unit

Each morning when I arrive at work I am aware of a distinct moment just before I step into the unit: as I put my key in the door, I take a breath, preparing myself for what is on the other side. I am deeply aware that I am stepping into a different reality, a sort of altered space in which the rules of my world do not apply. Some days it seems like I am a dignitary whose long-anticipated arrival has finally come. Several waiting patients may gently take my arm and escort me down the hall, questioning me about the day's schedule or my personal life, or making delusional claims of having 30,000 children. On one such day, it all seemed to be going relatively well until a woman with whom I felt rather close started calling me "Veronica." Other days I move through the unit alone, as if I were a stranger passing by on a city street. Some patients mutter paranoid motifs to themselves while others cluster in small groups, busy with secret cigarette exchanges which resemble drug deals. Still other days, sad and resigned patients shuffle by in their slippers and hospital gowns, mumbling a faint "hello" on their way back to bed. As I arrive at the art studio and face another locked door, I breathe again, this time as a reminder to stay present in the midst of extraordinary disorder.

Once at my desk, I am grateful to have a window nearby. The unit is on the top floor of the hospital and is one of the highest points in this section of Brooklyn, offering an unobstructed portrait of the sky. I try to make a practice of looking outward, watching the slow and steady changes in the atmosphere that would otherwise go unnoticed. The vastness of the sky slows me down and offers relief from the constricting environment behind the locked door.

The ritual closing the door that signifies the beginning of an expressive arts therapy group and protection of the sacred space is often rendered ineffective as patients may suddenly leave, frightened, finding the group's simple creative gestures too much to bear. For others, sleep arrives as a way out of the experience or as a side effect of medication. Some patients live with symptoms such as excessive talking, short attention span and delusional thinking, making it difficult for them to be part of a group. In addition to the disruptive moments of opening and closing the door, I struggle at times to find space for imaginative exploration. It often feels like we are playing with fire—the patients touch imagination and then quickly pull away, as though the flames are too hot.

In my work at Interfaith, I have sought methods of art-making that slowly warm the path into imagination. By moving very gently from isolation to short moments of contact, patients often begin to relax and open small spaces for creative surprise. Since interruptions and individual fears of expression can make this challenging, the groups I facilitate often require a combination of tight and loose frames. An initial tight frame helps to contain the fires of fear, assisting the group in relaxing. Once the group is more at ease, the frame loosens slightly, allowing the flames to breathe. This makes way for an exploration in play. As in dance-making, I have found repetition to be essential in guiding such a process. Performing the same action over and over, varying it slightly each time, serves as a slow, reassuring step toward the development of art and playfulness in the group.

Making murals, step by step

In working with the visual arts, I turned to the mural as a way to allow for moments of connection as well as to make room to explore with art materials. Initially, I struggled because these connections did not happen. The images the patients made remained isolated and distant from one another, even at my suggestion to draw connecting lines. This problem pushed me to find more algorithmic formats to guide the mural-making process.

I decided to approach the mural by offering concrete and simple directions. First, I asked the group to stand around a table with a large sheet of paper attached to it (step one). Participants each chose a pastel (step two), then reached out to a point in the center of the page (step three). At this beginning place, people were surprised and curious to be acting together in one motion, reaching toward each other. I was pleased to notice that although our intention was to create a mural, we had momentarily joined together in a choreographed dance of reaching in and going away, as each person drew a line back toward himself or herself (step four). The way we moved to make the mural suddenly became significant.

This "choreography" repeated itself several times (steps five, six, and seven), with each repetition encouraging a new line or energy (loopy, squiggly, jagged, etc.). The meetings in the middle became duets and trios as the reaching-in happened at different times. As people felt more at ease with the action and resulting mark on the paper, they began filling in the spaces between the lines quite naturally (step eight), becoming quiet and focused on the art-making. As the image filled out, a piece of art emerged that was developed and beautiful, full of color and varied line.

I have found that for people with a severely restricted "range of play" (or "*Spielraum*," Knill 2000), there is a need for a map of sorts, something to direct the markings on the page. What I have come to see is that algorithms carry beauty in their very predictability. Because we know what is coming next, we can let go of the worry of mistakes and the burden of artistic choice. Of course, art-making can never be fully predicted and choices are still available, albeit particularly limited in the hospital. Yet working with algorithms allows for a high degree of control while each new step gradually increases the possibilities for playfulness. In an in-patient environment, algorithms are supportive of a sticking-with-it attitude and a mural that is filled in and filled out, which can be immensely difficult to facilitate in this environment.

Studio and hospital: Stepping together

In the initial stages of its creation, my dance was about the simple action of a step. In order to accomplish the potentially mundane steps, a moment-by-moment presence and strong commitment to simple action was required. As the repetitions increased and my concentration waned, I had to allow for choreographic surprises where the familiar step could be energetically or spatially altered. What I have come to understand is that surprise within repetition, a belief in the most basic and simple action, and a strong-enough presence to stay with slow progressions all run parallel to my work in the hospital.

I often begin groups with a movement experience. Each time, I ask patients to begin by taking a deep breath. For some, a shallow inhalation is all that can be managed. When I guide them through movements, they first respond to my gestures. Then, each has a moment to create an original move. Every day I am asked to be present to see and feel the beauty in minute expressions of a solitary finger being raised, a repetitive, robotic circling of the arms, sometimes even a complete lack of movement. It would be easy to become frustrated and long for more developed or broader sequences of dance with the patients but, ironically, I recognize that I have taken a similar direction in my studio. By creating choreographic repetitions and potentially boring steps, I have been pushed to understand that it is not always the steps that make the work interesting, but how one attends to them. This gives the dance its life.

In my work as a choreographer, I had become bored with my own choices. Making an artistic decision felt burdensome and meaningless. This stopped the process of creation. I imagine this may be close to the patients' experience of the presentation of art materials or space in which to move. In order to move my body in the studio, as well as to offer formats for imaginative exploration on the unit, I needed to deepen my understanding of the importance of repetition through step-making. It was quite unexpected, in both venues, that when I allowed repetition to play a prominent role in the work, the steps began to flow, the art was enlivened and my ability to remain intensely alert to the moment naturally became sharper.

It also surprised me that an algorithmic format intended only for a piece of choreography found new life in a park in an impoverished neighborhood in Brooklyn. While I was pleased that the solo grew larger by the nature of the outdoor space and a neighborhood audience, it proved to be a first rehearsal of what I now see as an emerging duet between my dance and the work I do at Interfaith. It has been particularly meaningful to discover that my struggles as a choreographer, and the steps I took to move through my locked imagination, were already in dialogue, dancing with the daily challenges I met with patients. Like the sky I meditate on from my window, imagination can move slowly, making imperceptible changes with dramatic results. Other times the effect is quieter, like taking a step, or turning a key in a locked door.

Afterword

Since this article appeared in the 2004 issue of *POIESIS*, my choreography and practice as an expressive arts therapist have evolved. Shortly after completing the original article, I decided that the accumulated solo dance described below would be a duet. Dancing in relationship with a partner was a development which highlighted the nature of the work in therapy, and was an especially pleasing affirmation of the reciprocal influences between studio and clinical practice. As a duet, the dance opened up particular issues that were quite apt to the therapeutic meeting. The improvised choreography became about how the dancers met each other, where steps diverged or became a unison, when to wait, when to move, and about sensitivity to each other while also attending to one's own sense of time within a complex framework. Each of these elements is certainly an important consideration in any relational and arts-based approach to therapy.

In my continued clinical work, I have found that patients are often locked at either end of a spectrum of creative engagement that interferes with artistic discovery. Some patients tend toward unbounded and free-flowing energies, which lack containment and structure, while others are very rigid and have narrow conceptions that limit their capacity for surprise. In the step-by-step mural-making process described in this article, I have come to understand that such an approach is helpful to draw in people on both ends of this polarity with the added benefit of fostering relatedness. While the structure is the primary binding element, the therapist's well-timed delivery of each step is critical in allowing people to explore a moment-to-moment creative process. By giving just enough guidance, while holding back that which is not yet relevant, participants are supported to experience presence and excitement in the enlivened moment of not knowing. The hopes that I have for my patients are similar to those I hold for my choreography—to be well-timed, present, playful, and held together within a structure that ultimately unlocks a new sense of aliveness.

September 2016

References

Knill, P. (2000) "The essence in a therapeutic process: An alternative experience of worlding?" *POIESIS: A Journal of the Arts and Communication 2*, 6–14.

Knill, P. (2001) "Unlimiting limits: Principles of an 'oeuvre-oriented' expressive arts therapy." *POIESIS: A Journal of the Arts and Communication 3*, 70–75.

10

THE GARDEN OF PRAISE AND LAMENT

Expressive Arts Group Psychotherapy with Trauma Survivors in Exile

Melinda Ashley Meyer DeMott

For five years, from 1991 to 1996, at the Psychosocial Center for Refugees at the University in Oslo, Norway, I led a cross-cultural expressive arts psychotherapy group of traumatized refugees in exile. The group members came from different countries: Iraq, Iran, Turkey, Kurdistan (Iraq), Syria, Chile and Yugoslavia. They all spoke a little Norwegian and other languages, so they could translate for each other. There were four women and four men. The group was open: new members could join the group when there was a vacancy. The range of age was from 22 to 41. They had been in Norway from two to seven years. In addition to group therapy, all participants were in individual therapy with one of the group therapists. The group members presented the following symptoms: withdrawal, isolation, emotional lability, paranoia, impulsiveness, depression, regression, poor concentration, insomnia, suicidal ideation, short-term memory impairment, guilt, shame, apathy, low self-esteem, no hope for the future and depersonalization (exile from the body). Many of the participants joined the group and went into therapy because they were afraid of losing control and becoming violent and/or crazy. They exhibited somatic symptoms such as: eating disorders (bulimia and denial of food), back pain, headaches, pain in the whole body, stomach ulcers, eye problems and pain related to their sexual organs. The two group leaders were from North America and England and had both lived in Norway for more than 20 years. One was an expressive arts therapist, a psychodrama director and registered nurse (RN) and the other was a body-oriented psychotherapist and psychiatrist.

This project was the first group psychotherapy offered at the Psychosocial Center for Refugees. We were convinced that group therapy was the appropriate treatment to offer, but knowing their different cultural backgrounds and painful stories, we wondered if it was at all possible. What the participants had in common was that they felt like they lived in the dark and had very little trust in others. They had lost the ability to imagine and were stuck in the dark memories of the past.

A unique project

This project was unique in the sense that very few studies have researched on-going psychotherapy groups with refugees living in exile, and, in the field of expressive arts therapy (EXA), there are no comparative studies. Therefore, it was important to evaluate the project. This was done as a series of individual interviews in 2001. All the group members who showed up for an interview had participated in the group for a period of six months or more. They were very positive about being interviewed. Many said it showed an interest in how they were doing in life.

Over the course of the five years, altogether 20 people participated in the group. Three have repatriated (returned to the mother country) and one has died. During the autumn of 2000 and the spring of 2001, I interviewed eight of the remaining 16 about their experience in the group and their current situation. Of the eight interviewed, three were women and five were men. They all had different backgrounds. Five had been heavily tortured in prison, two were soldiers who either escaped from the military or police, and they still believed that their life was in danger. One woman, 19 years old, came alone to reunite with her mother who had lived as a political refugee for 17 years in Norway. Her father had been killed.

I am going to give my reflections and findings from the eight interviews I conducted five years later. I have chosen to focus on the role of the arts and of the group. But first I will discuss what it means to live in exile.

What does it mean to live in exile?

Exile is often reported as a more devastating experience than torture; it is a new trauma on top of the old. Responses to living in exile in addition to previous traumas include isolation, lack of self-esteem, apathy, numbness, depression and guilt. Since exiles have already lost so much, there is a strong fear of becoming attached and having to go through the pain of separating again. It seems preferable to stay isolated and live in a vacuum than to engage in the present and look to the future. Living in a different culture also breaks the continuity in one's life. Most refugees come from countries where it is dangerous to express one's opinion. In school, you are supposed to learn from textbooks and teachers. Here in Norway, you are encouraged to think for yourself, and teaching often occurs in group discussions. This can be very threatening for someone who has lived with the fear of being killed for expressing himself.

You may come from a country where the sun shines the whole year and find yourself in a dark, cold country where people love fresh air and are opening the windows to let the cold air in even though it is minus ten degrees. It is hard to understand, but it is part of the culture. Most refugees come from cultures where if you are invited to a party, you know there will be music, dancing and entertainment. In Norway, it is not uncommon that when you go to a party, people talk and drink and, when they are too drunk to talk any more, they go home.

Living in exile means that you are living involuntarily in a country. You cannot leave if you don't like the food, the weather, the music or the politics.

It is a totally different experience from when you know that you are only going to stay temporarily and know the date when you are returning home. The longer you live in exile the smaller the probability is that you will ever be able to go back home. Even refugees that can go home feel that they can't.

I have defined four different types of exile:

- *Political exile*—their experience is incongruent with the government in their mother country. The extension of their punishment is that they are not welcome in their own country.

- *Emotional exile*—they can go home according to the government, but due to going through radical cultural differences while living in exile, they feel it is emotionally impossible to return. Children from the mountains in Kurdistan, for example, can risk being mobbed because they have become so different while they lived in exile. Another example is a man who felt he could not return to Chile. When he was in exile, the police tried to find him, and when they did not succeed they tortured his brother instead.

- *Exile from the body*—clients report that they live outside of their bodies and observe their body as though it were someone else's. This coping mechanism of dissociating from the body is one of the most common among torture victims. Their body is numb and they have no affect.

- *Exile from culture*—all the participants came from cultures that were radically different from Norwegian in terms of language, religion, climate and social interaction. They were living outside of their culture.

Can the arts help trauma survivors to restore their imagination and the ability to engage in the present?

The expressive arts communicate from the senses to the senses. The arts are body-based. They open the senses. We touch each other by seeing, hearing, moving and feeling. Traumatic experiences such as suicide bombings, torture and organized violence have an enormous impact on the senses. The normal reaction is to shut down, to protect oneself from these overwhelming impressions. Working with the arts can help the participants to create a new way of communicating and help them to see each other, not only the "demons from the past."

The intention of the expressive arts group is to give the participants space to create and experience the present.

The field of play

We started by creating the field of play. Play has no beginning or end. It involves all the senses and demands total presence. *Play* is the opposite of *game* where rules and goals are defined and winning or losing is involved. Art operates within the "liminal" space where one is not clear about what the outcome will be (Meyer 1996, 1999). The participants do not have the skills or the talents of artists. Many have not touched a paintbrush since they were children. Communicating with a different and unfamiliar medium can give new perspectives. Elisabeth[1] from Turkey experienced the images she created and shaped as more powerful than words.

Elisabeth from Turkey

Elisabeth belonged to a revolutionary party. Her family was poor and lived in a small village. Her mother died when she was eight. At the age of 17, Elisabeth was arrested and sent to prison. Her sister and brother were tortured in front of her while she was interrogated. Her father died while she was in prison. At the age of 21, after four years in prison, she managed to escape. She was given the status of political refugee after three years in a reception center in Norway.

Elisabeth said:

> I experienced drawing as very helpful. When I draw, I don't control. When the control is gone, you come direct to the core of the issue, the sorrow, the happiness—whatever it is. Words are very limited. I found words through the images I drew. It is the images that make the words meaningful, not the words that make the image work.
>
> What I remember best is an image I drew. There are many women wearing black clothes and a war is going on. The women are carrying water and it's very quiet. It's a place where everything is left in ruins. Children are crying and the women are in deep sorrow. It is as though this picture is from an earlier life. I am stuck with this image.

These are the words she spoke at the time she made the picture in 1993:

> Here I am riding through the dry landscape; it is warm and the dust whirls up all around me. The women are carrying their babies; children walk alongside. Everything is happening on the same earth, Mother Earth. Death, corpses, funerals, grief, aggression. If only I could get back on the horse's back, so the journey could continue. But I am stuck in the grief. I am stuck

---

1 All names have been changed.

with the sadness and losses that were awakened in prison. The losses in my childhood, the feelings of loneliness, despair, hopelessness, powerlessness. If I get back on the horse's back, maybe I will just ride in a circle and have to go through it all over again?

I asked her how this image makes her feel now:

I feel pain. I experience the sorrow and the stillness. The women are patient. They are coping and supporting each other without saying anything. They have been very patient. I have respect for these women. They are wise and strong.

The picture of the women in black has stayed in Elisabeth's mind for eight years. She can't forget it. Perhaps it stays because it connects to her life and to the stories of many others.

Art as the container of pain

The group could work on the same picture for two or three sessions, sometimes group drawings, sometimes individual drawings. Finding the emotional expression through the art-work was often very challenging. On occasion the pictures could reveal the core of the problem for the client. Having the possibility to objectify a problem and work with it separately in a group context gave space to choose how much one wanted to share with the group. The whole story, if revealed too quickly, could invoke shame and guilt, and a participant might not return the following session (Meyer 1997).

The art-work was the main form of communication and helped the participants to understand what the group member was sharing, even though their Norwegian may have been poor. Art gave them space and permission to use their imaginations.

Storytelling through the performing arts is practiced all over the world and is one of the oldest traditions in human history. Today, where populations are becoming less homogenous, it is important that therapeutic approaches try to build bridges between people and cultures. Storytelling is one way to build such a bridge.

In telling a story through the arts, we often use "intermodal transfer," moving from one art modality into a new one: creating a poem in response to the image, music in response to the poem, movement in response to the music. In this way, we involve all the senses while staying with the image (Knill, Babra and Fuchs 1995). Intermodal transfer gives new perspectives on the image without moving into the literal reality. In this way, we stay on the surface before we go to the depth. We communicate with the image using all of our senses, trying to make sense out of our experiences with the help of our imagination.

Kadi from Kurdistan

Kadi came to Norway as a refugee with his wife and three children just before the Gulf War in 1990. They escaped over the mountains and two of the children almost froze to death. He had been tortured and arrested several times. Kadi said:

> If I could have been an animal I would have liked to be a bird, a dove...then I could have flown away whenever I wanted to. A dove can live anywhere. I have no hope today that I will ever experience this freedom. I am slowly suffering. I remember the picture I drew where the sky is black, a bird is flying and the earth is burning. You can't forget a picture like that. The bird has nowhere safe to land.

Omid from Iran

Omid was arrested because of his wife's political activities. He had a good business and was not politically active himself. He had to help his wife and his son to escape the country. She came with their five-year-old son to Norway. While Omid himself was getting ready to leave, they arrested him because they could not find his wife. He spent four years in prison and was tortured regularly. He has had several operations because of the damage that was done to his body. He works as a caregiver for the elderly today, and his wife has undertaken advanced education in data communication in Norway.

Omid said:

> I learned a lot from participating in the group. Now I know what to do when I am sad: I can go for a walk or scream. I have done that a lot and it helps. Going for a walk and looking at something in nature really helps. Movement and exercise helps the pain in the body and what is 'in there.' I learned how

to cope with the feelings. If I had not achieved this knowledge I would maybe not have been alive today.

I have more control. Movement helps me to be present and not think about the painful memories from the past.

Mercedes from Chile

Mercedes from Chile came to Norway when she was 19. At the age of three, she was put in an orphanage by her uncle. Her mother had to escape Pinochet's men; her father had already disappeared. Sixteen years later she was reunited with her mother. She had had only six years of schooling. When she came to Norway, she experienced it as being reborn, having to learn everything from scratch. Today she is studying to become a lawyer.

Mercedes said:

> It was no coincidence that I started to study law after all that had happened to me. Today I want to have influence and help others. I don't want to be a witness to injustice and not be able to take action. At least I want to have the possibility to do something...
>
> I enjoyed very much that we could express ourselves through different art mediums in the group. I could choose art, poetry, music, drama and so on. I had difficulties expressing myself through words. Drawing became very important for me; the pictures became a bridge out to the world. Even today when I am very upset I can sit down and draw and it helps. Sometimes I write too. Back then I was very lonely and had nobody to talk to, so drawing became an important outlet.

Imir from Syria

Imir from Syria escaped the military and fifteen years later still cannot go back to visit. Imir said:

> I remember the image of the circle. It's as though I am walking around in a circle I cannot get out of.

Stuck with the memory of one image

One of my observations was that several participants had one specific image they remembered having drawn. Five out of eight reported without hesitation that one image stood out in their memory. As a researcher and therapist I have made this observation before and found it very interesting. Many of my clients who suffer from chronic post-traumatic stress disorder (PTSD) are persecuted by certain traumatic events. These memories represent a threat of some kind, for example, no place to go, no place to hide, no exit and so on. Do these images represent one specific event, or are they symbolic of the state of being alive? The image certainly illustrated the problem, but these pictures were not literal. They were created with help of the imagination. Elisabeth said that she thought maybe the picture came from a past life. Perhaps we all have one image that tells "the whole story." My question is: can these pictures become obstacles in moving on? Janet (1909, quoted in van der Kolk and van der Hart 1991) said that memory is flexible, but when it gets attached to one traumatic image, it loses its role of restoring balance in the psyche. None of these images were drawn more than once. What these unique images have in common is that they carry the suffering but also the yearning it is calling for. Is the soul trying to send a message? What is the soul asking for? Shall we play more with these images, identify them earlier and stay with them, or should we abandon them and move on?

Dori Laub in his book *Testimony* (Felman and Laub 1992) refers to the "I witness" (the witness within) and the "outer witness" (the witness to the world). The trauma survivor is often stuck with trying to communicate exactly what happened, and this is a trap that many trauma survivors never get out of. The witness in the world can never perceive the event exactly the way it happened. However, the witness in the world can imagine what it was like through his or her life experiences and creativity.

It is important to abandon the literal trauma story and not try to communicate the event through one art form that stays with a single image, but through several. Here intermodal transfer helps the survivor to move the story through the senses and gain new perspectives. We go to a new medium together with the witness and begin to use the imagination to create a new "story," a story which also includes the images of the witness. In this way the art will function as a bridge to the world; it will take the person out of isolation and give them a sense of being seen and touched by another.

The meaning of the group

All the participants reported that one of the most important qualities of being in an EXA group was sharing their stories with others who had been through similar experiences.

Leonard

One feels more safe when one is aware that several of the participants have the same needs. It's easier to talk and share with people who have similar problems.

Elisabeth

Even though we were many, we were all given enough space. We were together and we shared impressions of each other's drawings. Some commented on things I had not seen. This gave me a new perspective and the image became more whole. I became more open for new and different perspectives when I heard a group member share a problem similar to mine. I reversed roles and tried to solve it. Distancing and approaching the problem from a new perspective helped me sometimes laugh and see that the problem was something I created or was not that big.

Omid

The best thing I remember about the group was that all the participants had similar problems and we got to know each other. I remember the man from Iraq; we could talk about being in prison. It was not only me who had problems, but many other people as well. It was not only me who was suffering the consequences of being imprisoned and tortured.

There are three reasons why it was helpful to participate in the group. It was good to be together with others and break the feeling of being isolated: the social aspect; secondly, it reminded us of sitting and drawing together in school: a good situation, doing something together. The third is that somebody cared about us: the thought that somebody cared, gave (us) hope.

Mercedes

When I started in the group I had very poor self-esteem. I did not know how to relate to other people and was too afraid to say "No" or mark my boundaries. One time, when the whole group was drawing on the same piece of paper, I became very angry, because one of the others began to draw in my space. I was able to say something. Back then it was very unpleasant, but today I know this was the first step in defining my boundaries and setting clear limits.

The group took the role of the witness. They used their senses to hear, see, feel and touch the story of the others expressed through art, music, poetry and drama.

The therapeutic factors of EXA working with trauma survivors living in exile

Judith Lewis Herman says in her book *Trauma and Recovery* (1992) that one of the most important treatments for people suffering from trauma and post-traumatic stress disorder is group therapy. My experience and research confirms this statement. But, at the same time, to get a group to function and not collapse can be very demanding for the very same reasons that group therapy is so important for these patients. I have listed the symptoms they brought to the group. Some of the most challenging were lack of trust in other people, withdrawal, depression, low presence, distorted identity and lack of a sense of time. Group and expressive arts therapy has a therapeutic effect on these issues.

In *Group Psychotherapy* (1975), Irvin Yalom divides the therapeutic factors of group psychotherapy into eleven primary categories. In addition to these, we found the following to be helpful:

- Each person is treated as an individual with an identity, instead of as an object.

- We identify the resources in the group.
- The arts can help clients to find an expression for their symptoms and learn to cope with these symptoms with each other's help.
- We help each person to be in the present—in the here and now.
- The group functions as witness to each member's testimony.
- Movement creates energy and gives a sense of life in the body.
- Through the arts and the group, we can gain new perspectives on our stories.
- Art-making is distancing and gives permission to play in the transitional space, increasing the range of play.
- Creating group rituals helps restore psychological balance.

In the interviews I asked, "When you think of the group what do you remember?"

Imir answered:

> It was the most important day of the week to come and participate in the group. When I came here I did not feel alone with my problems. The people around me had similar problems. I felt a freedom to speak about my experiences without being labeled as crazy or looked down on.

The role of the therapist

The arts are expressions powerful enough to become containers for the emotional pain of clients. Instead of the therapist becoming the receiver of the client's projections, the art-work takes on this role. Creating art gives the participants the necessary distance from each other. Through the art we can imagine how it is to be the other and we can relate from our own life experiences. If the listener feels forced to listen to the literal trauma story, he or she may feel invaded. As an EXA therapist, I always sense the "group body" and ask, "Is this body breathing? Is there enough movement and energy? Is this body alive and, if not, what will it take to help it come alive?"

Being a witness to other people's life stories is very enriching, but also challenging. Research has shown that having too much empathy or being over-engaged with traumatized patients can lead to "compassion fatigue." Compassion fatigue drains the therapist's energy and may lead to symptoms of burnout: lack of concentration, irritability, insomnia, lack of interest and accident-prone behavior, such as cutting yourself with the bread knife because you are not focused on what you are doing.

Perhaps the key to taking on the difficult task of witnessing other people's trauma stories lies in our own research into what we have witnessed inside ourselves. I am referring here to what Dori Laub calls the "I witness." When I hear someone else's story, what story is awakened in my own life? Perhaps I have to make my own life story available and experience playing with it? Then I can imagine where my life meets other's lives and I am able to provide a safe play space, a garden where there is room for both praise and lament. The plants in the garden must feel cared for and the uniqueness of each plant must be respected. Together they create a culture where all can grow. The therapist is the gardener who cares for this unique culture and has the humbleness and strength to take part in creating it.

References

Felman, S. and Laub, D. (1992) *Testimony.* New York: Routledge.
Herman, J. (1992) *Trauma and Recovery.* New York: Basic Books.
Knill, P., Barba, H. and Fuchs, M. (1995) *Minstrels of Soul: Intermodal Expressive Therapy.* Toronto: Palmerston Press.
Meyer, M.A. (1997) "Når livet vender tilbake." In *Flykt og framtid.* Oslo: Ad Notem Gyldendal.
Meyer M.A. (1996) Videofilm: *I eksil fra kroppen.* (21 min) Oslo: Melinda Meyer.
Meyer M.A. (1999) Videofilm: *Returning to life.* (50 min) Oslo: Melinda Meyer.
van der Kolk, B.A. and van der Hart, O. (1991) "The intrusive past: The flexibility of memory and the engraving of trauma." *American Imago 48,* 425–454.
Yalom, I.D. (1975) *The Theory and Practice of Group Psychotherapy.* New York: Basic Books.

11

PLAY, ART AND RITUAL

Working Therapeutically with Children and their Parents

Ellen G. Levine

The notion that therapies all have a kind of action that makes them "work" or that makes their action "therapeutic" is an interesting one. For example, Irvin Yalom (2005) speaks about "curative," or what he came later to call "therapeutic," factors in the practice of group therapy. These factors were reported by patients themselves at the conclusion of their group therapy involvement and are what make group therapy "work," i.e., be effective.

Perhaps for every kind of therapy there is a set of factors that makes it "work." When we turn to therapy with children and parents through play and the arts, we can ask the same question: when this work "works," what makes it "work?" Is there something unique in this particular work that can make it effective? Perhaps it is to be found in these very modes that we engage in, namely, play, art-making and ritual processes.

First, there is something important about play and the act of playing that contributes significantly to the effectiveness of the work in expressive arts. Play is the vehicle that carries our first interactions with the world and with others as humans. According to Winnicott (1971), playing is the activity par excellence that engages us generatively or creatively. It is what makes us feel alive and gives the fact of our existence to us. It places us in a not-knowing or open space where anything can happen. The back-and-forth quality of movement in play is a giving and receiving which is restorative.

Second, when working in the expressive arts, placing the emphasis on the art work and the doing or the making that brought it into being, rather than focusing on the interpretation, takes us out of the psychological realm. Looking through a psychological lens, we tend to see art-making as an expression of self. In expressive arts, rather, we see art-making as opening to the world and to unexplored territory. Searching for the form and shaping this form into a work is essential to art-making. When we are lost or stuck, this activity gives us back the sense of our capacity and agency. Just as playing is a basic human activity, so too art-making is an activity in which humans have always engaged. The arts, or *poietic acts,* are universal. The arts, in all their various and multiple manifestations, are common to every epoch and culture. Encouraging those who feel helpless to explore in the modalities of the arts is a way to build capacities and strengths. By creating simple and achievable challenges in the arts and exploring freely within that structure, we mobilize resources which are needed to deal with the challenges that life continually presents to us.

Ritual processes, in the same way as playing and art-making, engage us in activity that is part of what makes us human. Ritual has always been effective in carrying both the joy and the suffering of human experience. Ritual provides structure and a frame, employs repetition and involves a series of clearly laid out steps. Ritual work involves moving from the preparation phase into the liminal space and back again to a newly formed reality. In this sense it is linked to both play and art-making in making use of a transitional area of experience or liminal space for its generative and restorative possibilities.

In this chapter, I will tell two stories of work that I did, one with a boy and his mother and the other with a whole family. Through these stories, I hope to try to establish how play, art-making and ritual made the work "work." By "work," I mean, enable these clients to feel more empowered in their lives. I will try to show how the effectiveness of the work came through the client's willingness to engage in play, art-making and/or ritual structures.

The boy who found an oasis in the playroom with help from his friends

Bae was a 10-year-old Korean boy who came for the first time to meet me at the treatment centre where I work. Bae arrived with his single mother, the worker from the child protection services and a translator. Bae was rather quiet and withdrawn, a bit overweight and seemed physically lethargic. The mother suffered from severe depression and, according to the child protection worker, Farid, over the years had often been too ill or too tired to parent Bae in ways that would be effective for him. Bae was currently missing school regularly; he was way behind in his work, lacked friends entirely and slept in his mother's bed every night. He expressed a fear that his mother would die if he should be apart from her. In an early conversation that I had with Bae's teacher, she reported that when she asked the students about their goals in life, Bae responded: "To grow up and be a homemaker and take care of my Mom."

Bae's mother, Eun, wanted to talk to me privately at the beginning of the treatment in order to tell me her story. This story was filled with violence and extreme suffering: severe physical and emotional abuse visited both upon herself and upon Bae at the hands of the father who was an alcoholic (he had left several years ago, returning to Korea); there were several suicide attempts by Eun, who also suffered from alcoholism after the father left. Bae apparently witnessed one serious suicide attempt where his mother stood on the railing of the apartment balcony and was pulled back at the last moment by Bae's grandmother who lived with them at the time. Eun also told me about constant arguments and conflict between her and her mother that Bae overheard. When Bae and Eun came for treatment, the grandmother was no longer living in the same house.

This atmosphere of conflict and violence had obviously taken a toll on Bae, and his development was compromised as a result. In addition to failing at school, Bae was sad most of the time and would not do anything that the mother asked. Eun told me that she would go to the schoolyard during Bae's recess time and watch him wandering aimlessly around the yard, not engaging with the other children. She said that this made her very sad and that she cried all the time about it. She told me that she often let Bae stay home from school if he complained about being tired or not feeling well. She would also let him miss school when she did not feel well. Farid was working with Eun and Bae to get him to attend school regularly.

Both in sessions with Bae and alone with me, Eun emphasized her worries, her own sicknesses and how tired she was most of the time. She noted that she slept most of the day and was often asleep when Bae was at home. I worked quite directly with Eun to extricate Bae from her bed. In one session in which she was alone with me, she told me that she did not want to live. At this point, I alerted her psychiatrist and other support workers involved with the family.

I saw Eun as a very caring mother who was able to access help and services for both her son and herself. While I identified separation as a key issue for this mother and son, I also recognized how they had needed to be close in order to withstand the difficulties that their family had faced. Closeness, then, had both its positive and negative side. The treatment for the first few months included a mixture of individual sessions with Bae, joint sessions with Bae and Eun, and sessions including Farid. In terms of the relationship between mother and son, I had the image of the weaning of a mother and baby in mind.

In the sessions with Bae and Eun together, I focused on exploring their relationship through play and encouraging them to play together. Because of their closeness, I assumed that they would be able to do this. I was surprised to see how difficult it was for Eun to play at all. In Winnicott's (1958) framework, I wondered about Eun's early experiences of play, whether she was able to play and what that indicated about the quality of her early relationships. The toys made her sad, and often she cried throughout the session. A toy dinosaur caused her particular grief; she said it reminded her of Bae, explaining that the dinosaur was "becoming extinct" like her son. I coaxed her into playing with the dinosaur, and only because of my on-going support was she able to do so. In discussions and reflections after the play scenarios, without the benefit of the openness of the play frame, Eun often shifted from sadness to anger at Bae. She would challenge his ideas and became enraged when he had his own thoughts that were different from hers.

In his individual sessions with me, Bae made very good use of the playroom and the toys. He seemed to thoroughly enjoy the sessions and played with great gusto and enthusiasm, as if he were eating a very satisfying meal and drinking water after being in the desert for a long time. He was excited to come to the playroom every week.

After a quite shy and restrained beginning where he chose more structured board games, Bae moved into imaginative play with animal and family figures. There were fierce battles between domestic and wild animals, with the domestic animals ultimately winning. After a few sessions, Bae began a series of stories in which he enacted and narrated the scenes with the toys and I wrote down the stories. In these stories, which he came to call "Family Adventures," there was a family including grandmother, grandfather, mother, father and three children (a son, a daughter and a baby). Typically, the family went on dangerous adventures and risked their lives with wild animals and pirates. Ultimately, they survived, primarily due to the interventions of the knowing and wise grandfather. In the last story before a long holiday break, the grandfather died, and Bae said that his plan was that each week another family member would die. The only ones left would be the boy and the baby.

During this initial phase of therapy, Eun reported to me that Bae began sleeping in his own bed but that he was still unhappy at school. Eun began to think about changing his school. The school had several meetings which I attended and in which everyone seemed committed to help Bae stay at the school, develop more friendships and get extra help. The teachers reported that Bae was terrified of making mistakes and would not engage in visual art of any kind.

In the next four-month period of treatment, Bae continued to play Family Adventures. The story shifted somewhat to include a "security guard" who was attached to the family. The family would go on happy outings involving picnics and play, but soon dinosaurs or meteors would appear out of nowhere, crashing the family party and trying to destroy everyone. At first, family members were being killed off, with the grandfather being the last to die (he was brought back into the play after the holidays). In a further development, the family members and security guard used shields (plastic spoons and knives) to protect themselves by smashing the attackers and sending them flying off the table.

Bae's main enjoyment came from sending the toys off the table onto the floor. This more "aggressive" play made him laugh uproariously. The "normal" expression of aggression had been thwarted in Bae's experience. Certainly, he associated bad things with aggression, having been deeply affected by the violence between his parents in his early life. In the play space, the aggression could be safely explored. Making a mess or throwing things off the table would not hurt anyone or destroy anything and, therefore, we could enjoy it and play with it. Perhaps this helped Bae to be more comfortable with his own aggressive feelings.

During this period of the treatment, I met monthly with Bae and his mother together. We worked on several practical/emotional issues including:

- making sure that Bae attended school regularly
- improving Bae's peer relationships at school
- helping Bae to take more responsibility for himself (getting up by himself, getting dressed in the morning, making his own breakfast)
- creating more emotional space between Bae and his mother (allowing Bae to have his own thoughts/helping Eun to focus on her own desires and to simply listen to Bae's complaints without having to fix everything for him).

There were improvements in Bae's ability to accomplish some of these goals, especially on the days that he came to our sessions. Both Bae and his mother were proud to report this progress to me. Eun continued to believe that Bae should change schools because there were no Asian children at his present school, even though it was steps away from their home. Farid, the child protection worker, encouraged Eun to drop this idea, particularly because if it was difficult for Eun to get Bae to his current nearby school, we all felt it would be impossible for her to get him to a school farther away.

During the summer period, while I was away from the centre, Bae and his mother worked with an advanced student who had been observing the work from behind a one-way mirror. Bae continued to play Family Adventures with very similar themes emerging. In the joint sessions with Bae and his mother, the new therapist continued to help Eun "learn to play" with her son. They chose to play board games. Bae was helpful to his mother while also demonstrating some competitiveness. The therapist reported that they seemed genuinely to enjoy this joint activity.

When I returned from the summer break, I began seeing Bae and his mother again. I learned that Bae, with the help and support of Farid, was able to go to a summer day camp, and was feeling quite proud of himself for being able to do it. In the first month of school, Bae had been attending more regularly, and I noted that Eun seemed more alert and engaged. In an early school meeting, the teachers and support workers said that Bae was showing signs of progress in his subjects.

I had referred Bae for psychological and academic testing before the summer break, and he was picked up by a male psychology student.

After some initial anticipatory anxiety, Bae began to enjoy the testing meetings, perhaps mainly because he could spend time with an adult male who was kind to him. The testing revealed that Bae had major language delays, problems with visual/motor integration and significant lacks in all areas of academic skill. He was performing way below grade level in all areas. The testing also found indication of an anxiety disorder. Essentially, the testing confirmed what everyone had suspected all along. The results of the tests in academic areas helped to spur on the school personnel to find a more adequate educational placement for Bae.

In the play therapy sessions, Bae began playing with plastic food, organizing a restaurant where he was the waiter and I was the customer. I had thought about challenging Bae a little more in the areas that he needed to address: his fear of making mistakes and his refusal to engage in visual art-making. I had the idea to make drawings of the plastic food as a starting place. I began by making drawings of the food myself, and then I urged him to do likewise or even to copy my drawings. When Bae realized that he could draw the food, he began drawing these forms everywhere. He also began turning the food drawings into monsters. Once when I came to get him in the waiting area, I found him proudly drawing images of bunches of grapes from memory.

During this period, Bae also played with puppets. He chose four stuffed animals who were friends and had adventures with them, doing battle with many enemies. There are others who helped but these fuzzy friends could also turn into superheroes who helped themselves and each other. At the same time as Bae still enjoyed a kind of play that was appropriate for a much younger child, I noticed that he demonstrated an increased facility with oral language. As compared to the Family Adventures, the content of these stories seemed richer, more complex and imaginative. There were mean teachers who refused to die, evil donuts, insults (calling one of the friends a "fat pig"), good and evil magic markers. Bae was content with leaving the play unresolved from one session to the next. I saw this as significant in terms of his usual tendency to make everything come out fine in the end. I sensed that he was less anxious around this lack of structure.

In my work with Eun, I focused on helping her to see how much she tended to treat her son like a baby. She was able to begin to see this and to experience her own desire to help him be more grown up.

In a series of final sessions before my departure for the summer break, Bae had an imaginary birthday party. When he blew out the candles on his imaginary cake, his wish was "to be a good painter." Taking off from his impulse, I sensed his anxiety and moved into painting (which he had not yet done) by first inventing on the spot a kind of relaxation technique. It was a simple practice of just putting water on the brushes so that Bae could experience the feeling of painting without becoming preoccupied by what he was making and whether he was doing it "right" or not.

I started making random lines and circles with the water-soaked brush and he imitated me in much the same way as we made the drawings of the toy food. He seemed to enjoy this very much. We noticed that forms were starting to come from the brush because there were traces of dried paint on it. Then I put fresh paint on my brush and talked about how nice it felt to put the paint on. Bae picked up on my enjoyment—just making marks and random lines and circles, blending the paints. He started becoming curious about what colors resulted from mixing the paints and was delighted to be able to make orange and green, purple, brown and gray. He thought it was funny and exciting that I got paint on my sleeve, and was quite aware of getting paint on his hands and on the plastic cloth that covered the table.

We continued painting together, with me showing him various ways to do it: particularly scratching out marks, letters and figures with the end of the brush in the still-wet paint. At one point, he introduced what he called "a tornado" to the painting, and I made trees. He became quite excited about this. In several places, he wrote the name "John" on the painting and said that his mother calls him John sometimes but that he prefers his Korean name. When we both agreed that the painting was done, he told a story about the tornado that attacked the trees and about the sun that was trying to come out. He titled the painting "John's trees" and wrote this name on the painting.

Bae asked to do another painting and to start the same way: with water on the brushes first. He was really excited to do this and seemed very happy and relaxed. This time we mixed white with the colors and made round shapes. It was a colorful painting which Bae said he liked very much. His title for this painting was "Mixing Colors is Fun and Interesting." Before we started on the painting, Bae said that he thought he could do this at home, that he had a table to work on and he could ask his mother to get him some paints. He described the paintings as being in our "museum" and he helped me put them in a closet to dry.

In the next session, after making another painting, we began playing in the paint left over on the tray where we had been mixing colors. He enjoyed playing around in what became brown mucky paint. Bae invented scenarios while playing with the paint: he was chasing me and drawing figure eights. He seemed quite free, not worrying about messing (the paint was contained on the tray and he did not venture outside of this frame). At the end of this session, Bae needed to be prodded to help with the clean-up but was ultimately cooperative. When I asked him to carry my container of play and art materials out of the room, he complained that it was too heavy. I urged him to carry it and told him that I was certain he could manage it. After I said this to him, he carried it down the hall to the elevator and proposed that we have a race, that he would run down the stairs and I would take the elevator and see who got there first. He was quite pleased to have arrived before me. This burst of physical vitality was new for Bae who always seemed quite tired and lethargic.

In the last sessions before my summer break, Bae asked if I could teach him how to play chess. I took this as a very good sign, that he was beginning to want to pursue activities that were more appropriate for his age and also that could potentially engage his peers. He seemed happy to be able to learn the names of the pieces and the rules of how they could move. He was not upset that he lost the first game and stayed with the whole process quite patiently. In subsequent sessions, Bae was able to talk with me about the importance of "strategy" and how chess was about planning the moves ahead and anticipating what your opponent will do. This idea seemed to interest him.

During this time, we also planned to have an ending party in our last session together which would coincide with his birthday. Bae said that he would bring balloons and a pump for blowing them up. In planning for my absence over the summer months, I had the idea that he might really like to work with the male psychology intern who did the testing several months earlier. When it was arranged, Bae asked if David, the intern, could come to his party in the last session. I thought this was a good idea to help with the transition from me to the new therapist.

David stayed for the first half of our last session. During this time, we played various games with the balloons that Bae had brought. Bae was excited to blow up the balloons himself. David and I tied them off and then we showed Bae how to make whistling noises by letting out the air and then letting the balloon fly wildly around the room. Bae thought that this was quite funny. He invented a competitive game where you had to bounce the balloon as high as you could, and had a great time playing against two adults. After David left and at the end of the session, Bae and I decided to pop the balloons. At first, he said that he was scared to do it. After I did a few and showed Bae how to do it, he was able to pop the balloons and found it quite fun.

David subsequently noted that during the four months of treatment, Bae made progress, especially in terms of his self-confidence within the play mode. More and more, David said that Bae took the lead in the play and often spoke in a very strong and confident voice when he was playing characters. His emotional range within the play scenarios expanded. This contrasted sharply with his everyday presentation: that of a very meek, anxious and compliant boy. David concurred with me that talking to Bae in the therapy room about everyday events was usually difficult but, as soon as he moved into the play mode, he was lively, excited, exuberant, uninhibited and loud.

Prior to my return after this summer break, David and I consulted on Bae's progress. David was leaving the agency, as he was a trainee in psychology and finished with his internship. We decided that the next step for Bae would be to participate in group treatment with other children of his own age. He needed to develop his social skills and to make friends. Individual play therapy, while it had been effective for him, would not specifically help him to build these skills. Because her English was not good enough, we decided not to refer his mother to a parents' group. A new group for children with parents who were diagnosed with a mental illness was forming at the agency. It seemed that this would be something from which Bae could benefit.

According to the leaders of this group, Bae is currently playing well with the other children and interacting with them socially. However, in terms of the intended goal of the group (understanding more about the challenges of the "mental illness" of their parents), Bae seems particularly clueless. Of all the children, he seems least aware of his mother's challenges. There could be many reasons for this: the psychological testing revealed serious gaps in Bae's academic levels.

Perhaps Bae is somewhat delayed developmentally which would have ramifications for his cognitive capacities. The group leaders are still exploring how to approach this subject with Bae so that he can understand better.

After his involvement with this group, which is time-limited, the question will be where Bae will go next. On the basis of his individual needs, a good case could be made for the continuation of play therapy. It was clear that Bae made great progress in this format.

When we examine the key elements of this work with play and the arts, certain themes come forward. For this anxious and frightened boy who suffered due to the serious lacks in his mother's capacity to guide him and show him the way forward into the world, the play space is critical as a practicing ground for new and risky activities. This play space is held and facilitated by a caring adult who believes that the child can do many things, has resources and has capacities. This belief in the child's power to make and to do helps bring about stories, images and scenarios which by virtue of their concrete existence demonstrate to the child that he has abilities. These works prove and reflect back to Bae his growing capacity to take hold of the world. The therapists, by means of introducing challenges through the materials, are showing the way forward and encouraging Bae to join with them, to be courageous, to try new things. Bae seems like a starving, thirsty boy who is just emerging from a long time in the desert and who finds his oasis in the playroom.

Ritual and the arts: Call the Ghostbusters!

I was approached by two social work colleagues who were working with a family. One of the therapists was focusing on the mother and the other was working with the 11-year-old son. They asked me to join the team for some sessions of expressive arts work. They had a sense that working through the arts could be effective for the family as a whole but they did not really know how to facilitate this kind of work.

The F. family was South Asian, originally from Guyana; they were non-practicing Muslims. The family constellation consisted of the following: mother, Sharon; older brother, Michael, 20 years old, from the mother's first marriage; brother, Carl, 11 years old and eight year-old fraternal twins, Theresa (a girl) and Thomas (a boy). The mother suffered from a number of physical ailments, including severe seizures. About two years before the time of our work together, she was approached by a relative with a request to help out two of her nephews. They were young men, brothers, in their early twenties and they needed a place to live for a while. Sharon agreed to let them stay with her.

Later, Sharon learned that one of these cousins sexually abused Theresa on a continual basis for over a year and that both of them physically abused and intimidated the two other younger boys— also for the year or more that they had lived in the house. These experiences had occurred in various rooms of the house. At first, Sharon had not believed the stories but then became convinced of the truth and subsequently kicked the cousins out of the house. As a result, she was ostracized from her extended family.

After the cousins left, and until the time that I had contact with the family, the children had difficulty being in most of the rooms of the house; they all, especially Theresa, would not go into any of the bathrooms alone. Only Michael's room seemed to be a safe space. The mother felt that she could not move to another house. She had fought very hard to find this house, a subsidized townhouse with enough room for her whole family.

In the first session, as a way to begin the work, I met with one of the social workers and the family (minus Michael) for the first time in the clinic. In this session, I began to get to know everyone, to see what resources they had and what they might want to do together. When I asked what each person could do, the youngest boy, Thomas, jumped in and readily divided the family into different roles: he said that Theresa was the "specialist of art," Thomas himself was the "reading specialist," Carl was the "sports specialist" and Sharon, the mother, was the "specialist of pain."

Everyone identified the problem to be the house, and we started brainstorming about this: one child drew a picture of the house on a flip chart, mapping out the different rooms. I asked them what they thought we could do about the house. There were many ideas, and I decided to take charge of structuring the process. I had a growing sense that we needed to perform some kind of operation on the house, to "cleanse" it and to make it habitable again, and that the way to do this was to create a ritual structure for the cleaning and restoration process.

They also wanted to paint something on the walls of the house, to leave a permanent mark.

Ritual structures are able to frame and guide experience toward a desired result that can be used by individuals, groups or communities. When the ideas for what we could do together started emerging, I knew that they needed a kind of shape that had a progression from one stage to another and that this shape would help them transform both the experience itself and their relationship to it. I felt that this had to be a collaborative process which took account of all the individual needs and desires.

At the end of this session, we arrived at the structure and a frame for the work to continue. We decided that the therapist team would go to the house and do two more sessions there as the primary site for this work. First we would rid the house of the bad stuff that had happened in it and of all the memories that still lingered in the rooms. I suggested that we go into each room and put all the "bad stuff" into a box and that the therapists take the box away and dispose of it. One of the social workers suggested burning herbs and smoking out all the rooms of the house. I felt that perhaps this would not fit for the family since it was a practice taken from another culture. However, the mother said that she really liked this idea, so we decided to do it.

I also created a restriction for the work: we could not spend any money. I felt that this restriction not only fit with the fact that this family had very little money but also that it might stimulate them to be more imaginative in what they could create together. This challenge in the ritual creation could be achieved whereas the challenges that faced the family in real life were what we were trying to help them overcome. The idea is that if they could manage the challenge in the therapy work, then it would give them more ways and possibilities for coping with the life situation. We came up with the idea of using rocks and writing words on them, leaving a rock or two in each of the rooms after they were cleaned. At the end of this session, I left the kids with the task of collecting lots of rocks from the areas outside of their house.

When we arrived with the box and the herbs the following week, Thomas ran out to greet us. He was very excited, especially wanting us to know that they had worked hard to clean up the house for our visit. The children had collected the rocks and were anxious to begin. (Michael was not part of this session. He came in later and spent the time in his room.) First we went over the steps of the process:

we would write the words on the rocks and get them ready, then we would go into each of the rooms and put the bad stuff into the box. We would then burn the herbs, and Theresa would lead a procession back through the house to clean each of the rooms and all the hallways. Finally, we would put the rocks in every room.

Some of the words that were put onto the rocks were "love," "family," "rollerblades" and "gameboy" (Thomas's contribution), as well as everyone's initials. When we began, and as we paraded ceremoniously up the stairs to the bedrooms, everyone became quite focused and serious. First we went into Theresa's bedroom. Theresa told the stories of what happened to her. They were very explicit and graphic. She "threw" all these stories into the box, then we banged on the lid of the box. In this first room, I encouraged them to develop a chant and a song that we sang after we put the bad stuff in the box. This was a repetitive line sung with great force and gusto: "In the box, in the box, put that bad stuff in the box!!!" We repeated this in every room of the house, in all the bathrooms, bedrooms, the living room, dining room and kitchen. The activity of cleaning the house of all the "bad stuff" reminded me strongly of the team of "ghostbusters" from the 1984 science fiction comedy.

Each member of the family told their story of what had happened to them and to each other. The chant was strong and involved shouting and banging on the box. The kids seemed to really enjoy it; after a while, they began to take the initiative in starting up the chanting and shouting. After the smoking out of the rooms, Theresa surprised everyone by quietly, with no announcement, going into the bathroom by herself. We all applauded when we realized what she had done.

The rocks were placed in all of the rooms, then there was a quiet and sad period of time. Everyone gathered in Theresa's room, and her mother cried, saying how sorry she was that she had not believed the kids when they told her their stories. The children held her and cuddled with each other, and the therapist team went downstairs to give them some private time. It was obvious that a lot of work had been done and that everyone was moved and exhausted from it. When we left, the social work team took the box out of the house and disposed of it in the garbage outside the treatment centre. This was a final step that we had all agreed upon.

We had planned to paint a mural on the wall. When we arrived for this third session with the paints (and with a cake for a party afterwards), everyone was ready and waiting. Initially, Sharon had wanted the painting to be done around several large baby pictures of the children on the main wall of the living room. But she changed her mind, and we all decided to put the mural on the wall leading upstairs. She liked that wall because it could be seen from all directions from the downstairs. We then set about deciding what we would paint and who would paint what parts.

Someone suggested a huge heart as the centerpiece. As the "art specialist," Theresa was designated to paint it. Then her mother wanted two things: prints of everyone's hands (including Michael's for which he did come and join us) and places on the outside of the heart for the names of all the people who had helped and supported the family get to this point. The family had been involved with many different agencies over the last few years. Theresa wanted to paint stars and moons and Carl and Thomas wanted to write the words that had been on the rocks in the center, along with everyone's signature. We only had about an hour to carry out this project, and everyone worked smoothly together.

During the party afterward, the children said that they felt much better about the house now and noted that everyone was using all the rooms, both alone and together. Sharon said that it would still take her some time to feel comfortable alone in her own bedroom but that every time she looked at the mural now, she felt happy and appreciative of her family and what they had together now.

When I visited the family about a year later, Sharon showed me what had happened to the heart on the wall. One time, Carl had been very angry and punched a hole in the center of the heart. Sharon had placed a bandage over the hole and she told me, "I really like it now because this is much more like our family, the way things really are." She seemed quite content about that. She also noted that the whole house and all the rooms were still being used.

In reflecting on the work that we did together, some important themes emerged which point to the effectivity of this work. First, it seems critical that we took the house as the "client," and put it at the center of the action. By doing so, everyone could focus their attention outside of themselves. They were invested in the house, wanting it and wanting to make it habitable again. This pairing of commitment to the house and distancing from the problem itself by means of focusing on the house struck the right note for pushing the work along. Second, the art-making or the work consisted of creating a ritual with objects (the box which held all the stories and the rocks with words painted on them), songs/chants and the wall painting which was the culmination of the ritual process. The ritual was able to contain all the strong emotion, the graphic and disturbing stories, and the pain of what everyone had suffered. This seemed to last a year later when the wall painting gained even more poignancy by being partially destroyed. Third, the fact that the professionals and the family were a team together, co-creating the process as we went along, seemed to be another strong contributor to making the work effective.

In both stories, there are common threads which run through and which relate to the question of what makes the work "work." There are some very specific factors which contribute to the effectiveness of the work. First, the role of the therapist and the surrounding supports seems central: the extent to which resources and strengths are emphasized, the encouraging attitude which facilitates taking action and shaping into forms and the commitment to stay with it through all the ups and downs. Second, the forms themselves and the concrete manifestations are crucial: stories, paintings, songs, chants, painted rocks. Paolo Knill often speaks about the "thingly" nature of work with the arts. Beyond the things themselves, the creation of a sheltering space, an alternative world in which the arts enable distancing or "decentering," is important for the working through of difficulties.

Finally, in both situations, of central importance was the creation of a space for play and imagination. Both Bae and the F. family grew in their capacity to deal with the difficulties that faced them by entering and staying in such a space. In exploring the question of what makes the work "work" in expressive arts therapy, it could be said that play is the key in that it is at the base of art-making and of the creating and carrying out of ritual structures. These basic human activities help us to restore ourselves when we lose our way.

References

Winnicott, D. W. (1958) *Collected Papers: Through Paediatrics to Psychoanalysis.* London: Tavistock.
Winnicott, D.W. (1971) *Playing and Reality.* London: Tavistock.
Yalom, I. (2005) *The Theory and Practice of Group Psychotherapy.* New York: Basic Books.

Part III

EDUCATION

Untitled   Judy Nisenholt

CHANGE in the AIR
Elizabeth McKim

The creatures
Are trying out
Their new-
Found gestures
Every which way
Like penguins.

Nothing
Perfunctory.
Only these
Succinct
Hard won
Motions.
The architects of new meanings
Excite the frozen air
Exit with unexpected eloquence
Flapping their possibilities

Like Prayer Flags
Like Prayer Flags

Where I am
You are
In this fabulous tableau

Look ahead now.....
The creatures
Are taking
Their bows!

AESTHETIC EDUCATION
Learning through the Arts
Stephen K. Levine

What is distinctive about teaching and learning in the expressive arts is the emphasis on aesthetic education: learning through the arts. In most universities, the arts are separated from other disciplines. Professional training in the arts takes place in fine arts faculties, which the majority of students visit only through the occasional elective course. This separation reflects the traditional distinction between *theoria* and *poiesis*, theoretical and artistic ways of knowing. The arts are thought to be non-cognitive; at best, they employ a kind of technical and situational know-how, completely different from the scientific understanding that offers us an objective view of the world. Even Humanities departments, which concern themselves with the study of cultural works, do not usually use the arts themselves as a means of learning.

This radical distinction between science and art is itself an historical one. It was not until the beginnings of philosophy in classical Greece that the traditional mythopoetic transmission of knowledge was rejected in favor of a concept of reason grounded in the logic of non-contradiction. In this way, *mythos* gradually gave ground to *logos*: poetry, drama and storytelling were replaced by deductive thought. Ultimately, for Plato, the poets were to be exiled from the just city, since their work was thought to give rise to disorder and chaos in the soul and consequently in the body-politic. This Platonic conception of the deleterious effects of *poiesis* is clearly in contrast with the honored place that Greek tragedy traditionally held in the city-state.

In the late 18th century, the German poet and philosopher Friedrich Schiller challenged this exclusion of the arts from the realm of knowledge. In *On the Aesthetic Education of Man* (1965) Schiller set forth the view that human existence had become split between the body and the mind, sensibility and understanding. He saw aesthetics as a way of overcoming this fragmentation. The embodying of meaning in art, as well as the harmony of form in great works, gives us a presentiment of our own possible wholeness. Far from being irrelevant to education, aesthetics was now seen as what we might call the royal road to learning, unifying the different faculties of the mind and, potentially, the different strata of society.

Schiller was following Kant in the conception of aesthetics that had been developed during the 18th century. In this tradition, "aesthetics" refers to the study of the experience of works of art, the subjective states of mind that are produced by contemplation of such works. Schiller, in spite of being himself a great poet and dramatist, kept to this contemplative tradition. It is true that Schiller, following Kant, emphasized play as a means of bridging reason and sense-experience. Nevertheless, aesthetic education for him comes primarily from the contemplation of the works produced by play and not from play itself, despite its poietic nature.

Moreover, *poiesis*, the making of works, was thought to be the realm of genius. It is *aesthesis*, the experience of these works through contemplation available to all that is the means of leading the mind to that wholeness which had been torn apart through the development of a scientific rationality divorced from sensible experience.

An expressive arts approach to education presupposes a restoration of the central role of *poiesis* as a way of knowing. Students are encouraged to engage in art-making not as an illustration of a theoretical framework but as a way of discovering what had been previously unknown. This emphasis on *poiesis* as discovery accords with our understanding of its role in change-processes, whether in therapy, education, coaching, or conflict-transformation and peacebuilding. In order for individuals and groups to move from a restricted situation to one in which their range of play is enlarged, it is necessary for the imagination to be put into action. The arts are disciplines of the imagination; they take us beyond the actual into the realm of possibility. By decentering from the literal reality of our lives, we can engage a practice of the imagination that opens up new horizons and draws on resources that may have previously lain dormant. Furthermore, through reflective analysis on this process in a phenomenological mode, we can see possibilities for change that had been previously covered up.

Thus not only is *poiesis* or art-making restored to its central role in knowing, but *aesthesis* in the sense of contemplative understanding is also given an important, though secondary, role in the learning process. It is not enough to engage in art-making; afterwards we must step back and reflect on its significance. We call this mode of reflection "aesthetic analysis" to indicate that it is not an interpretation based on an explanatory framework but rather a phenomenological process of understanding in which we allow what shows itself to show itself without imposing meaning upon it.

This understanding of *poiesis* as the path to aesthetic education relies on a conception of art-making as central to human experience, not as restricted to those possessing genius or to professional artists. By engaging in poietic acts, students can discover their own resources for imaginative expression and thereby the possibility of helping others to do the same. This conception of aesthetic education also challenges the notion that the knowledge which the arts bring is primarily a matter of subjective experience; rather, the practice of the imagination can lead to the discovery of the truth of the situation in which we find ourselves.

Poiesis opens up the possibility of something new, and, in doing so, enables us to understand the past in a new light. As resources are uncovered, individuals and communities can develop a sense of possible action, ways of transforming themselves and their worlds. In this sense, we follow Schiller's conception of aesthetic education as a possible basis for the development of the individual and as an aid in helping to heal the fragmentation which is often experienced in contemporary life.

However, the goal of wholeness which guides Schiller's thinking can no longer serve as an unquestioned ideal for us. From the totalitarianism of the last century to the "war on terror" today, the search for unity can often become a means for repressing difference. Any movement toward integration and wholeness must also contain within it a tendency toward greater pluralism, multiplicity and differentiation.

Perhaps the concept of aesthetic education itself has to be deconstructed to allow for the beauty of the various. As Gerard Manley Hopkins wrote, "Glory be to God for dappled things… All things counter, original, spare, strange…" (1918) From an expressive arts perspective, we glory in the dappled things in all their beautiful multiplicity and variation. As Paolo Knill has often said when leading community art sessions at the European Graduate School, "Beauty is the *we* song of flowers." *Poiesis* is our way to that song.

References

Hopkins, G.M. (1918) "Pied Beauty." In *Poems of Gerard Manley Hopkins*. London: Humphrey Milford.
Schiller, F. (1965) *On the Aesthetic Education of Man*. New York: Frederick Ungar.

AESTHETIC RESPONSIBILITY IN EXPRESSIVE ARTS

Thoughts on Beauty, Responsibility and the New in the Education of Expressive Arts Professionals

Margo Fuchs Knill and Paolo J. Knill

> *The work of art gives daily life its dream—transcending our time— bound constraints.*

In the art- and studio-based learning frames essential in the training for expressive arts professionals in the Arts, Health and Society Division of the European Graduate School (EGS), students are challenged aesthetically both in studios and in seminars. Our students—artists and non-artists alike—are engaged in different roles in artistic activities and reflective discourse; but directly or indirectly, the curriculum at EGS must have a strong aesthetic component.

Questions about aesthetics and responsibility arise in respect to the arts in education. Aesthetic education, as we practice it, emphasizes a different kind of responsibility than we usually encounter in life, one that is respectful of and to the arts, namely an aesthetic responsibility (Knill 2005). The dilemma is that although we may be responsible for providing frames that encourage the emergence of the new, we cannot trick beauty into shining through; the work of art emerges in its own time. Yet we still want the sensory experience of beauty to arrive in order to help us make sense.

In this respect, certain questions arise:

- How can we avoid forcing the artwork to a specific educational purpose?

- How can we stick to the arts and go beyond pedagogical creativity exercises?
- How can we set the challenge of an aesthetic learning frame quite right: not too low or too high?

Teaching with aesthetic responsibility has to do with setting up challenging tasks. If we did not do that, the students would not have a sense of achievement that moves, touches and amazes—some of the attributes of beauty. The teacher needs to be able to confront; not everything goes. There is thus a responsibility to suggest the quite right challenge to help the student make the artwork "work."

The teacher therefore proposes a task that the learner is challenged by, yet is able to cope with. This is where aesthetic responsibility focuses on the principle of low skill/high sensitivity. We choose an art form or style that demands high sensory competency for the shaping of the artwork and an adequate level of manual skills so that even a non-professional artist can experience the process of art-making. For instance, making a collage demands high sensitivity to images and the skill to cut with scissors. It does not necessarily require training in an art academy.

The teacher's coaching lies in the interest of helping the emerging work of art to find its beauty. She guides the student to that very moment where it "works." And as the process continues, the more an atmosphere of longing for the work of art begins to arrive. This longing should not be confused with a goal-directed orientation. It is much more process-oriented, raising curiosity and grounding each shaping action in the present yet completely directed forward into the future.

Of course, we cannot prepare the student completely for the future. We cannot conquer the unpredictable scenes that will arise, nor simulate and role-play the unknown. However, in staying with the arts, we learn how something new is created and comes into our world. This fosters an atmosphere in which the unknown can be encountered more as an opportunity than as a threat.

To make this possible, the teacher needs to be skillful and artful in paying attention to the intrinsic forward movement that occurs when working with the arts. The artistic process needs to be attractive and nurturing so that it helps the student overcome fears of failure. The newness and strangeness of the artwork then becomes a resource that keeps both the teacher and students curious. Motivation through curiosity must be cultivated for everyone engaged in the learning process—teacher and students alike. We want to learn what the work of art—still unknown to us—may be, and what it may have to tell us.

To learn actually requires an encounter with something unknown to us. Working with the arts is in that sense a gift to any classroom, since the material to learn from is always new, as if it were just being created in that moment. Being a change agent constantly puts us into new and unexpected situations, just as working with the arts teaches us to live with the new and unexpected. Any change—wanted or unwanted—in educational, consulting or therapeutic contexts requires shape-shifting anew.

This kind of lived-through learning touches on existential issues and is not a "may be" nor an "as if." Therefore, we as teachers have a responsibility to give directions that are congruent with the art-based learning process. These directions guide the process in the tradition of the arts with clarity about the frame and the play-range of shaping. This commitment to the arts is an educational purpose unto itself.

Even though we cannot know the outcome of an artistic process, we can always rely on its unique newness and freshness. Validating this as a good enough learning base frees us from searching for imposed securities such as pedagogical creativity exercises or games that would limit our capacity to encounter the unknown.

> The arts speak without speaking—revealing and concealing, crisscrossing the tangible and the intangible, allowing our minds and senses to be here while there, and encouraging us to give the inconceivable a chance.

Reference

Knill, P., Levine, E. and Levine S. (2005) *Principles and Practice of Expressive Arts Therapy: Toward a Therapeutic Aesthetics*. London: Jessica Kingsley Publishers.

14

EDUCATION ON THE EDGE

Acts of Balance

Elisabeth Hösli and Peter Wanzenried

In many fields of education, we need more and more specialists in order to find a balance of values, to lead when there is a lack of orientation, or to help people find new perspectives in their lives. Classrooms with students from difficult family and cultural backgrounds, adult education with unemployed people, rehabilitation of young offenders, education in hospitals, projects in countries where violence and wars are dominant, all require teachers with a high degree of skill.

But what kind of learning is possible in these situations? It is not sufficient in these fields of education to have a strong capacity for social engagement. No matter what curriculum we follow or textbook we use, it is important to find both trust in our own spontaneous awareness and in the availability of special educational skills. Then education becomes more and more an art, a dance, and a losing and finding our balance again and again.

In the following stories, Elisabeth Hösli tells us about her work in difficult situations of multicultural education in order to show how this art of teaching and learning can work. In accordance with these examples, Peter Wanzenried points out four kinds of balance we have to be aware of.

Rafael

Nine years old, from the Dominican Republic.
Nine months in Switzerland.
Tall and strong.
Even in the first minute
he gave me the impression of being pressed,
like a pressure cooker under high pressure.

Full of panic for making mistakes?

Last February, I wrote:
"Doesn't communicate in German even after 2 ½ months;
is unreachable, like there wouldn't be any connection between him and us.
He paints in a restrained way,
and it looks like he is not in contact with his roots.
What does he have to tell?
Is my working method incompatible with his disposition?

My developmental desire for him:
To recover a relation to his own images and stories.

Often we've been quarreling and struggling for power.
I didn't feel good about it—
He probably didn't feel good either."

Then, last September, he began working with clay.
Free experiments, free play:
Knocking, tapping, beating, pounding, forming, folding, rolling, kneading…

Modeling with closed eyes:
Rafael acquires a delicate and tender expression.
Beside him, Ismail [another child in the class] is softly singing an Albanian song.

The following Friday:
Rafael's piece of clay turns out to be a volcano.
Some clay balls spew out of the volcano.
Manuel copies the volcano. From his volcano,
magma flows like water.
A man cries for help, runs away.
Rafael's volcano falls silent and disappears under the towel.
"Too bad, we have to stop now," he says.
"When will we play again with clay?"

Two weeks of vacation pass by.

"Do you remember last Friday before vacation?" I ask.
Immediately, Rafael remembers his volcano.
"Would you like to paint today?"

The children agree with enthusiasm.
My advice: "Paint, whatever you like to paint."

I cannot give further help.
Latifa and Leyla with their parents are knocking on our door.
Two new students for our class. They need my help and my time.
So the children start to work by themselves.

And what appears on Rafael's paper?
A volcano, "a sleeping volcano," as he writes later.

Next day: All the pictures are hanging at the black board.
A dialogue occurs between Rafael and Ismail:

Rafael: What did you paint?
Ismail: Beautiful colors.
Rafael: Why?
Ismail: Because I like them. And what did you paint?
Rafael: A volcano.
Ismail: Why did you paint a volcano?
Rafael: Because I'm interested in it.

I bring books and pictures of volcanoes, and pieces of lava.
I tell about the existence of dead, sleeping and active volcanoes.
Rafael writes to his volcano:
I painted a sleeping volcano. I like it.

Next step: "Look for the most beautiful thing in your picture? How does it sound? Which instrument goes best with it?"
Rafael plays to his sleeping volcano with high concentration and in a very delicate manner on the xylophone.
Beside it, he sings softly his own text he has written to the volcano.

"I'm shivering:
Would I be able to meet my own inner volcano in such a loving way?"

We listen to all the musical work.
We paint all the musical work.

While listening to his own music, Rafael is again painting a volcano.
This time, red "Zs" are floating out of the crater.
"My volcano is snoring," Rafael says.

Back to the clay.
Forming a work, which can be dried and burnt.
Rafael likes to form a volcano.
With love and patience, he is modeling and forming;
rapt, and with endurance.
He almost doesn't have enough time.
But at last, he shows me his work:
A wonderful – penguin!
Rafael explains: "I love penguins because they are aquatic animals."

A fiery thing wanted to be formed, an aquatic animal appeared.
Balance of elements?
Since then, Rafael seems to me to be more quiet and content.
Our relationship became more relaxed.

Every time he works with the arts,
Rafael is very present and alert.
He works and cooperates with intensity and seriousness.
He faces the challenges.
He tries, searches, and finds.

Summer seminar in Bosnia-Herzegovina

A 10-day summer seminar for teachers in Bosnia-Herzegovina. On July 17, the first meeting with the participants of the summer school, in a formal setting. I'm faced with benevolent, expectant, but tired glances. Sixty female and male teachers from Sarajevo and Gorazde. Two days later, I sit in the circle of the first group. After some hesitation, the people get into it— men and women, young and old. Interactive games follow, with the objective of making visible and experience-able the variety, the differences, and the things in common among human beings. Insecurity coupled with increasing cheerfulness characterizes the atmosphere. We have many opportunities for laughing or smiling. Whoever becomes tired, sits down at the fringe of the group. In the subsequent reflection phase, the correlation with democratic teaching and with their own everyday life is established.

The first phase is followed by a phase of individual working: creating a portrait of oneself. Describing what the important component of one's own identity is at present. Making a wish, a vision, an expression by a work of art, i.e., in a poem, a drawing, or a symbol. Insecurity again. But most of the participants get into it spontaneously.

Third phase: sharing. The works contain and conceal many emotionally delicate, unsayable things. The predominant symbols in all groups are the sun, nature, the sea—symbols of reconstruction, of variety in common, of peace. The artistic work permits the participants to express sensitive problems, unsayable and private things, while knowing that their intimate feelings remain protected. The numerous wishes and visions expressed seem to give power and courage to all of them for a moment.

The presentation of a portrait by one of the female participants causes all of them to be deeply moved. A woman who makes a slightly pert and resolute impression presents her work to her colleagues. From her attitude and from her determination, I gather that this presentation is important to her. On the upper part of the sheet I recognize text, on the lower one she has painted a dove of peace. "Peace I want, only peace," she says and starts to read her text aloud. Then her words are drowned by tears. "She tells about her son who died," Feras, the interpreter, whispers to me. Then the woman asks him to finish reading her text. What is written down is to be expressed aloud. Silence in the room. Tears, dry swallowing. "May we smoke?" a man's voice asks. After ten minutes of silence and smoking, a phase during which everybody has dealt with his or her own past, a woman asks me: "Elisabeth, tell us about Zurich!" The atmosphere relaxes. But I cannot tell about Zurich in this moment. So I suggest telling a picture-book story, which is accepted with enthusiasm. So my interpreter, sitting beside me, empathically and with a warm voice tells the story of *The Magic Bird* by Max Bolliger, the story of the reconciliation of the last dwarf and the last giant, who had spent their time harassing each other until they finally united in order to save a bird's life. Spellbound, the participants listen to the story and afterwards they leave the classroom obviously more relaxed and more hopeful.

The balance between education and therapy

No doubt in both educational and therapeutic situations we encounter human beings who suffer. A nine-year-old boy lives in a foreign world he cannot participate in. A woman has lost members of her family and her home. They both need help. In both situations, Elisabeth has to be clear that her frame of work is an educational and not a therapeutic one. On the other hand, she has to be aware that education here first of all means to take care of these souls. So she offers possibilities to let the soul speak in the way our ancestors did: by painting and playing music, by sharing stories and acting. And in this way it just happens. The sleeping volcano slowly wakes up and turns into a penguin. The story of the Magic Bird leads to hope for peace out of the sharing of tears and silence. Thus, a crisis may become an important step to personal growth if we dare to open the space to the unexpected— even in education. But school or an in-service training for teachers are not the places to work in depth on personal issues. The focus has to switch from the personal image of the sleeping volcano to pictures of volcanoes in books, to learning the foreign language by writing sentences in German describing the pictures. After a period of silence, the teachers in the training program have to go ahead to the next class. This is a first act of balance: between the special needs of these souls for individual care and the goals I am expected to reach.

We all have to be brave in order to maintain this balance. In these days, school development takes on a direction in which test scores become the only standard for quality in teaching.

The balance of dialogic encounter

Deep feelings are expressed in both situations and ask for an answer. So Elisabeth has to find the balance of dialogic encounter. It is not helpful to take over all that fear, aggression, sadness and hopelessness and to lose any distance to all the suffering in front of her. But it is also inappropriate to hide behind a mask of professional crisis management. It is necessary to walk the tightrope between blind identification and untouched distance. Dialogic encounter, "*Be-gegnung*" as Martin Buber called this educational relationship, means to face carefully what happens between us. It means to take my responsibility as a teacher, and at the same time to say "Yes" with compassion to whatever happens. Elisabeth tells us how she struggled for power with Rafael, and how badly she felt about it. "Would I be able to meet my own inner volcano in such a loving way?" she asks herself. She refuses to tell about Zurich just to relax in a difficult situation and makes a different suggestion instead. All these examples show that dialogic education is not the easy way of not setting any boundaries. It is the way of taking risks again and again, knowing that every act of education is a paradox in itself.

The balance of different languages creating our realities

All the people in the situation above are urged to find new identities.

Rafael, Manuel, Latifa, Leyla are moving to a new place in our multicultural world, and all the teachers in Sarajevo are starting a new part of their life stories after a complete breakdown of their homes. This is what happens—let us hope not as extremely—to many of us, students and teachers. And education has to support a personal development in this very world.

But how can we find new eyes to see that reality can also have other shapes? How can we find words to express a new point of view, one that is only on the way to its first appearance? How can we find metaphors to give sense to new experiences? How can we find orientation in a world where everything seems to fall apart?

In order to help grow up and live with broken identities in our postmodern society, education has to create spaces for dealing with the diversity of realities. Following the constructivist theory that the language we use creates the world we live in, we have to find a wide range of languages to express different approaches to this construction:

Language Creates Realities

Choose common everyday language
As you talk at home
In simple usual words
So we can find trust.

Choose language of explication
As science requires
In precise, unambiguous terms
So we can find definition.

Choose language of understanding
As arts allow us
In strong visual metaphors
so we can find meaningful communion.

Choose language of silence
As spiritual meditations
In awe and wondering questions
so we can find eternity.

Rafael's work on his volcano makes visible, step by step, how the translation from one expressive language to another works:

- modeling his expression by playing with clay
- finding a first form of a volcano
- adding color to it by painting
- comparing with volcanoes in books to understand their nature
- describing what he painted in a few German words
- finding the music of his volcano
- forming his final masterpiece: a penguin.

It seems magical how the transformation from one modality of representation to another leads to an unexpected place. Let us focus on the methods Elisabeth used.

The balance between process and work

Figure 14.1 shows aspects and phases of an intermodal learning process which we consider to be analogous to an artist's working process.

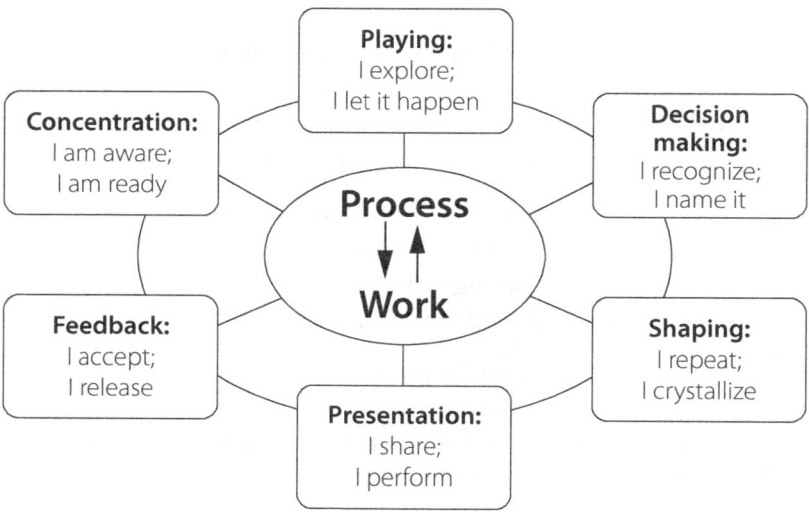

Figure 14.1 Aspects and Phases of Intermodal Learning

As teachers, we have to take care of the balance between all of these six aspects. We have to be aware of our own and our students' tendency to cheat: not leaving enough time for exploring and just fixing on the first idea is one way to escape. Not making any clear decision and just staying with all the ambiguity is the opposite. Having all work remain in progress as never-ending stories may be my weak point. Creating wonderful objects for a great exhibition without any meaning for the students might be another.

Education on the edge needs teachers who are good dancers with a high awareness of balance:

The balance between
the needs of the very moment and the goals they have to reach
in all their education

The balance between
going very close and staying at a clear distance
to all these thirsty souls

The balance between
the many realities from different approaches
all these individuals create

The balance between
the chaos and order that occurs
in all these works which may arrive

Let us dance
losing and finding balance
again and again

15

ART ASYLUM

Exploring Otherness through Play and Art-Making

Ellen G. Levine

One night a few years ago in a European Graduate School (EGS) Masters core group, I decided to use the three-hour class time for an arts-based reflection on the course material that students had just completed in the psychopathology subject course. "Core group" is the name we use for the group that studies together throughout the whole three weeks of the summer school program, and for the sessions devoted to reflection on the material arising from the four subject courses. These periods between the subject courses can also be used for group building and for an examination of the dynamics of the group in order to provide the students with a clear learning frame.

In the psychopathology subject course, we began by looking at the impulse toward classification and diagnosis of "mental disorders," particularly as found in the diagnostic manual used in North America, the DSM-5. The course then examined psychopathology from an arts based, phenomenological and relational perspective, one which puts emphasis upon encountering "otherness," that which is strange to us, and finding a way to be with and shape it. To think of psychopathology from an arts-based perspective means to consider how the arts have always been able to hold suffering within human life and how they can also uncover the resources with which people meet such experiences.

Our focus here was on how we work with psychopathology as expressive arts therapists. We explored the subject through the arts, as well as through a reflective discourse, using painting, writing and theatre as our media. The results that emerged from this research then became material for further enhancing and enriching our understanding of the subject.

While we had used the arts in the work of the course, I wanted to also use them in the core group time in order to continue to reflect more deeply on the material. That night, therefore, I posed the following questions to the students: what is the otherness in you and how do you encounter that otherness in another? How could we make an art studio together that would give us the freedom to be other than ourselves for a few hours? I then came up with the idea of creating an "art asylum," a space where the students could feel free to explore whatever they wanted, to play in a completely unstructured way, perhaps in strange ways. Using the word "asylum," the old term for a mental institution, was an attempt to play with the idea of the art studio as a place of retreat and safety where anything non-ordinary was possible—we could "go insane" for a little while, held in the safe container of the arts.

The students took on this challenge. They ranged freely around the room, engaging with each other in playful and strange ways. Years later, whenever I meet these former students, we reminisce about this evening and the special quality that was created in the classroom that night.

That night, students danced, sang, painted and engaged in improvisational encounters without instruction. The atmosphere was one of completely free and unfettered play. The picture below (Figure 15.1) captures one of the many playful moments we experienced in the studio. Through "going insane" within a safe space, the students not only explored some of the characteristics of their own psychopathology but also experienced how "otherness" can be a creative resource as well as an intolerable burden. I believe that this is one of the ways that the "freedom to learn" (*Lernfreiheit*) fostered by a creative, arts-infused atmosphere in the classroom provides an understanding that could not be achieved through more conventional means of education.

16

ARTISTS IN COMMUNITY

The Black Mountain College and the
White Mountain Graduate School

Sally Atkins

Black Mountain College was an experimental liberal arts college, located in a rural mountain area in western North Carolina. It lasted 23 years, from 1933 until 1956, and enrolled fewer than 1300 students. Nonetheless, it is considered one of the most innovative and fascinating experiments in the history of education and the arts. It had as its purpose the education of the whole person, with an insistence on the central role of the arts in that purpose. Many books have been written about the college, and many more have been written by those who studied or taught there. Recently a new museum was begun in Asheville, North Carolina, to showcase the college's continuing influence in the arts.

The European Graduate School (EGS) is an international professional graduate school, providing graduate and postgraduate education in the expressive arts, critical thinking and the philosophy of the arts, in the Swiss alpine village of Saas Fee. Despite differences in cultural and historical contexts and differing purposes, the two schools share some important similarities. Paolo Knill, founder and first Provost of the European Graduate School, has referred to EGS as the White Mountain College, with a nod to the artistic and experimental heritage of Black Mountain College. In this article I want to tell a small piece of the story of Black Mountain and to reflect upon the nature of community in which learning and the arts play a central role, as they did at Black Mountain College, and as they do presently at the European Graduate School.

My interest in both schools is more than academic. Black Mountain College existed near the town where I grew up. I was eleven the year it closed. Both Black Mountain campuses, the Blue Ridge Campus (the Blue Ridge Assembly of the YMCA) and the Lake Eden campus (Camp Rockmont) were places where I went on outings and picnics as a young person. I know the landscape of Black Mountain.

In the 1980s, as a young professor at nearby Appalachian State University I had the opportunity to meet the poet and potter, M.C. Richards, who had taught at Black Mountain. Her ideas about the arts, education, creativity, and community have exerted a continuing influence on my thinking. Her references to Black Mountain, both in her writings and in personal conversations, furthered my curiosity about the school. Furthermore, throughout my life I have been inspired by the innovative works of artists such as Merce Cunningham, John Cage, Josef and Annie Albers, Robert Rauschenberg, Jacob Lawrence, and Buckminster Fuller. Likewise, I have been touched by the writings of M.C. Richards, Charles Olson, Fielding Dawson, Michael Rumaker, and Robert Creeley. I have continued to reflect upon the impact the school must have had on these artists and writers.

Martin Duberman (1973) called his seminal work about Black Mountain, *Black Mountain College: An Exploration in Community*. Vincent Katz (2002) called his more recent edited work, *Black Mountain College: An Experiment in Art*. These phrases, "exploration in community," and "experiment in art," touch a yearning in me. Currently, as a core faculty member at the European Graduate School, I am intensely involved in teaching and living the experiment of academic community centered on the arts. So I approach the subject not as an outside observer, but as Duberman himself did. The issue, he says, is not whether the historian (I would add "researcher") should be known, but how. Like Duberman, I have attempted to place myself in relationship with the material, to let it touch me, tug at me, make me ever more curious. It continues to do so. The rich diversity of perceptions and commentaries about the Black Mountain experience continue to open to new and ever more complex questions about art, education, and community. This is a personal response to some of the stories written and told about Black Mountain, as well as a response to those stories currently being lived at EGS.

The nature of community

The word community carries multiple threads of history and associations. It has been used to describe groups as varied as those characterized by physical proximity, those based on religious or political ideologies, those formed around charismatic leaders, even those formed on a temporary basis in classes and workshops. Today, in our age of technological and economic interconnectedness, we often speak of the "global community" of the world. The word community also carries a connotation of a certain way of being together, one that is often romanticized and often held as an ideal in society. Thomas Moore (1998), in his book, *Care of the Soul*, argues that one of the strongest needs of the soul is to be in community and that a genuine sense of community is lacking in our society today. What the soul needs is not a collection of uniformity, but to be in connection with multiplicity and difference. Moore goes on to point out that a community is not a family but a group of people held together by a common purpose, shared values, and feelings of belonging.

What is of most interest here is the concept of community as it is applied to higher education. Parker Palmer (1997), the teacher and philosopher of higher education, offers a definition of community as a *capacity for relatedness* in human beings, relatedness not only to people but to historical events, to the world of ideas, to nature, and to things of the soul. This capacity, says Palmer, is what holds community together. It is rooted not in therapeutic, civic, or market models of community, but in the very relational nature of reality.

One of the most important qualities of true community, Palmer says, is the *capacity for creative conflict*. Conflict is the dynamic by which we test our ideas, in a joint effort to move forward, to stretch ourselves and each other. Palmer also says that community is the place where the person you least want to be with lives, and that when that person leaves, someone else quickly arises to take his or her place. Community is not opposed to conflict. Indeed, it is exactly the context in which conflict can be held within a compassionate fabric of human caring. Carl Rogers (1980) says that we grope for future forms of community, and that in this time it is especially important to listen to the contrary voices, those that express unpopular or unacceptable views.

Reflections on Black Mountain College

Black Mountain College began in 1933 when John Andrew Rice, a classics professor, and several of his colleagues and students left Rollins College in Florida amidst a storm of controversy regarding issues of academic freedom. Their desire was to create a new type of college—

an experimental liberal arts school with the arts at the center of the curriculum. There was no logical reason to start a small liberal arts college in remote western North Carolina in 1933. The market did not demand it, nor could the economy support it. It was a confluence of personal circumstances and opportunities that made it happen (Reynolds 1998). This was the same time in which the United States was struggling through the Great Depression and Europe was seeing the rise of Nazism, the closing of the Bauhaus, and the persecution of artists and intellectuals. Black Mountain survived the Depression, World War II, dissension and changes in leadership and faculty, until faculty disagreements and financial difficulties ultimately brought its "adjournment."

Some fundamental beliefs shaped its practices. The first was that living and learning should be intertwined, that education happens everywhere. While information, analytical skills, and reason were highly prized, they were not considered the whole of life. All aspects of living were considered important for learning. There was a strong emphasis on fulfilling the social responsibilities of a community without sacrificing individual freedom. Students and faculty alike lived on the campus, took each other's classes, created celebrations and performances, and made art of all kinds. They participated in the work program of the college, raising their own food, and building and maintaining the facilities of the college.

Rice's philosophy was to create a climate of freedom, to offer invitation after invitation (Duberman 1973). Especially in the arts, students and faculty were encouraged to try all forms, to experiment. One of the underlying factors at Black Mountain was a desire to see in a new and fresh way, free of previous restrictions. What was most encouraged was experimentation. Rice believed that there was something of the artist in everyone. He also believed that the whole community was the teacher. Rice was an innovative educational theorist, a colleague of John Dewey. He aspired to teach philosophy in a dynamic of query and pursuit, promoting constant questioning, and he was strongly opposed to a controlled pre-established syllabus or any bureaucratic control of the educational process (Katz 2002).

Josef Albers of the recently closed Bauhaus in Germany was brought in to lead the art department, which he did for 16 years. His philosophies of art-making and teaching were extremely important in shaping the foundation of the school. Albers saw art as revelatory and transformational, not just informational, and he felt that experimentation was more important than production. He believed that one should start not with theory, but with materials, and that free play was crucial in the beginning. Specific aesthetic forms were not taught. He believed that as one worked with materials and through experimentation an individual aesthetic could develop. His wife, Anni Albers, exemplified his ideas in her weaving, endlessly experimenting with new weaves, materials, and designs. Her presence at the college also served to bridge the gap between art and craft, which both Alberses felt was an unfortunate artifact of the Renaissance (Katz 2002). Albers was innovative and dynamic, and his presence drew other distinguished artists to Black Mountain. In the early years, the ideas of Rice and of Albers inspired continual experimentation and innovation.

The natural beauty of the setting was a factor in bringing both students and faculty to Black Mountain. Doughton Cramer (1990), a student in the early 1930s, put it this way:

> The college's setting was extraordinarily important to me. The mountains of western North Carolina are beautiful beyond description, and it is as if the atmosphere of the College was consciously a part of the living beauty. It made me sensitive to everything. (pp.80–81)

During the 1940s Black Mountain grew and flourished. It moved location to nearby Lake Eden at the foot of the Seven Sisters Mountains and began the continuous project of constructing the campus, primarily with student and faculty labor. May Sarton (1990), in a letter to a friend after visiting Black Mountain, offered a glimpse into the spirit of the college at that time. She wrote, "The thing that holds Black Mountain together and keeps it from the phoniness I feared is that they are building their new building with their own hands. It is something hard to describe in words" (p.80). Again, she comments, "There is continual dissatisfaction and improvement and clearing of fundamental issues going on. Every single person in the college feels responsible for it" (p.80).

Black Mountain reached its peak of enrollment during this time, partly due to the special summer institutes that became full-blown multi-disciplinary culture institutes (Patterson 1995). There were also internal and external difficulties. Rice had resigned amidst faculty controversy in 1937, and an unfortunate incident brought the sudden departure of a subsequent rector in 1945. Money was an ongoing issue. Faculty members were never paid more than a token salary, along with their room and board. Race was another divisive issue. Black Mountain was the first college in the United States to admit black students in 1945.

The 1950s were a period of decline from an enrollment standpoint, but still a time of inspiring innovation and remarkable energy from an artistic standpoint, bringing John Cage's first legendary "happening," and other multidisciplinary arts events. Under the leadership of the poet Charles Olson, Black Mountain became a vital center for contemporary writing. Olsen founded *The Black Mountain Review,* an arts magazine whose seven issues helped establish the Black Mountain writers, as well as others such as Allen Ginsberg and Jack Kerouac as important forces in American literature (Patterson 1995).

Michael Rumaker was a student at Black Mountain in its later days, under the leadership of Charles Olson. In his recently published memoir of that time, Rumaker (2003) writes that Olson's advice to students was always to take what feeds you. So there were many opportunities, to write with Charles Olson, to dance, however awkwardly, with Merce Cunningham, to improvise, thanks to Stefan Wolpe, on the various Steinways around the campus. Rumaker (2003) was also influenced by the setting of the college. He writes:

> I was learning not only the slowed pace of the school itself but also the slow time of the Seven Sisters Mountains, so that my movements, even my heartbeat became slower, yet, paradoxically, my eyes and mind became sharper, began to perceive...new ideas new ways of seeing and thinking...ideas and visions that seemed to stream everywhere, tumbling and echoing from ridge to ridge over all of the hundreds of acres of land that was Black Mountain, ideas and ways of seeing and being that would in years to come stream everywhere beyond its borders. (pp.143–144)

Black Mountain College was a group of creative people living and learning together. It held to the radical idea of college as community, always complex and imperfect, where both cooperation and conflict flourished with intensity. It existed in geographic isolation from the rest of the world. Imagination, inspiration, intuition, and integration were seen as fundamental to all learning. The process of artistic making was seen as a model for integrating vision, materials, imagery, and structure.

Black Mountain unquestionably became a nurturing ground for much that was later considered innovative in education and the arts. But, beyond the names of famous people who studied and taught there, it was, says Duberman (1973), really the story of a small group of people attempting to find some resonance between their ideas and their lives. It was a disparate group of individuals who committed themselves to a common purpose, who were resilient enough to hold the inevitable conflicts involved, and who sometimes were brave enough to allow themselves to be transformed by the experience. It was at its worst a series of bitter squabbles, but at its best a glimpse (not a sustained vision) of how both diversity and commonality can coexist and reinforce each other.

The diversity of experience that characterized the Black Mountain College cannot adequately be reflected in such a brief summary. I have attempted to capture the flavor of its story, particularly as it relates to attitudes and values about the nature of learning, community, and the arts. The writer, Fielding Dawson, in an interview with Joseph Bathanti (1995), said that the learning at Black Mountain was life-changing. It was facilitated not only by the living/learning community itself, but also and especially by the fact that all the teachers were doing what they were teaching.

Some of the most interesting commentary about Black Mountain comes from M.C. Richards (1973, 1989, 1990, 1996). Her experience at Black Mountain is reflected in almost all of her written works, and it is she who has written most clearly about the dynamic tensions that existed between the ideal and practical at Black Mountain. Richards (1996) said of Black Mountain, "She was born in controversy and died in controversy, splendid in the between, as she inspired and shattered dreams of liberation and fulfillment" (p.61).

Richards left the University of Chicago to come to Black Mountain to teach English in 1945. She was drawn by the vision of possibilities for education and community free from grades, tenure, and administrative bureaucracy and by the three-fold program of community life, studio arts, and intellectual discipline based on the imagination. Richards (1996) said of that time, "We were called to a new consciousness, and we felt the thrill of a new vision—something generous, resourceful, contemporary, witty, informed, visionary, and grounded in the daily work we chose to share..." (p.67).

She was devastated when the ideal didn't work out. She left Black Mountain and left teaching for a number of years. In those years following Black Mountain, the question she continued to ask herself again and again was why such intelligent, creative, idealistic, and well-educated people could not make community work. She concluded that the members of the community had not developed the habits necessary for the commitment to process. She also felt that, despite a real commitment to live in community, each of them carried shadows of adversarial ways, all in the name of armored idealism (Richards 1996).

In her later life Richards transformed her sense of loss into a sense of gratitude. She wrote of Black Mountain, "We did the best we could. We lit our little light on the darkling plain of higher education and human values and it has not gone out" (Richards 1996, p.67). She added, "There is a view of creativity shining through the fabric of Black Mountain which to me has the wisdom of the Fool—the wisdom of the Saint. It has affected deeply my own lifelong engagement with creativity as a Life Pat" (p.67).

Reflections on the European Graduate School

The story of Black Mountain College has been written many times from a multiplicity of different perspectives, by those who were there and by those who have studied it. To reflect upon the story of the European Graduate School is to reflect upon a work very much in process. EGS is still being created in the ideas and the lives of all who participate in this unique educational experiment. If communities are held together by shared values and a common purpose, where do we see the values that are shaping our community? Certainly they are expressed, both directly and indirectly, in the writings of members of the community. They are also expressed in how we live our lives together day-to-day in classes, in community meetings and lectures, in community art-making, on hikes, and at the dinner table. Many of the things we say and do echo the themes of Black Mountain. What follows are some of the shared values I have observed, filtered through the lens of my own perceptions.

A living/learning community

Paolo Knill says that EGS is, first of all, dedicated to learning for both teachers and students. We exist for the purpose of transformative learning. EGS holds a philosophy of partnership between students and faculty in learning, emphasizing cooperation, mutual recognition, and respect. Faculty are a learning community mirroring the students. Both faculty and students meet the relational difficulties of understanding each other. Knill emphasizes that we must take care of the group process so that we can learn from each other. "When you live together, eat together, you are forced to attend to the group process. You can't avoid it. You have to talk, to share. How well that's done, that's another question. You are forcefully exposed to each other" (Knill, personal communication, 2004).

The centrality of the arts

What holds us together is the common work, like an orchestra or choir, says Knill, and that common work is based upon the centrality of the arts in learning and in life. "Art is an existential of humankind. You cannot think *human being* without art" (Knill, personal communication, 2004). Stephen K. Levine (1997) sees *poiesis*, the creative act, as soul-making, the act by which we affirm our humanity. Majken Jacoby (1999) emphasizes the importance of caring for the individual, the group, and the art. She speaks of the necessity of giving form to our experience of the world. She sees art-making as a way of responding to the ethical demand we are given to take care of the life that is given to us. Margo Fuchs Knill (2004, p.16) speaks of the capacity of the arts to transcend the self in these lines:

Poetry connects the
never-ending selfish story of daily life
to a pearl row
moving the horizon to a further place
to learn the alphabet from another view.

The importance of imagination

Art is the discipline of imagination and play, the place where things happen, says Knill (personal communication, 2004). Stephen K. Levine (2000), in his editor's introduction to the second volume of *POIESIS*, speaks of continued commitment to the "practices of the imagination." He proposes that the power of imagination lies in artistic practice, the life of the soul. He argues for an artistic conception of knowing, as knowing and making were once united in the Greek concept of *poiesis*. He suggests the possibility of *poiesis* as a living experience today. In the same issue of the journal, Paolo Knill (2000) says that it is imagination that enables us to experience the world beyond the bounds of literal reality. Also in that same issue, Ellen G. Levine (2000) says that imagination requires *eros*, the motivating force that drives humans to go beyond themselves, to create new worlds.

Research and experimentation

"True wisdom happens by constant research, by constant questioning of any canonized thing" (Knill, personal communication, 2004). Research, says the historian Paige Smith (1990), is the pursuit of truth in the company of friends. At EGS, this kind of research is ongoing at all levels. Knill sees the class as the laboratory for research that feeds the progress in the field. Curricula and syllabi must not be rigid. Most universities make a syllabus that canonizes the field, and then it cannot progress. At EGS, says Knill, we have a vision of education that is beyond any canon, embracing art, philosophy, and with a stubborn phenomenology as a base. Knill is passionate in his belief that we should always be pushing the boundaries of knowledge, experimenting with both ideas and methods.

He believes that in this climate of experimentation there is something like a chemistry: people are drawn to each other. Perhaps, he says, it is the chance to experiment with how higher education can function, to experiment with the vision faculty and students hold about higher education. That and a passion for the work create a bond something beyond friendship. Perhaps this idea is akin to Duberman's (1973) reference to faculty seeking a resonance between their ideas and their living.

Transdisciplinarity, transculturalism, and creative conflict
The community of EGS embraces transdisciplinary and transcultural learning. In this way, the school crosses many boundaries and serves as a bridge between worlds. Differences that exist among community members at EGS are vast: language, culture, history, politics, and academic disciplines. Yet EGS is a meeting ground, even for some whose countries, historically or currently, are at war with each other. At EGS, such differences offer both richness and challenges. These challenges often become the subject of action and reflection. The multiplicity of EGS, when held in the ritual container of community art-making, offers the possibility of the experience of *communitas*.

Summary

Community is a complex and moving phenomena. I have only scratched the surface in my study of Black Mountain College. Likewise, I am still a beginning learner/participant in my understanding of the philosophical and theoretical ideas and practice emerging at the European Graduate School. My perspective on both schools is both informed and limited by my own cultural background as a Southern Appalachian woman, trained primarily in the discipline and discourse of American psychology. Yet as I study both schools, I am inspired. Each school, in itself, is an act of artistic making, a work of art.

Twenty years ago, in the midst of the woods where I walk every day, there was an open field, full of grasses and wildflowers. Then small pine seedlings began to sprout in the open area, where sunlight was available. Now there is a pine forest. Tall pines arch over the trail, their branches forming an arc like a cathedral over the soft carpet of needles which line the path there. Mary Emma Harris (1987) says that Black Mountain was not an institution but a process. At the European Graduate School, we too are a process, and we are in process, changing, still seeding the open spaces with new growth, still opening to what has yet to emerge. Mervin Lane (1990) said that it is the spirit of the enterprise at Black Mountain that has had a "long-range resonating effect" on the arts, on education, and on American culture. I wonder what long-range resonating effect may be wrought by what we make here at EGS.

References

Bathanti, J. (1995) "Spatial and energetic: A conversation with Fielding Dawson." *North Carolina Literary Review* 2, 2, 113–122.

Cramer, D. (1990) "A Hike to Craggy Dome." In M. Lane (ed.) *Black Mountain College: Sprouted Seeds: An Anthology of Personal Accounts*. Knoxville, TN: University of Tennessee Press.

Duberman, M. (1973) *Black Mountain: An Exploration in Community*. Garden City, NY: Anchor.

Fuchs Knill, M. (2004) *To day*. Toronto: EGS Press.

Jacoby, M. (1999) "The Necessity of Form: Expressive Arts in the Light of the Work of K.E. Logstrup." In S.K. Levine, and E.G. Levine (eds) *Foundations of Expressive Arts Therapy: Theoretical and Clinical Perspectives*. London: Jessica Kingsley Publishers.

Harris, M. E. (1987) *The Arts and Black Mountain College*. Cambridge, MA: MIT Press.

Katz, V. (ed.) (2002) *Black Mountain College: Experiment in Art*. Cambridge, MA: MIT Press.

Knill, P J. (2000) "The essence of a therapeutic process: An alternative experience of worlding?" *POEISIS: A Journal of the Arts and Communication* 2, 6–14.

Lane, M. (ed.) (1990) *Black Mountain College: Sprouted Seeds: An Anthology of Personal Accounts*. Knoxville, TN: University of Tennessee Press.

Levine, E. (2000) "Eros and imagination: An essay/review." *POIESIS: A Journal of the Arts and Communication* 2, 28–31.

Levine, S.K. (1997) *Poiesis: The Language of Psychology and the Speech of the Soul*, 2nd edition. London: Jessica Kingsley Publishers.

Levine, S.K. (2000) "Editor's introduction." *POIESIS: A Journal of the Arts and Communication* 2, 4.

Moore, T. (1998) *Care of the Soul*. New York: HarperCollins.

Palmer, P. (1997) *The Courage to Teach*. San Francisco, CA: Jossey Bass.

Patterson, T. (1995) "Black Mountain College: The success of its own accident: An opinionated, encapsulated history of Black Mountain College." *North Carolina Literary Review* 2, 2, 16–32.

Reynolds. K.C. (1998) "Socrates and serendipity: Ungainly beginnings of an improbable college" *North Carolina Literary Review* 2, 2, 32–44.

Richards, M.C. (1973) *The Crossing Point: Selected Talks and Writings*. Middleton, CN: Wesleyan University Press.

Richards, M.C. (1989) *Centering in Poetry, Pottery, and the Person*. Hanover, NH: Wesleyan University Press.

Richards, M.C. (1990) "Excerpts from 'Black Mountain College: A Golden Seed.'" In M. Lane (ed.) *Black Mountain College: Sprouted Seeds: An Anthology of Personal Accounts*. Knoxville, TN: University of Tennessee Press.

Richards, M.C. (1996) *Opening our Moral Eye: Essays, Talks, and Poems Embracing Creativity and Community*. Hudson, NY: Lindisfarne Press.

Rogers, C.R. (1980) *A Way of Being*. New York: Houghton Mifflin.

Rumaker, M. (2003) *Black Mountain Days*. Asheville, NC: Black Mountain Press.

Sarton, M. (1990) Excerpt from unpublished letter to Rosalind Greene, November 1940. In M. Lane (ed.) *Black Mountain College: Sprouted Seeds: An Anthology of Personal Accounts*. Knoxville, TN: University of Tennessee Press.

Smith P. (1990) *Killing the Spirit: Higher Education in America*. New York: Viking.

Part IV

SOCIAL AND ECOLOGICAL CHANGE

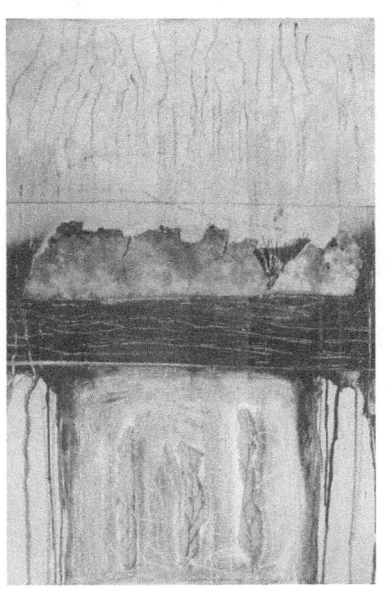

Degradation and Preservation   Ellen G. Levine
(mixed media on cardboard)

Cedar Fire Fragment

Judith Greer Essex

From 30 thousand feet it boiled,
The black and toxic
Wooly plume
      Choke smoke and ash. It

Sucked up a fragment of a photograph
Which rose into the filthy cloud
And was swept away by the roaring winds
      Over the chaparral
      Down, down the canyons
      Out to the coastal cliffs.

In the heirloom photo, my great Grandmother
      Mary, the Mormon, stood stiffly.
      Her high button collar and her leg-o-mutton sleeves,
      She looked stern and mature, but tiny.
      She was 12.

Now the tiny remnant fluttered.
      Fluttered like a translucent insect wing.
            Falling
                  Falling

One hundred year old treasured tissue
      Drifted out of the sky
            And floated down,
                  Downy
                      Down

Into the cauldron of the hissing sea.
All that remained of that part of me.

17

COMMUNITY ART

Communal Art-Making to Build a Sense of Coherence

Paolo J. Knill

Prologue

Some years ago I was asked to mediate, by means of communal art-making, a small college department that was polarized about how to go through a change in the leadership structure. It was Fall and the foliage was over, leaves tumbled and there was an early snow flurry. When I arrived at noon, I was informed that the community I would work with included the students as well as the old and new leadership. In addition, I was briefed about a preparatory meeting where the whole community had collectively wished to clarify the goal for the weekend with me. They also were very clear that they wanted to start in the afternoon with a community warm-up.

After the introductory routine, I started by saying something about the Fall. Later I asked the eighty participants to walk in the large studio. The steps are one of the prime acts of dancing. They became the center of my attention: sensitizing the feet to their grounding, and the neck, shoulder, and arm to the rising force received from the ground. Letting go of the breath brought the image of the wind. The first improvisation was about changes in a drifting walk dance, coming and going on a path that "happens" without planning it and without colliding with the wall or other dancers: "Perturb this drifting, shape the dance by making conscious changes of directions, turns or halts, and play between the two ways of dancing (drifting and shaping)." I played the piano, and the intensity of the dance increased. Dancers began to take some of their layers of Fall gear off. In a second take, I gave them the image of falling leaves and explained through illustration how the wind is the force that makes the erratic movements of the leaves that sometimes fly skyward and chaotically change direction. "We are not literally leaves—we are dancers; we can, as dancers, however, learn from the movement characteristics of leaves for our improvisational score or choreography. So let us shape all the directions, also the up and down, forward and backward, unintentionally and as if the impulse came from outside, carried out by a force similar to the wind. Lower the level more and more toward the ground where we will end." I asked some musicians to play with me, accompanying this "Rite of Fall."

This warm-up brought everybody together in the excitement about the unpredictability of directions. No one knew who they would meet in this flying mood which had a promised resting end on the floor. Live music resonated with the dance. This invigorating experience brought all levels of the hierarchy and parties with different opinions together and helped afterwards, in no time, to clarify the task for the weekend in such a way that everybody was willing to participate.

We will see later in this paper how the session continued.

Introduction

The term "community art" is a strange construct, considering that there is no art to be thought of without communities. The word, coined by therapists and educators connected to the arts and creativity, stresses the setting of "community" as something special and different from the usual one with individuals and groups. In the beginning, community art was done more or less in the tradition of "warm-up exercises," to tune in or engage the audience. This happens with scores similar to folkloric dancing, singing, or ethno-drumming, free dance and voice improvisation. This style of community art is still used for communities that are put together for a short period of time, like audiences or transient communities of gatherings such as conferences, educational settings, festivals, reunions and cruises.

I want to focus in this paper on community art that is commissioned as an event in task-oriented communities and therefore is shaped according to certain criteria. This kind of community art has the objective of strengthening the resilience of the community to establish and retain well-being. Resilience is understood as the ability to activate resources and mobilize coherence (Schiffer 2001). One could also say, metaphorically, that community art is designed to strengthen the "immune system" of the community, so that members, or member clusters, can respond early to conflicts before they escalate.

Schiffer also demonstrates, that "affective-sensorimotor" experiences (as they are present in the arts and play) are of primary importance for a sense of coherence and therefore for mobilizing resilience. This supports the use of the arts in activities that are expected to strengthen the resilience of communities. We need, however, to understand more about the structure of communal art-making, in order to find useful ways in scoring community art projects that serve the envisioned purpose in question.

We will look from two perspectives at communal art-making as it is practiced in community art. The resulting distinctions are gained from observation of communal art-making in a variety of communities, ranging from 30 to 300 members and with both transient and permanent characteristics, for example, task-oriented symposia, educational institutions and the private sector.

Community art as an alternative experience of worlding

All art-making creates an imaginary space that is distinct from everyday reality with its situational restrictions and rigid routines—*the habitual experience of worlding*. Art-making is, however, still part of the same world; we distinguish the difference therefore with the term *alternative experience of worlding*. Although this experience has constraints as well (imposed by the artistic frame, by restrictions of material and by the structures of the art discipline), these challenges act like openings to increase the *range of play* beyond the usual one, even "beyond imagination" (Knill, Levine and Levine 2005, pp.81–88).

In the imaginary space of communal art-making, things are surprising, unpredictable and unexpected, yet describable in their particular logic. These things happen differently than in everyday routine. People communicate with those with whom they usually have little contact.

Someone may play a leading role by contributing a new turn in an improvisation; this person may not have much influence in the usual organization of the community. People will receive opportunities to act, move and speak in ways that they have not previously experienced with each other. This difference expands the "range of play" of the rigid routine, often experienced as distress in everyday life.

One dance improvisation follows a score that asks dancers to connect with at least one other dancer in such a way that they can dance together for one round along a circle before separating or connecting with another cluster of dancers. This goes on until the whole ensemble becomes one connected company. During this improvisation, new connections are made between the dancers. The criteria of connections focus on a choreographic solution that makes aesthetic sense. Therefore it will have to be repeated. Decisions about the music, usually improvised by members of the community, as well as changes to the choreography, are in the foreground. This is an alternative focus than the one in the everyday work situation, and it facilitates new relational explorations.

There is a convincing logic and stringency experienced when a communal work of art is completed. Therefore, reflections about alternative experiences of worlding through art do not contravene the necessary logic of habitual experience within the community.

To guide a community into an alternative experience of worlding and later back into everyday life must be part of the score of community art. A characteristic of all the "In and Outs" of the alternative experience are aspects of intermodal decentering and range of play (Knill *et al.* 2005).

- By *decentering*, we name the move away from the restricted thinking posed by tasks, which results often in rigid reasoning and stressful acting that increases the pressure around unavoidable conflicts or even "dead end" situations in everyday work settings. Decentering is a move into the opening for the surprising, the unpredictable, the unexpected provided by the artistic experience within the logic of imagination. A centering follows the decentering, guided by the change agent, relating the two in an effort to find ease. It is helpful first to validate the artistic work that emerged in the decentering phase, as well as how that work was achieved, before experiences are compared and/or consequences discussed.

- In providing a *range of play,* we contrast the situational restrictions experienced in the art-making with those of everyday life. The phenomenon of *play* is the "doing as if," the "open-endedness" in the circularity of the here and now which results in a freeing up from the pressure to achieve a specific defined result, such as occurs in the attitude of *games.* This distinction has proven to be helpful in the design of community art scores. If game-like scores are chosen, the everyday habitual competitive attitude may be called into action, and decentering becomes difficult. Certainly, art projects also pose a challenge toward their completion. These challenges, however, create enough openness and options for surprising unexpected turns, which give a sense of freedom when directed with an attitude of aesthetic responsibility.

Community art: A decentering method providing a range of play

The complexity of the imaginary space in community art presents itself concretely and in a "thingly" way. During the shaping process, material interventions are concrete and placed particularly "on the surface." These interventions can serve the purpose of grounding, bringing participants closer to the here and now of the alternative experience of worlding. We may suggest to dancers to use more space to listen to the music or ask musicians to add voice to the instruments.

The in-and-out/to-and-from of the decentering experience and the reality posed by it is discernible through the here and now of the artistic work, its beginning, process of becoming and completion as a "thing." In its graspable presence, it offers many options to help distinguish between the different realities. The distinctions of stage, studio space, the audience space and the habitual experience of worlding are concrete and sensorimotorically explicit.

The idea of widening the range of play by engaging imagination is a common concept in the practice of *conflict resolution.* In such a practice, conflicts are seen as situations that lack choices and that give participants a sense of being locked into the matter of conflict. Community art therefore gives a community an opportunity to leave the zone of conflict with an opening to options for new actions and thoughts.

Systems theory argues that an intervention simultaneously perturbing and widening the range of play may be effective for a surprising auto-poetic process of improvement of a system. The impetus for discovery and fear is in balance in such a play. Communal art-making can be seen as a discipline of play where the probing of the participants is a kind of perturbation and where self-organization happens within the range of play defined by the frame's and the discipline's restrictions (material, space, time and means). The community art leader is a player in the system who does not play the habitual game of the everyday community.

The limits that define the frame of an art discipline, with respect to space, time, material and method of shaping belong to the tradition of art-making. Therefore, interventions with respect to limits and frame are easily accepted and understood. These interventions and those made during the process of the play may possibly restrict the range of play, but usually they do not restrict the act of playing and its content; on the contrary, they make the playing less threatening. Furthermore, those interventions help to distinguish between the realities of the habitual and the alternative worldings as they occur during the decentering.

The accomplishment in art-making is literally enabling and has the merit of beauty with the "Aha!" of an aesthetic response. Consequently, communal art-making is also a learning experience which provides an individual, as well as a social, enabling and a situational coping. The effect of this experience is cognitive and physical. We can observe it in the change of emotion, mood and tone of the participants. This coping process can also be seen as training, or "exercise," to cope with the situational restrictions and individual frustrations in everyday task-oriented communal life. Within a cognitive frame of reference, the coping experience in the communal learning process of community art confronts beliefs within the scope of: "We are not able to accomplish anything," "We have too little resources," etc. A community art process, however, includes more levels than only the level of cognitive argumentation.

- *It is a rich exercise with repetitive experiences of accomplishment.*
  In a typical work-oriented practice of community art, a blues improvisation with a chorus might be worked on. With each repetition under a competent leader, participants get more and more excited to get into the groove of it. This is a true repetitive experience of accomplishment.

- *It is a psycho-physical concrete experience that allows emotional and cognitive reasoning.*
  All artistic experiences are concrete and close to the psyche in their emotional resonance. In the example above, the blues will also eventually have an improvised text that links to this experience. Discussion between the repetitions, under expert leadership, is cognitive, even though it is focused on the communal art-making.

- *The communal artwork can touch or move the community members. All the senses are engaged, and therefore the art-work makes sense in its beauty.*
  The resulting work, e.g., the blues mentioned above, does not only make sense in terms of cognitive learning, it also makes sense in its beauty. It can be remembered as a touching, moving, regenerating, nourishing experience—a kind of "soul food."

- *It is also an experiential field of discovery that motivates curiosity. Discovery in this way is one of the fundamental sensorimotor and cognitive learning experiences.*
  The method of community art, in its improvisational character, is built on leadership that engages curiosity and motivates discovery. The discovery of the blues riff, the words that work and the rhythm that makes the community to create a dance, have many fundamental sensorimotor steps that will be cognitively reflected upon later in this essay.

In the traditional understanding of coping, exercise has a fundamental position. In the practice of community art, however, the process is guided with an attentive, supportive and open attitude. This openness gives the hidden a chance to be met and to be utilized as a resource. With this option come new perspectives, fantasies, ideas and images for alternative ways to act or respond (Knill 2002).

Communal art-making as a contribution to the culture of communities

When we look at how task-oriented communities try to release some of the individual and social stresses created by workloads, we can usually find two offerings designed for that purpose:

- entertainment events
- opportunities for relational reflection.

In the following section, I will sketch the specific needs addressed in these two activities; later I will elucidate the standpoint that comprehends community art as a culture, bridging these two isolated attempts at coping with the everyday task. Community art then is understood as a culture that fosters innovative thought and action by mobilizing resources and activating imagination.

Entertainment events

Task-oriented communities, like companies and institutions, have traditionally used entertainment events to ease habitual hierarchy and protocol and sometimes also to blend the boundary between workplace and private life. Such events may range from bowling and soccer games to extended parties (New Year's Eve, for example) and company trips. These events are founded in game-like social traditions; they offer some expected fun and distraction. They do not, however, provide an opening to an imaginative space that has a potential for new, alternative experiences. The positive effect of such events in the life of a community should not be underestimated. What has proven to be lacking over and over again in these events, however, is an opportunity for members of the community to reflect on their relationships within their task. To facilitate such reflection, in the second half of the last century, companies and institutions hired consultants who were trained in one of the group encounter or counseling techniques that became popular at that time.

Opportunities for relational reflection

In the beginning, confrontive models that had been developed for therapeutic or encounter group settings, like group dynamics, Gestalt therapy and related styles, turned their focus onto conflicts and their roots in the individual, personal biography. These confrontive models worked for groups with the task of doing therapy; however, they lowered the performance of the group in other tasks. Later systems-oriented, person-centered, theme-centered and other similar approaches were favored because of their focus on the social aspect of coping in groups (Nellessen 1997).

Toward the end of the last century, the systems-oriented approach prevailed and often was modified with resource- and solution-focused methods. These approaches support the activation of resources, as well as aspects of resilience. Therefore, they strengthen the system's coping mechanisms in fulfilling its mission.

When we consider the size of communities, it becomes evident that these methods of reflection are limited to small clusters, groups or teams within the communities. In addition, the exclusive focus on words makes the process lengthy and cumbersome, giving the taste of "more of the same," more of the verbal communication that goes with being "on the job." This is especially true for large groups. We need to recognize however, that the format of the resource- and solution-focused methods of reflection, in the tradition of systems theory, can have great merit within community art projects of larger communities. This merit becomes evident during the evaluation of the experience, when we organize the feedback and reflection in smaller groups and then report back to the full community.

Community art as a bridge
The need for a bridge
Communities soon recognized that traditional entertainment and separated opportunities for reflection stay isolated from each other and are not very helpful in the attempt to create new innovative and resourceful behavior. The tension in everyday work increases because of the fact that the fun of the event is over. Often issues become more severe in an atmosphere that does not provide a space to work on communication and relationships.

Attempts at bridging

In an attempt to connect an experiential event with reflection and a counseling opportunity, it became fashionable to offer "new games," "outdoor-bound/extreme sport" activities, etc., combined with counseling, reflection and coaching. Soon, however, the limits of these activities also became evident. Although these attempts truly gave an alternative challenge, they didn't offer much of a surprise in the outcome. The game-like characteristics are close to the problematic issue at hand. Even though they are different from everyday activity, they have a predictable strategy for solutions. Therefore, they create a reality similar to the stress-producing work process that needs innovative renewed strategies as well as structures and products. It is like having to win a game, without having a chance to invent it.

The bridge: Community art

The art projects undertaken by a community need spatial and temporal frames, selected materials and envisioned directions of forming. However, the act of creative shaping in the arts includes innovative strategies and shaping techniques that follow the surprising developments of the emerging product and therefore lead to a constant revision of the planned outcome. Each process becomes an innovative endeavor to find the optimal response to a complex dynamic between resources, objectives and actions taken, leading to emerging patterns within a defined frame and a feedback loop with shaping strategies and changing structure of material and environment. All of this takes place in the frame of a discipline of artistic play that includes an audience that witnesses and evaluates the work according to certain standards:

- The resulting artistic product works as a whole when it can be considered as "being on the way."
- It can be followed in its particular way.
- It is unique in its character and has a recognizable style.
- It has surprises that belong to the sense-making logic of the work.

When we consider this in the context of decentering as explained above, we recognize the parallels to the experience of the task-oriented challenge of a community. The complexity we are confronted with in everyday processes calls for innovative solutions that consider the dynamic interdependence of frame, material, structure, strategies, visions and emerging patterns such as environmental ones, etc. The problems are unique in their characteristics, and although the way to solve them needs to be congruent with this uniqueness, working styles may be similar.

It is therefore conducive to use the artistic process rather than games as a decentering method because they offer the complexity that games do not have unless we reinvent them each time and leave the envisioned emerging goal up to the process of completion. However, then we need a criterion of evaluation that most likely also has an aesthetic connotation, which is in essence a kind of artistic process.

Community art, therefore, bridges the uniqueness of the complex reality of a community in its challenges to reach objectives connected to its tasks with the uniqueness of an artistic "time-out" experience. Community art also offers pleasurable innovative explorations, which are close to the pleasure of "entertainment events." In addition, the community, with its striving for a unique artistic result, combines the everyday experience of having to achieve satisfying results, with an innovative, playful attitude. An artistic "work" that can be examined, reflected upon and evaluated with respect to the community's task and relationships can result.

Community art with its decentering characteristic, similar to brainstorming, circumvents the deadlock created by "more of the same" thinking which focuses on the problematic issues and is patterned around "more of the same" strategies and approaches. The didactics of community art follow the potential for surprises in the intermodal decentering, which brings a play range similar to brainstorming, yet steps out of the ordinary grammar and logic of conversational language. However, artistic shaping is "language" as well, a kind of language that also needs words and that ends in surprising new conversations.

An example of community art

Here we continue the description of the community art project begun in the Prologue of this paper:

In the task for the weekend, to which everybody was committed, we agreed to entrust ourselves to a learning process that would lead, in the end, to the election of a mixed task-force, representing all parts of the community, and providing a clear guiding vision for the future of the department. The learning process has four parts. First, we collect an inventory of concerns and resources about the issue at hand. In the second phase, we concentrate and work intensely on a piece of community art that brings us away from our habitual reasoning and position to a place of shaping and attending to an emerging work of art, of which we do not know the final form or outcome. We will, however, make it work to our satisfaction. In a third part, we look at the work and see what we did to make it work, how we did it and where and how we overcame obstacles. Finally, the work might open different discourses in response to it. In the last part, we harvest reflections from this process to formulate a guideline for the task-force and create a guiding vision. In this case, we organized the community into three dance/theater ensembles, all three composed of members of the different student cohorts and hierarchical levels.

The community art score furthered the imagery of the wind and Fall, already explored in the warm-up at the opening of the weekend. This time, however, we explored the birds in the preparation. The choreographic idea was drawn from the movement of the birds and their gathering for migration. The first exploratory improvisations served the search for shapes that show the birds' mastery in keeping the flight on course, while the disturbing erratic wind was utilized as a force to stay aloft. How can the dancer's body, which does not literally move like a bird, create an experience for everybody sensing exactly this "mastery of keeping the course lightly?" The answers were explored through improvisations.

After these explorations, I noticed an increasing ensemble of musicians gathering around the piano. Before the design of the next take was started, I made the score of music the first item. In the end, we had four ensembles, one of them responsible for the music of all the three "migration-dance-ensembles." In the next take, the dance ensembles wanted something that would allow the dancer to gain expertise in shaping the landing and take-off experience in the dance. Finally, we had three clusters of chairs on the stage which, when used by the dancers, brought the image of a bare tree in Fall that fell prey to a flock of birds. The dancers wished for music that was more contrasting, instead of music that illustrated the birds acoustically. The more takes that were made, the more the choreographic changes brought the dance/theater performance of the community into a convincing form. After the musicians found their music idiom as an ensemble, several members of the dance ensembles and one member of the music ensemble were selected as coaches to give the audience expert feedback. The result of the intensified coaching was astonishing. Soon we saw dance choirs moving in formations that sometimes seemed similar to flocks of birds swarming up from their place of gathering. In the final takes, a new dance choir came into existence: that of the winter birds that stay over. They had to find a choreography that clearly showed their difference through "the shaping of the space," the phrase we would use as dancers. Finally, the coaches suggested using the lights, so that toward the end, the dancers disappeared in the dark like birds fading on the horizon. The last take received passionate applause from the ensembles and coaches. The question: "Are we onto something now that might go on the road later?" was positively responded to by all the participants.

    The three original ensembles sat down separately in the studio, in different places, to honor the work in its dance/theater manifestations. The community art-work was considered outstanding because of the complexity in the choreography and the dynamic structure of the different ensembles, with the music as a unifying partner and the different dance choirs developing across all the ensembles. It was important to shape a choir together that successfully gave the impression of flight information and of utilizing the wind to stay aloft. "It was not the speed of propulsion that allowed the dance to be seen as a flight that goes far. It was the attention to the direction and the synchrony of the movement as a whole," said one dancer. How it was achieved was reported with an astonishing awareness of probing and sensing. The importance of grounding in landing and taking off, and even in the flight, was the common support that made it possible to give an impression of air and wind as a dancer. The explorative takes—aimed at getting these shapes distinct from others like landing, take-off, or resting in sailing or sitting—were described in detail and appreciated. Of special interest was to hear about the resources that helped to overcome deadlocks, fatigue, boredom or other frustrations. What helped to persevere was curiosity, physical engagement, options to participate in different ensembles or choirs, loyalty to the peer ensemble, realizing that sometimes it works, sometimes not, noticing that there is something emerging, etc.

The title "Gathering for Migration" was chosen, and a conversation about the beauty of the last image took over when we all were together. We spoke of the peace of the wintering birds, huddled together, and the four formations on the horizon, with the long stretched wings in a flow during the slow song, full of longing and directional determination. The difference of mood and physical presence was noticed when compared with the beginning, and astonishment was voiced about the unusual clustering of dancers in the final ensembles and dance choirs: "I never have worked so intensely together with these people before. Some of the members I did not know before, and others I even avoided in the past." At this point, we closed for the day by making posters that highlighted the characteristics of "Gathering for Migration" and graphically ordered the statements that lead to the analyses of the artistic process mentioned above.

On the second day, we started with a warm-up and then visited all the posters, before sitting down to remember our opening inventory. With a speculative mind-set, we began to harvest statements and images from the posters which brought us a step closer to the vision and guideline for a task-force. For the moment, the major visionary gain was summarized in the following way: "It is more important to find a directional determination for a vision, a kind of vision for the path rather than for the goal. The guiding principle seems to be that each participating cluster of the community, regardless of its position, must have a place in that directional determination without having to participate in the same manner. In addition, the organizational structure may allow different paths and different possibilities of governance to be explored and finally installed in the institutional choreography. We might also learn from the music that a contrasting accompaniment may be of more help to get to the organization that works than imitative support."

This first outcome was drawn as a mind-map from the principal visionary words "directional determination" on a poster. After a break, we went into a second community art project.

Didactic principles of community art

The example above serves as an illustration for this section of the paper and may be reread afterwards for the purpose of better understanding the principles involved in guiding community art.

A basic principle is to follow a didactic that circumvents the fear of failure and the narrow understanding of art that sometimes results from negative experiences with the arts in education or everyday life.

It is helpful, therefore, to first research the community and evaluate its resources and needs:

- What is the experience the community and its members have with communal work, games, the arts and the like?

- What are the goals of the community; what are you commissioned for?

- What is the organizational structure and governance of the community?

- What are the artistic resources of the community:
  - musicians, drummers
  - dancers
  - people with directing experience, etc?

- What are the physical conditions:

- room size and possibilities of use (equipment, lights, furniture to be arranged, etc.)
- availability of material and musical instruments?

• How will you plan the leadership according to the research you have done:
  - Will you be using a community member as a co-leader?
  - Will you be bringing a co-facilitator?
  - What is the role of the co-facilitator or observer?
  - How will you plan the event as an open sketch in terms of the scores, yet be detailed and strict in the time management?
  - How will you prepare for the educational aspect that must govern the introduction of community art?

The following didactic principles assume that the boundary conditions mentioned above are established.

The two pillars of attention

The two pillars of attention support the process-oriented learning with an approach that is based on systems theory. At the same time, the discourse needs to be lead in the language and tradition of the art studio and performance stage, using the method of improvisational scores, scripts and choreographies or artistic concepts. This includes not only the naming of the activities but also the addressing of the participants as a company, ensemble, choir, actors, etc. The feedback culture is primarily grounded on the concreteness of structure, form and physicality of shaping, with a process-oriented learning attitude, rather than on the basis of individual psychological considerations.

The first pillar: The here and now
Where are we in our "coming here"?

We want to anchor the community in the here and now of the world in which we are in, looking at the time, considering the calendar or time of day:

- season, holiday, day of the week, birthday, special event, etc.
- morning, evening, noon, beginning, ending, halftime, arrival, departure, return, etc.

We also want to look at the "space" we are in, considering the culture or lifespan of the system:

- customs, language, history, the news, birth, life and death of systems or individuals, etc.

Where are we in our "going to"?
We take aspects of the theme that is envisioned by the community or the world it is in:

- the theme of the symposium the community has chosen, the theme of the task negotiated in advance, the theme of the institution (e.g., corporate identity), etc.
- the season, the graduation, the reorganization, the celebration, or the vacation that is approaching, etc.

The second pillar: The I and the we
How do we provide space for the individual to get ready for communal work?
The tuning-in and warming-up need to prepare the individuals in their body-mind continuum: we awaken the senses, focus the mind's attention on what is physically present (space, things and people), build a sensorimotor awareness of the shaping capabilities that are envisioned.

How do we motivate for the ensemble work?
We introduce exploratory improvisation for small self-chosen or accidentally created ensembles, while using strictly studio language for the motivation of shaping. Through the leader's guidance, the envisioned artistic work has to take precedence over individual concerns not connected to the here and now of the improvisation. Therefore, the aforementioned preparation of the individual is of primary importance.

We use words for traditional formats of improvisational ensembles that stress the cooperative attitude: "ensemble" for music improvisations, "company" for dance or theatre, etc.

- The imagined format may be an ensemble or company production, wherein everybody has an equal input into the improvisation. The facilitator is like a "director" from outside, hired to help to get there.

- The ensemble or company may want a "soloist," a "protagonist" or solo ensemble. If so, then those performers get special attention from the director and the ensemble.

- There may be a person or team from the ensemble who wants to be the "arranger" or "choreographer" for a particular piece. Then the director assists these persons and the ensemble will follow their lead.

The two levels of readiness

While we guide the community with our attention on both of the pillars mentioned above, we need to always consider two levels of readiness. These considerations influence our didactics of leading the community.

The first level: The readiness of body and mind

- Grounding through the senses.
- Kinesthetic awareness connecting, watching and seeing, hearing and listening, moving and being moved: in short, sensing and making sense.
    - Shaping of the ordinary material, sensitized in a way that it becomes special and interesting.

The second level: The psychic readiness

- Be aware of negative experiences with the arts in the biography of individuals or past experiences of the community.
- Avoid sophisticated formalistic jargon and refrain from judgmental remarks.

- Avoid group pressure and address the individual within the common project.

- Consider the method of "low skill/high sensitivity" by introducing structures that ask for low manual skills but that require a high degree of aesthetic challenge, for example, making a sophisticated installation or minimal music improvisation while referring to the art world of today. Refusal to participate with the remark, "This is childish!" is then less likely.

The guidance of the process

The basic concept of resource-oriented consulting considers the client as the expert of the field where the problem occurs. What then is the expertise of the leader of a community art project? Besides being an excellent facilitator and counselor, the guide needs to act out of what we call "aesthetic responsibility." This expertise is related to the methodology of "low skill/high sensitivity." It focuses more on the sensory awareness in the making and perception of the artistic process and less on the formalism of certain styles. The leader is attentive in seeing and hearing whatever presents itself; the leading is always close to the sensory experience: on the surface and concrete ("Sense the pressure of the earth on the soles of your feet, listen to the sound of your breath, see the other dancer moving," etc.). We must be the experts of the challenging process. If we are not the experts of the professional domain of the community in its workplace, then we need to guide the challenging community art process to a satisfactory result in empowering the community and intervening for the emerging work, the artistic solution. What we do is offer an alternative challenge, that we help solve by enabling the members of the community to engage all their resources, focusing on the process. Here are some guidelines:

- Always guide in a manner in which you feel comfortable.

- Intervene or suggest without too much deliberation; rather, act with sensitivity, like an artist, in the moment. Do not plan for a solution of the problem at hand, otherwise you will be in a "dire straits" situation yourself. Be attentive to what emerges in the forming, and probe when you see an option in the moment of the process.

- Basic principle: Always create a window of opportunity. This entails a "frame" and a "task" that is challenging but manageable, because it is opening to exploratory play, at the same time restricting the material to be shaped and framing time and space to experience greater comfort. This has to be done in such a manner that curiosity is motivated, and anxiety (like the *horror vacui*) gives space to the respect of the work that emerges.

- Rules for the frame and structure: **Less is M.O.R.E. M**aterial that is easily manageable, simple shaping **O**rganization, **R**estricted frame, giving simple and clear directions for playful **E**xploration.

- Rules for the process: Low skill/high sensitivity. Participants need to experience an aesthetic satisfaction and success that is more connected to the sensory experience of the emerging form than to the virtuosity of manual skill. Anthropologically, these traditions are found in the art of making a flower arrangement, installation art, art brut, poetry slam, "sound sculptures," "wash-board" rhythms, etc. It is advantageous to start with what the participants are familiar with and expand from there by sensitizing the familiar thing through motivating their curiosity (walking is a ground material of dance, the voice is the base of vocal music and so forth).

- In the performing arts, we offer short time-frames and work toward an improvisational piece of art. These time-frames are called "takes." If a structure starts to emerge, we have to stay with it.

- The language we use in guiding the process must stay in the tradition of the chosen discipline of art (in theater, for instance, we talk about roles, characters, props, backdrops, scenes and plots or scripts).

- In the process of probing, you may like to follow the **EESS** rule: Give options to **E**xplore, and permission to **E**xperiment, stay in **S**imple language that is **S**pecific and concrete (on the surface).

- The communal artwork results from the acts, ideas and explorations of the community. The facilitator's task is to be alert and to observe attentively and in detail, so that they can give descriptive feedback as an aesthetic response.

- Staying in close contact with the participants and explicitly demonstrating what you explain verbally is helpful.

- Discussion should be avoided; rather, take up one of the suggestions and make a quick decision, explaining that we can look at it later and try other suggestions too and see what works by doing it. Art is done in the act and not in the discourse before it.

- The motivational forces are *curiosity* in the phase of exploration and *functional satisfaction* in the repetitive act connected to the mastery of an improvisation. Curiosity needs a framed play-range in order to explore within it, and functional satisfaction requires a frame to repeat and get feedback about the "takes."

- As a leader, you need to understand that you can only guide communal art-making with the necessary enthusiasm when you yourself are alert and extremely curious about what will emerge and how you will be surprised. You are the one who has to create the atmosphere of hope for the success of the work. Remember that what we do does not have the hope; it needs to be created.

Joining community art with music

The music is in a dialogue with the dance or text; it is an equal partner. To achieve improvisational skills, one has to observe the following:

- Be attentive to the movements, gestures, architecture, choreography, light, shadow, etc. Stay on the surface of the things you perceive. Do not go behind things, explaining them, or guessing their meaning. Be a partner to the thing, the dance, the theater, the performance happening. Remember, silence is part of music.

- The music improvised is not there to lead or to illustrate. It goes with the emergent; it nourishes, goes with or against; it is just another creation in the ensemble working together for one performance.

- A good way to start on an instrument (e.g., piano, flute, kalimba, marimbaphone) is to use a pattern and allow it to develop or spin off or change, like the way a dancer develops a step or movement pattern.

- The music may well be without a beat, a-metric like a sound painting. This gives maximal freedom to the dancers. When you use a beat, stay first with a simple beat ("mother beat"), unless you have a drummer supporting it. Give freedom for the ornamentation to the others. Remember that a beat is not mechanical; it is alive; it has a lag and a drive that keep it dynamic.

The feedback culture

We always stay on the surface in giving feedback, say concretely what we have observed and do not categorize it or make interpretations about what could be "behind" it. We make sure the one to whom it is addressed knows exactly what we are talking about. We need to find out if we are understood before we go on talking too long. It is all right to use illustrative imagery to clarify our observation; however, be careful that it does not explain the observed in a reductive way.

- Speak from your own perspective: "I have seen or heard…" Stick to the material, structure or form.

- Try to formulate positively and from a position of aesthetic responsibility toward the emerging work.

- Do not judge or focus on the things that failed; anchor what works.

- The leader needs to model the feedback culture for the participants.

Epilogue

Over the years, some community scores come up again and again, they become like available friends. You will notice that they grow into their own particular character, so that when you call them for help, they surprise you enormously. May you have the grace to allow them to hatch unexpected and sometimes strange works to open your sense-making anew.

References

Knill, P. (2002) "The essence in a therapeutic process: An alternative experience of worlding." *POIESIS: A Journal of the Arts and Communication*, 2, Toronto: EGS Press.

Knill, P., Levine, E. and Levine S. (2005) *Principles and Practice of Expressive Arts Therapy: Toward a Therapeutic Aesthetics.* London: Jessica Kingsley Publishers.

Nellessen, L. (1997) "Der Preis der Konsolidierung." In O. König (ed.) *Gruppendynamik.* Munich: Profilverlag.

Schiffer, E. (2001) Wie Gesundheit entsteht: Salutogenese: Schatzsuche statt Fehlerfahndung. Weinheim and Basel: Beltz.

18

THE PULSE OF HUMANITY

Carrie MacLeod

At the turn of the millennium, the United Nations' Human Development Index rated Sierra Leone, West Africa, the "world's worst place to live." Unthinkable atrocities of enslavement, exploitation and torture invaded media headlines and the world was finally summoned as an audience after ten years of civil war. The Canadian government offered support to humanitarian organizations in the form of post-war rehabilitation and reconciliation programs for the widespread population of amputees, war-wounded casualties and former child soldiers. The scope of these initiatives led me to confront a central question that has been at the forefront of my awareness for years: How can an artistic process be of service to humanity in a country ravaged by war and oppression? My journey to Sierra Leone led me to the place inside of myself that prompted this question again and again. I did not find the answers I was looking for.

It is late in the afternoon and the penetrating African heat is sizzling within the barbed wire fences of an overpopulated refugee and war-wounded camp. This place feels like the symbolic waiting room for all of humanity. On some level everyone here is waiting for death, waiting for life, waiting to go home and waiting for peace. A blanket of sickening memory from ten years of civil war extends to the perimeters of this temporal space. This constrained humanity on the edge of survival has made its way into the marrow of my bones, and I am wondering what my place is here. I don't feel like I can trust my natural instincts in approaching an arts-based project. How can creative expression be welcomed in the wake of a human massacre where hands are dismembered and mutilated to ensure a physical silencing of the voting public?

The familiar media phrases "Ethnic Cleansing," "Genocide" and "Blood Diamonds" all become synthesized into a living reality when I look into the eyes of a former child soldier. He was abducted at the age of eight into the rebel army and can't remember his name or where he is from. The symbol "RUF" for Rebel United Front is engraved for life on his chest. War has been waged on all levels of body, mind and spirit and his scarred skin is permanently branded with terror. While standing in the presence of this scared human being I can feel the weight of my own aloneness in the breakdown of our shared humanity. I have an inner knowing that this nameless child somehow belongs to all of us. I remember why I have come.

I am working side by side with a local playwright and griot storytellers who have firsthand experience of the intricate dynamics that shape this post-war society. They witnessed the widespread abduction and indoctrination of child soldiers by the RUF, and have a visceral resistance to the national slogan, "Forgive and forget." In a communal context such as Sierra Leone, forgiveness is not something that simply happens on an individual level. Nor can forgiveness be captured in one sentiment or simplistic slogan. Rather, forgiveness is an ongoing collective and cultural process that happens over time through poetic and performative acts. The loop of forgiveness comes full circle when audiences become active witnesses to what is otherwise unrepresentable outside of this ritual frame.

Our collaboration and integration of the griot traditions ensures a culturally responsive process and intergenerational continuity. They are hesitant to plan too much in advance, and their ability to cultivate a flexible creativity is both a gift for the youth and a vital ongoing lesson for me. I learn that disorienting and disruptive conditions call for improvisation at every step of the way. The transition from devastation to the generation of a renewed social system comes with many uncertainties. Ambiguity becomes the guiding creative force in the chaos of this transitional holding tank of humanity. The spaciousness that comes with not knowing allows just enough room for invention.

The challenge for us in the camp is to cultivate a creative space where youth can feel safe to reconcile disturbing memories from the past, envision new playgrounds of possibility in the present and prepare for their immersion into a post-war society. The inclusion of intergenerational participation ensures wide exposure and greater transparency around the social ostracism faced by. Lingering stigmas associated with the labels "child soldier," "victim" and "perpetrator" follow the young like a dark shadow. Misunderstandings from these polarized labels continue to threaten the fragile stability of the displaced communities. Creating an affective platform for increased agency and voice amidst clashing perspectives feels like an insurmountable task. The former child soldiers face abandonment from family members, humiliation from their communities, personal agitation and horrific flashbacks from being forced to kill and engage in a war that is not their own. Their forced conscription locks them into prescribed identities with little scope to create alternative narratives. For many, it is unfathomable to imagine possibilities beyond the dangerous borders, military checkpoints and guarded compounds.

Despite these ongoing restrictions, the youth are curious about the arts activities we are offering. However, they are willing to participate only under certain conditions. The saturated media presence after the war has taken a visible toll on them. International correspondents often sought highly sensationalized stories and asked for stories that served their own agendas on terms that worked for them. Although working with past events in a verbatim manner is not our approach, the youth are still suspicious of our underlying agenda. Many are hesitant to disclose their real names and instead assume alternative nicknames acquired from rebel commanders. Pairs of eyes struggle to meet ours as their gaze moves towards the ground to ensure their continued anonymity. In response to this hesitancy to disclose themselves, we look for non verbal body language and cues from the surrounding environment for hints on how to proceed. Our intentions to begin with playwriting are reassessed in the midst of this thickening silence. In the legacy of warfare sometimes there is nothing left to say, but this does not mean that all has been expressed. I do not understand the layers of meaning behind the weighted silence here, but soon learn that this apparent emptiness is a catalyst for what is to come.

It takes several days for youth to experience playing as a permissible and safe activity. Scrambling for creative ideas is an extreme contrast to scrambling from rebel commands. They have only known the unforgiving game of daily survival for years and the idea of rediscovering free play is a novel concept. I sense a collective exhale as laughter emanates from the group after symbolic signatures are scrawled in the sand in imaginative and exaggerated ways. In the midst of unfathomable suffering, I am reminded how humor opens up the possibility to see beyond the confines of this intense environment. Some carve out shapes of houses and symbols of animals, while others take this space to experiment with acrobatic explorations. These markings are drawn in clear, bold strokes. Swift movements communicate a multitude of untold narratives that linger from a long lineage of war. Even though many are still unrecognizable to themselves after years of conflict, the momentum of who they are becoming is gaining renewed traction here. This artistry creates the possibility to imagine life beyond glazed eyes and rebel scars. The montage of symbols sparks an improvised dance score as the lines in the sand inspire newfound reflexes in the body. Although the hollow corridors between the makeshift tents appear to limit the range of play, we can only start from where we are and work with what we have. As to our delight and surprise, their imaginal play range stretches far beyond the physical limitations here.

To encourage a sense of curiosity, we ask the youth to retrieve discarded materials from around the camp. The question for this treasure hunt is simple: what attracts you? A long strand of rope fuels the most intrigue in a pile of unmatched sandals, a broken antenna, fishing lines and old tires. Before much deliberation, this simple rope is effortlessly passed from one person to the next and instantly transforms into gun, a shield, an ocean wave, a raging fire, handcuffs and a military tank. In the beginning, most of the symbols are intimately linked to war images. As the energy around the rope escalates, other residents join in to gather and cheer as each person instinctually crafts their own connection to this transforming object. The shape of the rope slowly shifts from recognizable interpretations to imaginal explorations. When drumming is spontaneously added into the circle, the rope takes on its own life force as it recoils into new shapes.

A griot storyteller moves into the center of the circle and catches the words that loosely spill from moving hands. Leftover scavenged tires and fishing lines soon become improvised instruments to accompany this growing chorus of call and response. Each voice is distinctive as traditional parables are layered into the mix of polyrhythms. These are the unscripted stories of coexistence that are fused into oral tradition and composed in the body. There is unhurried assurance that carries these strange distortions into orchestrated inventions. The growing audience becomes a second chorus and is not confined to passive spectatorship. They are quickly taken into the circle by this strong undercurrent of movement, music and ecstatic commotion. Song and story are inextricable in Sierra Leone culture, and dance provides the impulse for both. A verbal recapitulation of traumatic events does not necessarily lead to cathartic release; some truths retold only deepen the wounds. Memory is multimodal and lives on in the fluid spaces between flesh and bone.

Community regeneration arises in its own time through the raw materials of daily life. Stigmas are unhinged from past strongholds as new systems of meaning are generated through the freedom of improvised forms. The arc of this mythical plot is not prodded or coaxed from outside sources, but is playfully invented and interrogated from within. There is a living pulse that moves through this insurmountable loss as site-responsive compositions change the face of this community. The path to peaceful coexistence seems possible in this fleeting moment where tradition encounters innovation. The collective energy gains momentum as the resilience of being fully alive finds its rightful place here. I begin to understand how the human condition is not simply a "given" in the displacement of war, but actively responds to the given conditions. Unsettled histories resurface without apology when the body generates meaning in motion.

The simple passing of the rope evolves into a series of place-based performance scenes depicting the upheaval of social and cultural anchors. There aren't references of blame and shame here as the bodies juggle the textures of sound and sensation. At the center of this peripheral existence, moving bodies speak volumes and partial limbs courageously etch out a new history in the making. This stark image of amputated limbs is a visceral reminder that the pulse of performance can still survive regardless of harsh circumstances. Even seemingly non-descript and derelict spaces can be transformed into enchanted places of play and possibility. Invitations into the circle leave imprints of generosity in this place that is largely defined by scarcity. There is temporal reprise in the camp when time is marked through rhythms rather than unmarked hours. It is a mystery how the simple exchange of a rope can catalyze just enough momentum to spark a series of original performances in the camp. These creations become rare lifelines for re-presenting what is otherwise unrepresentable. Despite the tangible legacies of war that overshadow this place, the imaginal impulse is alive and refuses to be defeated by the past.

Acts of improvisation lead to the creation of a culminating performance entitled *The Face of Peace*. The plot is inspired from lingering images of peace passed down from generations who still remember what life was like before the war. Images of peaceful coexistence are now juxtaposed with a montage of the injustices that continue to prevail. This paradox is reconfigured in the blending of poetic fact and fiction until it lands in the collective body of the ensemble. A refrain emerges from this push/pull tension and becomes a welcome place of return and reprise. This creates momentum as gestures and sounds find their own systems of meaning through repetition. Composing fictional narratives give the youth permission to articulate the immediacy of their experiences from a necessary distance. Imposed wartime identities are destabilized when remembering has permission to decenter from vivid memories.

Cultural norms and values are commonly communicated through performative practices in Sierra Leone, and such practices are the visible backbone of reconciliation in society. Pre-formed ideas of retribution find their way into communal performances of transitional justice. The strong physicality generated in performance holds a vital barometer for society that is active, playful and woefully persistent. Acts of embodied listening and questioning spark an enlivened nexus of reconciliation, justice and coexistence. However, these are not utopian gatherings of assumed cohesion, but multi-vocal spaces that can simultaneously hold those who are excluded and exalted. The youth adamantly oppose the notion of creating an idealized community given the underlying tensions that still shape their lives. One of the actors poses a daunting question to the ensemble: "*When* will peace come?"

A chant begins to arise in unison from the crowd: *We want peace, we want peace*...This free play between vocal registers becomes the opening ritual for every workshop, and a sense of belonging that we couldn't have "tried to create" arises. Like any call and response African song, a lyrical harmony immediately filters through the air, "We *are* peace. We *are* peace now." These words reflect an embodiment of the Lomé Peace Accord in real time. In the hollow corridors of the war-wounded refugee camp, there is nothing missing here. Peace is not a far ideal to be achieved, but is subtly aligning itself along the margins where unfamiliar realities encounter familiar traditions. Opening up a place for the imagination allows space for shaping the raw realities without imposing solutions. Peace processes are first scripted from the body and then translated to the page.

I see how the embodied performances here serve as restorative and retributive mechanisms alongside the more reductive Truth and Reconciliation Commission (TRC). These smaller performances of transitional justice reveal culturally fluent truths that cannot surface through verbatim testimonies alone. The locals are skeptical of imposing premature closure on histories that are still unsettled within the context of the TRC's model of "redemptive" statement taking. Although the commission collected more than 8000 statements from victims, witnesses and perpetrators, fitting memories into pre-given categories was not a redemptive or cathartic experience for everyone. This framework holds the potential to catalyze healing or humiliation depending on who is speaking for whom and why. The impact of giving testimony within predetermined parameters is vastly different than artfully accessing a living testimony through the senses. Culturally fluent memory practices are more likely to surface when memories that refuse to be edited out of formal archives arise from body language.

Identities in motion are malleable and live beyond the histories that have defined them. Improvisational truth telling highlights the malleability of identities as they open up to the possible and improbable. In the midst of this imported chaos, another kind of viewing punctuates the drone of displacement here. The space between performers and spectators creates a live conduit for the exchange of undocumented experiences. Whether harrowing or hopeful, experiences of both opposition and integration find a pivotal platform that offers a welcome reprise from imposed victim discourses. The politics of remembering finds a welcome reprise when memory is a poietic act grounded in the senses. These provocative acts bring renewed visibility to otherwise elusive spaces of survival.

Silenced and forgotten narratives surface when the body becomes a living archive in truth-telling processes. Communities come with their own kinesthetic responses to injustice beyond linear explanations. The symbolic weight of traumatic events cannot be fully held in rational ways after decades of war. Memory is mobile, malleable and multiple and expands beyond linear forms of recall. The timing of memory is not something that can be regulated from the outside, but manifests as a percussive rhythm that stops, starts and stalls in its own time. However, this instability still has a role to play within the unpredictability of improvised performances. A task in this post-war context is to ignite the lost threads between a remembered past and an imagined future. The performing body serves as a conduit for history in the making when memories aren't fixed and can't fit into a neat chronology of events. Performative memory offers a vital entry point into the creation of collective memory, and the tyranny of memory becomes powerless when creative invention reigns.

Given the collective impulse to return to the body, it is clear that we need a sensory map to navigate the spaces in between memory, history and identity. Image-based body tableaux reveal the unspoken limits of forgiveness and an unwillingness to forget atrocities from the past. Forgiveness comes with codes of conduct that are bound by a cultural cosmology. Simple gestures expose what is intolerable when basic human rights have been violated over and over again. Through movement patterning, we witness vengeance arising from the blurred interpretations of the "innocent" and "guilty" amidst forced abductions. Heated responses surface in the uneven choreographies and expose what still remains unresolved. The legacy of these visceral imprints challenges the correlation between "reconciliation" and "solving things" once and for all. There are no answers to be found here. There is nothing to solve in this moment. The pacing of priorities in a post-conflict environment is not based on a provisional formula. Rather, there are vital questions calling for a timely and embodied response in spaces that continue to evolve. There are some truths that reside more in the questions than in the answers. Such questions literally and figuratively remain out of reach when the body remains absent from these lived inquiries. Yet, to be unmade in the making involves risk; there are repercussions from traversing in unmarked terrain. These living legends may more likely lead to subtle intimations rather than final renderings.

Although tensions are magnified in this post-war climate, these issues are not limited to conflict-laden environments. Belonging, identity, peace and understanding are all central to our existence. Paying attention to what manifests in war zones can be an accurate barometer for relational dynamics elsewhere. I am also aware how the outward waging of war in some way mirrors the war that dwells within the borders of my own imagination. I intimately know the offender and defender who are at war with possibility and impossibility, hope and hopelessness, and the fear of life and death. As the universal rhythms of living and dying are infused into the scripts of the former child soldiers, it occurs to me that the message being written is a wake-up call to a much larger global audience. I feel the pull to pay attention here in order to understand my place in this complex labyrinth of our shared humanity and inhumanity.

The UN advocates that war zones inhabited by children be protected as "zones of peace." I would also add that in order for there to be zones of peace, "zones of imagination" also need to be protected for all ages. A safe space to remember and imagine provides the groundwork to open the borders for peace. We talk about wanting peace, belonging, identity and understanding. We want what we already have. We already belong to the infinite realms of our own imagination.

The performers in this camp are my greatest teachers when it comes to fully understanding this. The finite image of an amputated hand pounding down to hit the skin of a drum is a stark and unforgettable image. Yet in this moment, the finite reality of this tortured hand is home to an infinite realm of creative possibility. In this absence there is an intimate knowing of an even truer embodied presence. The drum becomes the accomplice in the unspoken path to reconciling the body, mind and spirit with the world. This is the first time that I have truly experienced the inexhaustible pulse of humanity. The stories pulsing from these absent hands may become some of the most urgent social narratives of our time.

While immersed in a rhythmic trance, one of the amputee drummers abruptly stops and looks down at my hands with awe. After moments of stretched silence, he boldly asks,

"What will you do with your hands?"

This question instantly shakes me into my own presence.

I look down at my hands for what feels like the first time. Even the subtle movements in my fingers transform into tiny kinesthetic miracles. In this moment my heart opens up to the sheer immediacy of simply being alive in my body. All desires to be anywhere else disintegrate and I simply am with my hands in their immeasurable complexity and beauty. This question leaves a resonating imprint on my soul.

What will I do with my hands?

With these hands I will write the rhythms of this story into the world.

With these hands I will share the vision of the amputee who can still feel the infinite pulse of energy running to the ends of his absent fingers.

With these hands I will hold a breathing space for living art forms to arise from the silence when all else has fallen away.

With these hands I will engage with the world beyond the answerable questions and remember that my fingers are instruments of my imagination, and therefore instruments of infinite peace.

WHAT DO YOU CARE ABOUT?

Arts Therapies in Support of Civil Courage
in a "World Gone Slightly Mad"

Rosemary Faire

Introduction

This paper draws inspiration from protest arts, deep ecology and critical psychotherapy to inquire how the arts therapies could play a part in restoring the World to its place in the therapy of the Psyche. In it the writer will describe her search for a middle-ground between her roles as a music/arts therapist and as an environmental community arts activist, a search which has led her to a workshop framework in which art-work-centered expressive arts therapy combines with community arts ritual. The writer suggests that such work can serve to counter the an-aestheticizing effects of "too much bad news" in the daily media, overcoming apathy and despair to contain and make communal our responses to world-dis-ease through the arts. Mobilizing such responses may be necessary for a truly healthy democracy.

Although examples are given of protest songs which express a political viewpoint, the writer would ask readers to distinguish between the "polemical" content of the songs themselves and the purpose of this paper, which is to highlight the potential role which arts therapies can play within the broader socio-political context.

My question

As global citizens, how do therapists support their own sanity when the daily news media contain so much evidence of dysfunction on national and international levels—enough to perhaps numb individuals into resignation and even despair? While therapists may spend their working lives supporting people with recognized forms of personal and family dis-ease, it could be argued that many in our population who pride themselves on their "normality" continue with agendas that are (to say the least) environmentally and socially suspect. We may even to our horror discover that inadvertently "we" support "them," even ARE "them," especially through our inaction. The question the writer has been grappling with is: How can the arts therapies help both arts therapists and concerned-but-disempowered citizens to find our voices and re-engage in the democratic process?

Art in protest

In 2003, Fran Healy of the Scottish band Travis described in a radio interview his process of writing his song *The Beautiful Occupation* after hearing George Bush's State of the Union address in January 2002. He had felt almost helpless, and sat down with his guitar. He said it was a song to himself, asking himself "what can you do…you can only go on your guts."[1]

The Beautiful Occupation is part of a long tradition of "trouble songs" (Estes 2002; Ma'anit 2003; Marqusee 2003) and other forms of protest art. Do these serve parallel functions at a community level as psychotherapy serves the individual and family:

- to allow disenfranchised "voices" to emerge
- to allow the "shadow" side to become conscious
- to develop insight
- to explore new possibilities
- to restore hope that change is possible?

James Hillman, in his famous critique of modern psychotherapy (Hillman and Ventura 1992), has called for "therapy as an aesthetic activity" (p.128), whose role is in "de-anaesthetizing" and awakening aesthetic sensitivity and civil courage in the citizen. The therapy room

---

1 The Hope CD, containing Healy's song and others from famous songwriters, was put out by War Child to raise money for children in Iraq (www.musicbrainz.org/release/01f862e4-a74a-45ec-9214-ba414e3f222b).

could be "a cell in which revolution is prepared" (p.38) by "redefining self as the interiorization of community" (p.40).

The arts therapies are ideally suited to contribute to such a metamorphosis in psychotherapy. Natalie Rogers (1993, p.221) states, "I believe that those of us who are midwives to the creative process play a crucial role in today's troubled world." She describes her own strong response to the Gulf War and a poem that "poured out" of her, mobilizing her into public radio and letter writing.

Lacunae in psychotherapy/arts therapies?

The professionalization of an occupation born on a growing edge of society is fraught with the danger of it being re-assimilated into the existing power structures and serving to maintain them (House 2003). The worst case scenario is that psychotherapy (including the arts therapies), has adapted so well to the status quo that it becomes a vehicle for interpreting people's concern and outrage at the dysfunctionality of the world in terms of the individual's "lack of fit" or personal neurosis, to be "expressed" in therapy so that the person can go back into the world (pollution/dehumanizing job/traffic) and "feel OK" about it (Wessan 1994).

James Hillman has been exposing this danger for twenty years. In his 1982 essay "Anima Mundi: The return of the soul to the world" he wrote, "To place psychopathology solely in personal reality is a delusional repression of what is actually, realistically being experienced" (Hillman 1982, p.93). In his own psychotherapy practice he encountered "problems that are no longer merely subjective... sickness is now 'out there'" (p.96).

In the book *We've Had a Hundred Years of Psychotherapy — and the World Is Getting Worse* (Hillman and Ventura, 1992), Hillman referred to "aesthetic disorders of the environment" and asked "what about the world's soul?" (p.51). Ventura also asked, "What is the real price we pay for how we live?" (p.46). The world's soul had been written out of psychology by focusing solely on the individual's subjectivity as the place where healing is needed. In Hillman's opinion, the myth that inner growth produces worldly power has been a disaster for political intelligence and democracy. "Every time we try to deal with our outrage over the freeway, our misery over the office and the lighting and the crappy furniture, the crime on the streets, whatever — every time we try to deal with that by going to therapy with our rage and fear, we're depriving the political world of something" (p.5). Therapy as a self-centered project fails to acknowledge that the self is an "interiorization of community" (p.40), a gap in the field, Hillman and Ventura argued, which needs to be addressed. "We're not attacking therapy so much as trying to extend it, reveal its blind spots and begin the enormous task of redefining its premises" (p.53).

Ecopsychology, green psychology and deep ecology

The emergence in the 1990s of ecopsychology (Roszak 1992; Roszak, Gomes and Kanner 1995), ecotherapy (Clinebell 1996) and green psychology (Metzner 1999) has continued to point to the need for the redirection of some of psychology's energy toward broader social and environmental issues. One guiding principle of ecopsychology holds that "there is a synergistic interplay between planetary and personal well-being...the needs of the planet are the needs of the person, the rights of the person are the rights of the planet" (Roszak 1992, p.321). Clinebell (1996) uses the word "ecotherapy" to refer to "both the healing and the growth that is nurtured by healthy interaction with the earth" (p.xxi). Metzner prefers the term "green psychology," arguing that, "Those of us in this field (including Roszak) do not mean to advocate the creation of a new sub-discipline of psychology... Rather we are talking about a fundamental re-envisioning of what psychology is, or what it should have been in the first place – a revision that would take the ecological context of human life into account" (Metzner, 1999, p.2).

These developments in psychology draw from the deep ecology movement, which, since the early seventies, has been challenging the anthropocentric world view and offering an alternative, ecocentric, philosophy. The term "deep ecology" was coined by Norwegian philosopher Arne Naess to distinguish between "shallow" environmentalism founded on materialistic science, and a new form of environmentalism based on a deep respect and concern for non-human beings (see Sessions (1995) for a comprehensive overview of this field). Environmental activism which recognizes the value of deep ecology is concerned not only for the physical world, but also for the Anima Mundi, the World as part of Psyche.

Joanna Macy's "Despair and Empowerment" work brought together deep ecology with Buddhist practices (Macy 1983, 1991; Seed *et al.* 1988), and she has continued to develop effective ways to support citizens to voice their concerns in community (Macy and Brown 1998). Bill Moyers also contributed to such citizen empowerment by broadening the concept of activism to include not only those "rebels" on the front line, but all those who work toward social change and engaged citizenship (Moyers *et al.* 2001). Kellen-Taylor (1998) has called for the incorporation of deep ecology themes and methods into what she calls "ecological expressive therapies."

As a student of both Joanna Macy and the expressive arts therapist Paolo Knill, it has been a natural step for this writer to attempt to envisage the ways in which the art-work-centered Expressive Arts Therapy, as developed by Knill (Knill, Barba and Fuchs 1993), Levine (1992) and colleagues, lends itself to the emancipation of the Anima Mundi. The therapist holds back from psychotherapeutic interpretation of the art-work, entering with its creator into the realm of poiesis, where the art-work can itself reveal its significance. Within this frame, the de-souled world can once again be en-souled and speak to us of its suffering without the fear of being reduced to projection and neurosis. And if the work asks to go further than the confines of the therapy space, community art rituals offer a vehicle for this sharing which can inspire others who resonate with the same concerns.

Ecological self—transpersonal self—an integrative model

Communities are defined by circles of self-identification—the series of overlapping and concentric circles of identification beginning with family, friends, colleagues, neighborhood. The widest circle of identification is known as the "ecological self" (Bragg 1996), defined as the experience of being part of the community of living creatures on this planet, and the extension of compassion and concern for life beyond the human community. The ecological self could be viewed as an aspect of the transpersonal self, grounding it in an embodied spirituality.

In bringing together both ecological and transpersonal world views, Ken Wilber has eloquently critiqued the limited scope of both the "Descenders" (some deep ecologists would view rationality and science as retrograde steps) and the "Ascenders" (who would transcend the body and earthly concerns toward spirit) (Wilber 1995). Unlike Hillman, Wilber is a developmentalist. His integrative model aspires toward balance and inclusiveness, warning against "absolutism" which occurs when one world-view negates all others (Wilber 2000). Wilber's differentiation between hierarchy (which can be dominating) and holarchy (which is both inclusive and transcendent) (Wilber 1997) allows for the notion of individual and social progress without necessarily placing value judgments on earlier stages as being inferior. Wilber's description of four "quadrants" of valid inquiry (spanning individual and collective, interior and exterior dimensions), each with its own criteria of "proof" (Wilber 1997), provides an alternative to the polarization that can so easily occur between scientific/medical vs. artistic/spiritual approaches to the arts therapies. Wilber's model could inform a critical arts therapy which supports both personal insight and socio-political engagement.

Community arts therapy

In the remainder of this paper, I would like to give a personal account of my own community arts therapy work and self-support work, and so I will be writing in the first person.

Since my earliest experiences of environmental community arts events on the Central Coast of NSW, Australia (Cameron 1997; Faire 2004; Henkel and Canin 1994), I have been excited by the possibilities at the interface between community art and the arts therapies, particularly in facilitating the clarification and sharing of concerns among communities about social and environmental issues.

Below are three examples of my own explorations of the forms that community arts therapy might take.

"Soundasations"

Short for "Sound and Dance Conversations," Soundasations is a monthly music and movement improvisation ritual which has been evolving over the last twelve years in Sydney (Faire 2002). As a co-caretaker of these leaderless gatherings, I have witnessed the holding function of the therapist being created by the community itself and the organic unfolding of supporting structures for improvisation.

For example: sound makers begin softly, listening to one another; a rhythm gradually emerges which entices dancing and miming; sound makers, watching the movers, amplify their gestures in sound and this feedback "looping" spins off into a spontaneous song; the song ends, the conversation comes to its end, and there is a pregnant silence.

Participants of these gatherings were asked in an informal survey I conducted in 1995 to list key words or phrases which sum up what these gatherings mean to them and to describe memorable moments. From their responses I drew together five meaning-clusters, summarized by the following terms:

- Play—freedom—spontaneous—improvising—exploration
- Community—kinship—tribal—communication—connection
- Earth—ancient—ritual—sacred
- Deeper self-expression—healing—safe
- Fantastic—spectacular—joy—fun—ecstasy.

Transpersonal/ecological themes (earth—ancient—ritual—sacred) were particularly prevalent in descriptions of gatherings which had occurred outdoors in parks. Participants described "archetype emerging through dance," "singing the earth" and "feeling myself being danced by the drums."

One meaningful moment was described as follows:

"I felt like I entered a timeless, space-less dimension united with people gathering in such places to celebrate the earth and the spirit, the fire and the trees, the whole cosmic cycle – it was like bringing together Aboriginal and European tribal energies and creating a new energy of our own time. It was a wonderful contradiction to the alienation and sense of disconnection I sometimes experience living in the big city."

Disturbing themes from current world events (such as nuclear testing or the plight of refugees) have often incorporated themselves into the spontaneous songs, dances and dramatic enactments. It has been very interesting for me as a therapist to watch my community creating a container for itself in which it has been safe to unleash and artistically explore powerful feelings of a political nature which tend to be socially disenfranchised.

The Council of All Beings

A deep ecology workshop developed by Macy and Seed (Seed *et al.* 1988; Kellen-Taylor 1998), the Council of All Beings is a series of structured processes which support participants to imaginatively enter into, and speak from, non-human perspectives about current global problems. Arts therapy methods have been incorporated into these processes to deepen the experience, although again the community itself forms the container, and facilitation of processes is shared by group members. During the process of "Evolutionary Remembering" (Macy 2003), participants imaginatively embody the movements and sounds of our animal and human ancestors, giving rise to direct experiences of ecological self. Making a mask of an "ally" in nature and then moving, sounding and speaking from behind the mask during the council process also enables us to glimpse beyond our human-centeredness. Drumming together and singing songs of dissent help to re-inspire those who feel isolated and despairing by connecting them with the broader activist community.

The Council of All Beings structure was adapted to explore the theme of reconciliation, using creative arts therapies in a workshop called Towards Creative Reconciliation held at the NECTA (Network for Exploring Creativity in Therapy through the Arts) conference, *Hand in Hand*, in July 2000 (Faire *et al.* 2000).

"What are you concerned about?"

In December 2000, I co-facilitated a workshop entitled "Expressive Music Therapy: Empowering Engaged Citizens and Communities" at an Education and Social Action Conference. Participants wrote and shared "trouble songs" about their concerns (Faire and Langan 2004). The following year I developed this further into the "What are you concerned about?" workshop open to both UTS Music Therapy students and members of the general Sydney community. The structure of the workshop is diagrammed in Figure 19.1.

THE GROUP PREPARES...
Self care and confidentiality agreements
Broadening "activism" (Moyers *et al*. 2001)
Brainstorming of concerns about the world

BEGINNING INDIVIDUAL EXPLORATIONS...
"Creativity contour map" to establish comfort zones and growing edges in various arts modalities (Faire 2003)
Somatic grounding processes (Faire 2002a)
Constructing "cairn" of natural objects representing concerns (Macy and Brown 1998)

"DECENTERING" THROUGH ART...
Individual time for art works to emerge (Knill 2000)

↓

ENCOUNTER WITH ART WORKS...
Groups of three: facilitator supports dialogue between creator and work, scribe notes dialogue (Knill 2001)

GROUP RITUAL...
Opening ceremony
Individuals share in community through art
Closing ceremony

CLOSING WORDS

Figure 19.1 The structure of the "What are you concerned about?" workshop

Participants shared their current concerns about community, environmental and global issues and the feelings associated with these concerns. Arts modalities were then used to express these concerns, and after a process of dialogue with them, the art-works were shared with the group in a ritual designed by the participants. The highly creative and individual forms and themes that these art-works contained are summarized in Figure 19.2.

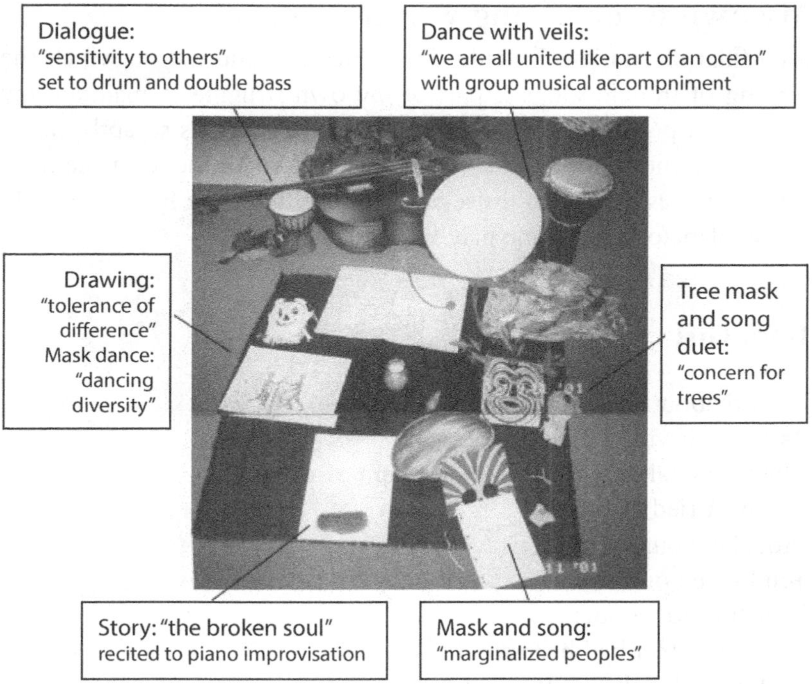

Dialogue: "sensitivity to others" set to drum and double bass

Dance with veils: "we are all united like part of an ocean" with group musical accompniment

Drawing: "tolerance of difference"
Mask dance: "dancing diversity"

Tree mask and song duet: "concern for trees"

Story: "the broken soul" recited to piano improvisation

Mask and song: "marginalized peoples"

Figure 19.2 Forms and themes of art-works that emerged

I was inspired by the sincerity and vulnerability of these works and their creators; they showed me how much creative energy is locked inside us when we despair of being heard and making a difference to the world's suffering.

I have lately been encouraged by the emergence in the music therapy discourse of socially-oriented community music therapy (Kenny and Stige 2002),[2] which has the potential to serve both individual and community in "giving voice to experiences that have been silenced" (McLeod quoted in Stige 2002, p.242) and in which (echoing Hillman) "therapy may be considered an emancipatory practice" (Stige 2002, p.243). I was also recently inspired by the "music and social action" workshop of Phil Nunn and Simon Ronk (2002), youth workers in Sydney, which gave rise to a group song called "Too Much Bad News."

---

2   Also see www.voices.no.

My own trouble song writing process

As a final illustration, I would like to describe the way in which the writing of trouble songs is part of my own struggle to maintain my sanity as a person and a therapist in what Wilber has so aptly called "a world gone slightly mad" (Wilber 1997). I will focus on the most recent of these songs to insist on being written. The lyrics are fairly self-explanatory and some may find them shocking:

Iraqi Girl

I heard about you on the radio
As I was driving home.
They were talking about a photograph of you
Being carried by a man
Probably your father.
You looked quite faint
Which is no wonder
Since your feet had been severed
And were dangling from your legs.

Iraqi girl.

They talked about how that photo
Was too strong to put in the newspaper
It might put people off their breakfast
So they cropped the photograph
They cut off your feet
So that people—the "over 50% of people"—
Who approve of this war
Could eat their breakfast
Without facing your horror.

Iraqi girl.

Afterwards I found myself wondering:
Which cut was the most obscene?
Which cut was the most obscene?

I wondered if you had survived
Or what future lay before you

Even if you had.

If you had been here in Sydney,
They would have rushed you
To Royal North Shore Hospital
And your feet would have been
Sewn back on with microsurgery,
Or at the very least
You would have been fitted with
Prosthetic feet to walk on.

I wonder what lies before
An Iraqi girl
With no feet?

When I first played a recording of this song to a friend, I was told that it was too strong and that no one would want to hear it. I sent it to an activist song site but received no reply; so I gave up. Then, about a month later, I heard Fran Healy being interviewed about his song *The Beautiful Occupation*—this inspired me. I heard about a Truth Mandala workshop based on the work of Joanna Macy (Macy 1998), the focus of which would be to share our feelings in the aftermath of the war in Iraq. At that workshop I found people who were willing to hear my song. I felt grateful that some people could bear to face the strong emotions I had expressed.

Since 2003, I have continued to pursue my passion for expressive arts therapy's capacity to foster citizen engagement. My current focus is in supporting climate change awareness and activism.

Final comments

What determines what we care about? For me, this process is mysterious. An image comes to my mind of a tiny Tinker Bell-like fairy which flies on ahead of me with a glowing light, beckoning me to my next "growing edge." At times when this light has been almost extinguished by being overwhelmed at the one-way media bombardment of bad news, my artistic responses have been a way to venture out again from under my paralysis.

In a postmodern world, the political nature of therapy is undisputed. Aware that the trap in individualizing pathology is a failure to recognize and treat social dysfunction, arts therapists are growing ever more mindful of social contexts.

All of us have been led to engage with the arts therapies because we care about something. Whether as a "calling" or as a "profession," and whatever our client groups, the arts therapies also offer therapists and clients the possibility to respond as artists to global events and to share our protest art and trouble songs in the community, thereby contributing toward a more inclusive democratic process. I would like to suggest that a radical community arts therapy which questions the status quo and explores alternatives is essential to counterbalance the tendency for the arts therapies to become part of the consolidation of power by professionals in a society in which we are all increasingly giving over our decision-making to "the experts."

Note: This paper began as a presentation at the Australian Music Therapy Association's 29th national conference Music Therapy: Creating Connections, Strengthening Communities, held in Brisbane, July 2003. I am currently engaged in climate change activism through Citizens' Climate Lobby Australia, and am supporting climate change activists to form Active Hope groups, based on the work of Joanna Macy and Chris Johnstone, and arts-based peer support groups, through the Sydney Climate Wellbeing Network. www.resilienceintransition.net.au.

References

Bragg, E.A. (1996) "Towards ecological self: Deep ecology meets constructionist self-theory." *Journal of Environmental Psychology 16*, 2, 93–108.

Cameron, N. (1997) "A Practitioner Speaks: Interview with Ronaldo Cameron, a Pioneer of Community Dance in Australia." In H. Poynor and J. Simmonds (eds) *Dancers and Communities: A Collection of Writings about Dance as a Community Art.* Sydney: Australian Dance Council, Ausdance NSW Inc.

Clinebell, H. (1996) *Ecotherapy: Healing Ourselves, Healing the Earth.* Minneapolis, MN: Fortress Press.

Estes, C. (2002) "Who's afraid of music?" *Yes! A Journal of Positive Futures.* Summer, 38–41.

Faire, R. (2002) "Soundasations: Sound and dance conversations: The story of an evolving community improvisation ritual." *MCA Music Forum 8*, 2, 34–35.

Faire, R. (2004) "Environmental community arts: Refinding natural connections – a personal history." *Voices: A World Forum for Music Therapy 4*, 3. Available at www.voices.no/index.php/voices/article/view/189/148, accessed on 02/12/17.

Faire, R. and Langan, D. (2004) "Expressive music therapy: Empowering engaged citizens and communities." *Voices: A World Forum for Music Therapy 4*, 3. Available at https://normt.uib.no/index.php/voices/article/view/187/146, accessed on 11/20/16.

Faire, R., Weiss, B., Nicolson, A., Hitchman, K. and Allan, M. (2000) *Toward Creative Reconciliation: Telling Stories of an Australian Ecology of Culture.* Rainforest Information Centre, Nimbin, Australia. Available at www.rainforestinfo.org.au/deep-eco/web/Web6/rosey.htm, accessed on 01/23/17.

Henkel, C. and Canin, J. (Producers) (1994) *The Homage story: A Community Celebration Lives On.* [Video]. NSW, Australia: Hatchling Productions.

Hillman, J. (1982) "Anima Mundi: The Return of the Soul to the World." In *The Thought of the Heart*. Woodstock, CT: Spring Publications.

Hillman, J. and Ventura, M. (1992) *We've Had a Hundred Years of Psychotherapy – and the World's Getting Worse*. San Francisco, CA: Harper.

House, R. (2003) *Therapy Beyond Modernity: Deconstructing and Transcending Profession-Centred Therapy*. London: Karnac.

Kellen-Taylor, M. (1998) "Imagination and the world: A call for ecological expressive therapies." *The Arts in Psychotherapy 25*, 5, 303–311.

Kenny, C. and Stige, B. (2002) (eds) *Contemporary Voices in Music Therapy*. Oslo, Norway: Unipub forlag.

Knill, P.J., Barba, H.N. and Fuchs, M.N. (1993) *Minstrels of Soul: Intermodal Expressive Therapy*. Toronto: Palmerston Press.

Levine, S.K. (1992) *Poiesis: The Language of Psychology and the Speech of the Soul*. London: Jessica Kingsley Publishers.

Ma'anit, A. (2003) (ed.) "Sounds of dissent: The politics of music." *New Internationalist*, August, 359.

Macy, J. (1983) *Despair and Personal Power in the Nuclear Age*. Philadelphia, PA: New Society.

Macy, J. (1991) *World as Lover, World as Self*. Berkeley, CA: Parallax Press.

Macy, J. (2003) *The Council of All Beings*. Rainforest Information Centre, Nimbin, Australia. Available at www.rainforestinfo.org.au/deep-eco/Joanna%20Macy.htm, accessed on 01/23/17.

Macy, J. and Brown, M.Y. (1998) *Coming Back to Life: Practices to Reconnect our Lives, Our World*. Gabriola Island, BC, Canada: New Society.

Marqusee, M. (2003) *Chimes of Freedom: The Politics of Bob Dylan's Art*. New York: New Press.

Metzner, R. (1999) *Green Psychology: Transforming our Relationship to the Earth*. Rochester, VT: Park Street Press.

Moyers, B., MacAllister, J., Finley, M.L. and Soifer, S. (2001) *Doing Democracy: The MAP Model for Organizing Social Movements*. Gabriola Island, Canada: New Society Publishers.

Nunn, P. and Ronk, S. (2002) "Music and Social Action Workshop." In *Education and Social Action Conference Handbook*. Sydney: UTS Centre for Popular Education.

Rogers, N. (1993) *The Creative Connection*. Palo Alto, CA: Science and Behaviour Books Inc.

Roszak, T. (1992) *The Voice of the Earth: An Exploration of Ecopsychology*. New York: Simon & Schuster.

Roszak, T., Gomes, M.E. and Kanner, A.D. (eds) (1995) *Ecopsychology: Restoring the Earth, Healing the Mind*. San Francisco, CA: Sierra Club Books.

Seed, J., Macy, J., Fleming, P. and Naess, A. (1988) *Thinking like a Mountain: Toward a Council of All Beings*. Philadelphia, PA: New Society.

Sessions, G. (ed.) (1995) *Deep Ecology for the 21st Century: Readings on the Philosophy and Practice of the New Environmentalism*. Boston, Ma: Shambhala.

Stige, B. (2002) *Culture-Centered Music Therapy*. Gilsum, NH: Barcelona Publishers.

Wessan, L. (1994) "What's really bothering you, Lisa?" *The Ecopsychology Newsletter 2*, 6.

Wilber, K. (1995) *Sex, Ecology, Spirituality: The Spirit of Evolution*. Boston, MA: Shambhala.

Wilber, K. (1997) *The Eye of Spirit: An Integral Vision for a World Gone Slightly Mad*. Boston, MA: Shambhala.

Wilber, K. (2000) *Integral Psychology: Consciousness, Spirit, Psychology, Therapy*. Boston, MA: Shambhala.

20

WHY ECO-PHILOSOPHY AND EXPRESSIVE ARTS?

Per Espen Stoknes

Eco-philosophy examines what it would mean to acknowledge the *inherent value* of each being for Western society's thinking and practice. It is the turn from a human-centered (or anthropocentric) world view where non-human beings only have value for human use, to one that is nature-centered (or eco-centric) where other beings have their own, inherently meaningful existence. Since Norwegian philosopher Arne Naess introduced his concept of "deep ecology" into international philosophy, this field has mainly followed analytical and political modes of speaking and acting.

What is too often left out of academic eco-philosophy is our human sensuous and bodily relationship to the earth and how it speaks to us in a multitude of manners and voices. In response to this, a new generation of eco-philosophers are working to expand this "deep ecology" into a "depth ecology" which starts from the realization that we're not *on* the earth, or somehow discussing nature from outside of it, but instead we are always already *inside* its depths. We are speaking from, to and *through* it as much as about it. As David Abram formulates the dimension of depth: "The curious nature of this dimension is such that, unlike 'height' and 'width,' which seem entirely objective aspects of the perceived world, the dimension of depth is wholly dependent upon the position of the viewer *within* that world!" (2005, p.470). What is needed then, is not only a human ethics to guide our actions, but a *wild ethics* that starts from this realization (Abram 2010).

Having worked for years with both expressive arts and depth ecology, the two approaches have always, to me, seemed clearly to be complementary. In expressive arts, we start from the realization that the images of the imagination have their own will, their own "inherent value." We try to see the world from their point of view, by entering into dialogue with them or trading roles with them. More and more, too, the expressive arts are practiced outside, or if inside, with natural materials readily available for art-making, thus recognizing the primacy of the lived, natural earth. The philosophical underpinnings of this eco-centric work within expressive arts has, however, been lacking. The new eco-philosophy as presented by David Abram (1997, 2010) offers a huge contribution here.

On the other hand, eco-philosophy has offered us beautiful writings and concepts about how to recognize the inherent value of each being in nature. Its criticisms of the human-centered and ego-centric worldview of our society have been groundbreaking. However, the field has not developed a practice of how to help and coach fellow human beings to engage in a full and sensuously lived relationship with the more-than-human world. The principles and practices of expressive arts can offer a remedy to this.

In the practice of expressive arts, we are interested in the wild, undomesticated side of beauty. When teaching, coaching or counseling, the general approach is to invite students and clients to engage more fully with a more primordial, animistic style of perception. When making music, we ask: what rhythm does the music itself call for? When painting: what colors does the image itself desire at that very spot? When walking together along the path, we try to notice which particular leaves beckon to us, which branch reaches out unexpectedly to snag our awareness? What does *it* want to say? *This basic move, the decentering from the egoic concerns to the imagination of the earth, seems to me exactly parallel in the two approaches.* We typically invite the world itself to speak through the very materials that surround us: we may discover a collage where a rusty can juts from the smooth silence of clay. Perhaps by moving a rotting log, we invite its contorted, twisting branches to engage three round stones in conversation. Sometimes the things resist us or startle us with their audacity: the unexpected lewdness that a certain ocher pigment, applied just so, brings to a cerulean canvas. Who are we to claim that we create these conjunctions by ourselves, *ex nihilo*, as though they are not also instances of the ongoing collaboration that matter undertakes with itself?

Giving voice and speaking to and from such creative encounters, helps to revive that primary layer of lived experience that David Abram calls the "oral culture." This is where the tradition and practices of expressive arts can have a practical, revitalizing effect also on the environmental movement and social change: our work with the arts promotes an increased sensitivity to the world, which is a useful tool in social and communication situations where our unification with the earth might have been forgotten. By encouraging both activists and those in power to engage with the arts—in whatever way they can—we loosen the hold that our habitual instrumental and technological attitude has over our mind, and let the body explore again the speech of things and of the land. This brings with it the attitude of wildness: an attentive wonder that draws us into the mystery, the unpredictability, the many voices of the more-than-human world around us that have been silenced for too long.

References

Abram, D. (1997) *The Spell of the Sensuous: Perception and Language in a More-Than-Human World*. New York: Vintage Books.

Abram, D. (2005) "Depth Ecology." In B. R. Taylor and J. Kaplan (eds) *The Encyclopedia of Religion and Nature*. London and New York: Continuum.

Abram, D. (2010) *Becoming Animal: An Earthly Cosmology*. New York: Vintage Books.

21

NATURE AS A WORK OF ART
Towards a Poietic Ecology

Stephen K. Levine

> *Not only handicraft manufacture, not only artistic and poetical bringing into appearance and concrete imagery, is a bringing-forth, poiesis. Physis, also, the arising of something from out of itself, is a bringing-forth, poiesis. Physis is indeed poiesis in the highest sense.*
>
> Heidegger (1977, p.39)

Can a philosophy based on *poiesis* contribute to ecological thinking? Does it even make sense to talk of nature as being like a work of art? In order to begin thinking about these questions, we first have to deconstruct the concept of nature itself. Too often "nature" is understood as a transcendental signifier, something that in its pristine essence underlies all our making and doing. The goal of ecological practice is envisioned as a "return to nature," a doing away with all the depredations that humans have wrought upon it. The concept of "wilderness" is a corollary to this way of thinking. Wilderness is pure and good; but civilization has ruined it.

In fact, "nature" is always a product of "culture." The two concepts belong together. Moreover, human beings are poietic "by nature"—we are shaping animals. Our instincts are not pre-adapted to our environment, as other creatures' are. Rather, we must shape the world around us in accordance with our needs. Thus, even "wilderness" is what we make by declaring an area to be territory off-limits to human use. It is "marked" as such and delimited; often it continues to be affected in accordance with our designs—trails are laid down, controlled burns are set, etc. "Nature" is something we make, not something we find. We cannot "get back" to nature, but we can shape it in a way that makes sense to us.

Often, however, our shaping does not "make sense," i.e., it is not pleasing to the senses. If the need according to which we shape the surrounding world is one of maximizing profit, then we run the risk of making the world "senselessly." Good illustrations of this form of shaping can be seen in the work of Edward Burtynsky, photography that vividly displays the ugliness of our designs.[1]

As we shape the world, moreover, we also shape ourselves. We form our way of life by affecting the world around us. Thus, we draw petroleum from the earth to fuel the cars that we use as transportation. We then become "drivers," i.e., beings who move by means of machines that have required fossil fuels to work. It is impossible to overestimate how deeply the automobile has affected our existence. Our whole way of life, our economy as well as our ecology, is based upon it. If we ever were to shift to other forms of transportation, we ourselves would become different beings.

What can *poiesis* contribute to ecological thinking? First of all, we must understand what we mean by this term. In Greek, the word *poiesis* means *making* in general. All forms of production are comprehended by it. At the same time, *poiesis* can also refer to the particular mode of making in which something is made so that it can appear *as* made. The poietic work, what we call "the work of art," shows itself, and in showing itself it shines forth as what it is. This showing manifests itself to the senses. Thus the statue is meant to be seen, the music to be heard, etc. The work is sensible; it can only be apprehended by the senses. Beauty, then, can be understood to be the sensible manifestation of appearance.

The traditional philosophical antipathy to the arts is easy to comprehend from this perspective. If philosophy aims to go beyond appearance toward essence, beyond the way a thing *seems* to be toward the way it *is*, then *poiesis*, which aims at appearances, can only be an inferior mode of existence. For Plato, the arts deal with the changing world of the senses, whereas philosophy seeks the unchanging object of the intellect. The chaos of sensible appearance is a hindrance to true understanding, itself based on the unitary nature of unchanging truth. For Plato, then, *poiesis* is the enemy of truth.

From this point onward, what Plato called "the ancient quarrel between poetry and philosophy" is weighted on the side of philosophy.

---

[1] www.edwardburtynsky.com

Even in Aristotle's thinking, in which *poiesis* is understood as a kind of knowing, i.e., knowing by making, it is seen to be inferior to *theoria*, the kind of knowing that does not depend on the senses and which can grasp pure form by the intellect alone. The tradition of philosophy either denies *poiesis* any insight into truth or considers it to be subordinate to intellectual understanding.

It is not until Nietzsche that *poiesis* is restored to its central place as our fundamental mode of being and knowing. For Nietzsche, even philosophy is something *made*, and as such can be considered art, in spite of its own self-understanding. Nietzsche's rehabilitation of *poiesis* implies a greater valuation of the sensible world as well. He even accuses the philosophers of a "hatred of the earth" in their attempts to reach a realm of existence beyond the world of the senses. Philosophy's "Being," for Nietzsche, is only another name for what religions call "God"—the eternal principle beyond the ever-changing world of sensible appearance.

It is possible to see Heidegger's phenomenological ontology as a continuation of Nietzsche's fundamental project of restoring *poiesis* to the center of human existence. Heidegger's task is to think what is *as* it appears to us; the opposition between essence and appearance, intellect and sense, being and becoming, is overcome once we give up the idea of an eternal unchanging world behind the world of appearance. Rather, being *shows* itself; the task of philosophy is to grasp its mode of disclosure.

However, the temporal manifestation of truth means that it appears in different ways in different epochs of history. We are historical beings. We live in worlds that are illuminated in different ways at different times. The philosophical understanding of truth as unchanging essence is a mode of disclosure that reveals the world to us in a particular way, but this understanding itself is historical and subject to revision.

In *Being and Time* (1962), Heidegger tries to think the way in which our own existence manifests itself within the perspective of time. At this point in his thinking, Heidegger saw our temporal mode of being concealing itself as what it is not in our everyday, on-going life, in which one moment seems to follow another. It is only when we are shaken out of our complacency by an experience of dread (*Angst*), an experience in which everyday concerns fade away and we suddenly realize that we will die, that our existence is revealed to be what it is. If we do not try to escape from this moment of insight but instead hold onto our mortality resolutely, then we can choose to exist "authentically," i.e., to grasp our possibilities in a way that is proper to our own existence as finite beings.

From the beginning, Heidegger's thinking was oriented primarily toward Being; his analytic of existence (*Dasein*) was a way to grasp our own being as a pathway toward the understanding of Being itself. As his thinking developed, however, it underwent a "turning" (*Kehre*) in which he attempted to look directly at the way in which Being is disclosed. In his essay, "The Origin of the Work of Art" (1971) Heidegger considered the primary manifestation of Being to take place in the work of art, i.e., through *poiesis*. For Heidegger, *poiesis* is understood to be a mode of disclosure proper to finite beings who live their temporality within a historical horizon. Art does not reveal eternal essences; rather a work is of its time; indeed, it shapes its time by disclosing possibilities that were previously hidden.

Since art is itself a mode of showing, it is particularly suited to the disclosure of Being, a disclosure that is always historical. The work reveals the world in a new way; it shows the possibilities of our historical existence. At the same time, however, this setting-forth of the World is only accomplished by what Heidegger calls a setting-back into the Earth. There is something in the work that resists manifestation. The work itself is a struggle between World and Earth, between manifestation and hiddenness, a struggle that is put into place in the figure (*Gestalt*).

Heidegger's concept of "Earth" is difficult to understand, primarily because "Earth" refers to that which resists understanding. In one sense, it refers to the "material" of the work, that out of which the work is made. However, Heidegger does not intend the opposition between World and Earth to be understood as one between "form" and "matter." Thinking in terms of form and matter implies a violent imposition of a structure upon an inchoate material; this kind of thinking is still within the framework of the Will to Power, which, as Nietzsche saw, was the fundamental project of philosophy—to master the world by understanding it.

"Earth," therefore, is not to be understood or mastered; it is that out of which knowing and willing emerge. There will always be something that is unknown in the art-work; this is what makes interpretation both possible and necessary. Nevertheless, an interpretation proper to the work does not seek to go beyond its appearance to an underlying essence; rather it tries to let what shows itself show itself from itself— i.e., to let the work manifest itself more fully. "Earth" is what prevents the work from being subject to a totalizing knowledge; it is also what enables us to go continually further in our understanding of the meaning of the work.

Heidegger's thinking of *poiesis* remains to some extent within the tradition of philosophy, even though he aims to deconstruct aesthetics as that tradition has configured it. The works to which Heidegger refers still possess the "aura" which, as Walter Benjamin tells us, is in decline; they are the "great works" of high culture that the discipline of aesthetics has always prioritized. For the most part, Heidegger is only interested in the works that can change the world, the founding works of an historical epoch that compel us to understand our existence in a fundamentally different way.

In the field of expressive arts, as it has been developed at the European Graduate School and elsewhere, the Heideggerean notion of *poiesis* has been extended to apply to other modes of change, both individual and communal. Expressive arts in all its forms (therapy, coaching, education, conflict-transformation and peace-building) relies on an essentially *poietic* mode of understanding: we shape ourselves by shaping the world. The arts have that special capacity to take us into an imaginal world that enables us to see new possibilities in our daily lives. The role of the change agent, then, is to help others shape this world of the imagination in a way that affects them, that touches, as we say, their "effective reality" (a concept analogous to H.G. Gadamer's notion of "effective historical reality," that history which affects our understanding of our own existence). The sign of this effectiveness lies in what we call the person's "aesthetic response," that sensory-emotional experience which is literally "breath-taking," which makes us stop and compels our attention to what is happening in the moment. It is akin to what Aristotle tells us is the beginning of philosophy: the sense of wonder. It is also, we might say, an experience of beauty.

The responsibility of the change agent is to help the other person find their aesthetic response, that which feels "just right," the "felt sense" of what is needed at the moment. "Aesthetic responsibility," then, is an essential component in all actions that aim to bring about change. Change agents cannot "produce" or "make" change; what they can do is to help others find the possibilities for change and the resources that are needed to accomplish it. Art-making then becomes an analogue for everyday life; we shape our world as we shape our works—and our works are one way we shape our world.

This shaping, again, is not a willful imposition of form upon the materials of a life. Rather it is a letting-be, analogous to the ways in which images appear in art-making. Heidegger calls this *Gelassenheit*, letting something show itself as what it is. How can the individual or community take what has been given and allow it to find the possibilities proper to it? We cannot escape the historical context in which we exist, but we can act in such a way that we can discover new possibilities for meaning and beauty to emerge.

What would this perspective mean in ecological thought and practice? Can we speak of an "aesthetic responsibility" toward the earth? This would imply that it is our responsibility to shape the world a way that "makes sense," i.e., that is pleasing to the senses, that, we can even say, is beautiful. We have to overcome the traditional opposition in aesthetics between "interest" and "beauty," between what we need and what we value for its intrinsic form. "Beauty is but the *promise* of happiness" (Stendhal, p.32). Ecology thus takes place within what Marcuse called the "aesthetic dimension," the world that is manifested to the senses. It "makes no sense" to think of an "an-aesthetic ecology," a world in which sensible appearance is secondary to instrumental goals. We suffer in such a world, and we make others suffer as well.

A *poietic* approach to ecology would not begin with an abstract blueprint; "planning" is too often the imposition of an idea upon an environment unsuited to it. Rather, we must ask, what does the earth need? What possibilities are contained within our surroundings that can be developed in a way that touches our effective reality? This approach presupposes that there is a fit between the human and the environment, an *a priori* between what used to be called "man" and "world." Despite all evidence to the contrary, it rejects the notion that the human being is essentially destructive and that the only way to "heal" the environment is to remove it from human concerns, to, in effect, de-humanize it.

Certainly much of what we have done to the planet has been destructive; we cannot ignore the depredations that we have wrought on the world around us and on the creatures within it, including ourselves. But can we not see this violence as a consequence of our unwillingness to accept our limited place within the world, an attempt to become "masters of the universe," to go beyond our finitude and ascribe unlimited powers to ourselves? The earth then becomes, as Heidegger tells us in his writings on technology, a "standing-reserve" (*Ge-stell*) for human purposes. Nature is treated as a "natural resource," i.e., something at our disposal without an inherent existence of its own.

We need to deconstruct the opposition between the "natural" and the "human," an opposition which leads to the alternatives of a dream of unlimited control over the earth, on the one hand, and the vision of a nature "pure" from human contact on the other. As finite historical beings, we are "thrown" into a world we have not ourselves made, yet it is within our power to choose those possibilities which exist within this world in order to develop it in a "suitable" way, a way that is fitting for the habitation of finite beings.

This would mean, however, that we would have to acknowledge our own *poietic* nature, our existence as creatures that shape ourselves by shaping the world around us. It would also mean acknowledging our aesthetic responsibility for the way in which we shape this world. How can we affect the world in a way that makes sense, a way that is pleasing to the senses, a way, indeed, that brings forth beauty? A *poietic* ecology would have to take these questions seriously without falling into the trap of a romantic conception of the natural.

A romantic view implies a world without the human or, at best, with a humanity that lives in "harmony" with the world without disturbing it. The pastoral image of the shepherd is sometimes used to evoke this: the human who dwells in pastoral simplicity by "tending" what is given to him. The metaphor of "shepherding," however, does not begin to grasp the human situation. We are not shepherds living harmoniously in pastoral simplicity, we are builders and shapers who form both urban and rural communities in which to dwell. We *work* the materials that are given to us; we do not simply receive them. But this does not mean that we can disregard them, that we can simply bend them to our purposes. We are not creator gods; rather we take what is given and *respond* to it. In doing so, we give it a new form. We transform it in accordance with its own possibilities.

There is a truth to the romantic view, however, that we need to pay attention to. The romantic image of nature "in itself" points to the hidden character of "Earth" of which Heidegger speaks. Beyond all our projects, there is something that fundamentally resists our capacity for mastery. "Earth" is what remains beyond our power; at the same time, it reveals itself as capable of transformation in specific ways. This quality of "Earth" shows itself in all our projects; in whatever we do, we encounter the limits of our power. We have to take account of the consequences of our shaping activities. In this sense, there is no "free lunch" in a *poietic* ecology. No technology, no matter how "sustainable," will be consequence-free—after which the process of shaping will begin again. Of course, this does not mean that we cannot choose between technologies, taking into account both their effectiveness and their destructive potential, but it does imply that there is no technological fix for our environmental concerns, nothing that will provide a "final solution" to our relation to the environment.

What, then, might be the perspective of a *poietic* ecology? The following are some of the principles that it would embody:

1. The human being is a shaping animal. We exist by shaping the world around ourselves.

2. In this process, we shape ourselves. We always exist in a particular historical world, and we take the form appropriate to this world.

3. Nevertheless, we are not determined by the world in which we live, or by the form in which we find ourselves at any given time. Rather, we exist in the mode of possibility; we can choose to shape the world and our own existence in ways that are not yet actual but that are contained potentially in what is already given.

4. Human existence is finite. Not only do we come to an end, as all beings do, but we can grasp ourselves *as* finite. This implies that we can respect our limits and recognize that we are not the masters of the world around us, or even of ourselves.

5. To shape the world in a way that is appropriate to human finitude would mean to develop an attitude of *respect for otherness*. "Earth" will always be beyond our power. In this sense, our proper attitude toward it is *awe*.

6. As finite beings, we are in the world in an embodied way. We live in a sensible world, and we experience the world primarily through our senses. This is a receptive capacity, but at the same time it has a shaping aspect to it. We see what we look at,

and we look at what engages our attention. Sensing is not passive, but neither is it pure activity—it is a responding to what is there.

7. Sensing has a cognitive capacity; our senses "make sense" of the world. It is not the case, as Kant thought, that the senses are "blind" and that it requires the logical intellect to impose categories upon sense data for meaning to emerge. Rather, there is a "pre-formation" of meaning in sensible experience; this provides the material on which the intellect works by developing its potential significance. In English, as in the Romance languages, "sense" means both sensory capacity and significance; the two are not divorced.

8. If we are to live in a world that makes sense, then this world must be appropriate to our senses. It follows that we have a responsibility to shape the world "aesthetically." *Aisthesis*, in its original sense, means pertaining to the senses. Aesthetics, then, refers to the way we sense the world; *poiesis* to the way we shape it according to our senses, i.e., aesthetically. Thus we can say that we have an *aesthetic responsibility to the world*.

9. Beauty is what pleases us aesthetically. It is what touches us through the senses and takes our breath away. The beautiful may not be harmonious and perfect in its form, as traditional aesthetics would have it. Rather beauty, within the framework of a *poietic* ecology, is seen to emerge from the awe with which we regard the world and the beings within it. A *poietic* conception of beauty has some of the quality traditionally ascribed to the sublime—that which surpasses our finite capacity to grasp it. Beauty could thus be said to be the apprehension of "Earth" in the world.

10. The arts have a special role to play in this framework. As modes of showing, they can reveal the ways in which we have made the world ugly; they can confront us with our an-aesthetic and destructive acts. At the same time, they can point towards what is possible. In their imaginative explorations, the arts show us what *can be*, not only what has been. The vision of beauty provided in art can serve as a guideline for all our shaping acts.

11. To speak of a *poietic* ecology is to imply that nature can be considered as a work of art. This could be seen as a romantic attitude, were it not that within this framework, art itself is not understood to be the imposition of form upon matter, as it is in the traditional ontology that underlies Romanticism without its knowing it. If the work of art is itself a struggle between "World" and "Earth," between revealing and concealing, and if "Earth" is essential to the work as its bearing ground, then to consider nature as a work of art is not to imply mastery over the environment. Rather, this perspective points to a different attitude toward the world around us, one in which we accept our responsibility for shaping the environment in a way that respects its otherness as well as our own capacity for affecting it.

The implications of a *poietic* ecology for environmental practice remain to be worked out. Nevertheless, we can point to many examples where this framework has implicitly been employed. Any time when we see, for example, the development of a landscape that takes into account its natural contours and the particular materials which make it up, we can see a *poietic* ecology at work. Similarly, when urban redevelopment is designed in terms of the culture of the people involved and their way of life, there is an element of *poiesis* at work.

I am particularly fond, in this context, of Rousseau's image of the contrast between the French and the English garden. The French garden, as he describes it, is developed according to an abstract plan. It has a formal quality which is appropriate to the social position of those for whom it is designed. The English garden, on the other hand, looks wild, as if it has developed "naturally." In fact, it has been carefully tended to, but its shaping has taken into account the "natural" capacities of the land and the plants that can grow there. In Rousseau's eyes, this "natural" chaos is much more beautiful than any "artificial" order. "Nature" here, of course, means not that which is wild and untouched, but that which has been shaped in a way that respects its otherness. Perhaps we should understand Rousseau's concept of "natural man" in the same way: "natural" human beings those who shapes themselves in accordance with their own capacity for beauty—in the words of Hölderlin as quoted by Heidegger, they "dwell poetically upon the earth" (1971, p.227).

Human existence is *poietic* by nature, and nature is what we shape through *poiesis*. If we can accept our responsibility as shaping beings, our aesthetic responsibility, while at the same time respecting the limits of our powers as finite beings, then perhaps it will make sense to see nature as the work of art that it always has been. And then, perhaps, we can honor the earth, for in our relation to it, to paraphrase Saint Paul, "...we live and move and have our being."

References

Heidegger, M. (1962) *Being and Time*. Harper & Row: New York.
Heidegger, M. (1971) "Poetically Man Dwells." In M. Heidegger, *Poetry, Language, Thought*. Harper & Row: New York.
Heidegger, M. (1971) "The Origin of the Work of Art." In M. Heidegger, *Poetry, Language, Thought*. Harper & Row: New York.
Heidegger, M. (1977) *The Question Concerning Technology and Other Essays*. Garland Publishing: New York.
Stendhal (2009) *On Love*. Hesperns Press: London.

Part V
RESEARCH

ROCK, from 4 perspectives (2004)   Kelly Lycan

AMONG
Elizabeth McKim

All these others, all the way home, she listened
To remarks among swirled conch shells
On city windows calling, caterwauling
Old time remedies, leading bass violins, leased
Barbershop poles, subterraneous particles

Among barn owl's scarred remains

Speech of hand/ shake /eye/blink/ghosts
Of good by/problematic/ equations/faraway/tsunami
Devastated countries/defunct auto parts/burnt
Out architecture/molded memories/ hemp
Woven belligerently into battle trenches
Aromas and scents/ lingering inside winter
Coats/moldy/match books/newly ground/whole
Bean coffee/damp heat of sex, of skin, of root
Of rutabaga, of casual encounter, sudden
And serious, she loved the clean casual
Squeak of things she lived among:

Voluptuous sap nighttime repair
Tracks of wild and skittish creatures
Stunning cries of former times
Old ways, now…turning
Here and there
She listens
Among…

22

THE OPEN SPACE OF ART-BASED RESEARCH

Shaun McNiff

Like so many other people I found my way to the arts in therapy through experiences with artistic knowing and healing; the pattern is archetypal. The work grows from our experiences with the intelligences and transformative powers of artistic expression; we get to know it personally and want to bring it to others. As Michael Polanyi (1967) suggested, sometimes we might know things that we cannot tell. I do not disagree, but in my experience it has had more to do with artistic processes being a number of steps ahead of knowing and the reflecting mind.

Artistic discovery tends to emerge through acts of expression; the process delivers the insight, the sense of direction. I learn how to carefully watch, listen, and witness what the expression has to say about itself and the problems I am addressing in my research. And what happens can never be planned in advance or accessed by pre-existing procedures. Of course, we still have to deal with how to tell or present what we learn from the engagement. I will address that later in this essay.

My definition of research is a simple one—a systematic process of inquiry where the methods are designed in relation to the question asked or the problem examined. I define art-based research (ABR) as the use of artistic expression in various art forms by the researcher, either alone or with others, as a primary mode of inquiry—in contrast to the more conventional use of artistic expression to generate "data" for examination by other disciplines (McNiff 2011). Art-based research is thus a mode of inquiry used to address situations that can be best explored and understood via empirical artistic explorations. In my experience, virtually everything we do in striving to serve others in the applied arts fields can benefit from this kind of firsthand inquiry, focused on both knowing and perfecting practice.

Creating form or following formats

In the applied arts fields, we tend to lose contact with our "base" when determining how to do research. The major challenge facing art-based research today is its lack of adoption by the fields and people who have the most to gain from it (McNiff 2012). In the practice of formal research, we lose faith in the essential dynamics of artistic knowing that shaped our calling and we take on the adjunctive role that we oppose, trying to justify and explain artistic processes through other disciplines.

Professions based upon the arts as ways of knowing universally contradict themselves in the practice of research. A research course in most applied arts graduate programs will exclusively follow social science methods. Within that domain, a one-sided focus on quantification has generated an appropriate support for qualitative methods; where the former separates individual variables from their environments for analysis and measurement, the latter argues that complex environments are better studied within a context of reciprocal relations. Since applied arts professions have been associated so closely with psychology and human service professions, we have been subsumed within this dualistic and restrictive way of thinking about research, and our work has generally been incorporated into the burgeoning area of qualitative methods.

With all due respect for the quantity-quality discourse happening within the social sciences, artistic inquiry cannot be limited to this. When we partner with social science, we need to deal with the tensions that arise, and hopefully in a creative way. But there is a fundamental conflict within the relationship if art is always expected to follow rather than lead when the situation may call for the latter.

In *Art as Research: Opportunities and Challenges* (McNiff 2013), I urged contributors to explore and define the challenges we face in advancing art-based research. I asked why the majority of people and institutions in the applied arts fields do not become involved. As reinforced by authors contributing to this issue, a primary factor is a desire for acceptance within the system where one hopes to work. However, I find that even when supported in pursuing art-based research, most continue to resist it, so we cannot attribute blame solely to outside forces. While struggling with the questions in an essay for the new book, I crystallized my sense of what may be a fundamental cause when I wrote, "What is unique and perhaps most challenging about art-based research is that it does not advocate set methods of inquiry" (McNiff 2013, p.110).

Art is infinitely variable and this extends to art-based research. No wonder people hesitate. It is easier to choose from the ever expanding menu of sanctioned qualitative methods than venture into the unknown. Although the way of art may bring considerable chaos and difficulty, it is the only route to the formulation of a truly individuated mode of inquiry. Where some cannot do without this open space of possibility, most avoid it.

Of course I seek a liberating and guiding structure in my work and do everything I can to help others find it in the research that I supervise—structure liberates expression, as I repeatedly discover. But the way of art, and the discovery of artistic form or structure, requires that we let go of pre-ordained procedures. There are a few cases when everything falls together effortlessly in the creation of an art-based study, but in my experience this is not usual. It is more likely for artistic inquiry to involve a creative crucible, which I have learned may be a necessary condition and a prerequisite for gaining access to the kinds of complex problems and processes addressed through the arts.

We also need to restore James Hillman's call for critical and ongoing assessment of our professional language. He felt, "A field must have a language of its own; in fact, a field is its language" (1978, p.203). In calling for more sensitive and imaginative discourse he said, "Although not fashioned in schools, this language will be fashioned and schooled" (p.207), and he encouraged a closer correspondence to the poetic basis of the psyche—again, paying attention to our art base.

In addition to fields becoming their language, the same applies to persons. In my experience with art and healing, I see this repeatedly. I am healed and transformed by what I do, what I see and witness, hear and feel, and read. Disturbances are created in the same way. Thus I encourage the pursuit of research that enlivens and deepens our professional and personal commitments and which corresponds to the dynamics of artistic transformation, healing, and renewal.

Although I have consistently adopted a pragmatic respect for designing research methods in response to particular questions—which can result in studies using conventional case studies, interviews, and surveys, as well as art-based inquiries—I have to say that art-based inquiries have the most potential to shape future practice in the applied art fields. We can embrace the open and undefined space or artistic possibility, shape it through our research projects, and accept the risks of artistic experimentation.

These expressions are telling more than we know—Ah POIESIS!

As I read the articles published to date in the *POIESIS* journal, and reflect on what I have experienced in art-based research over the years, I envision the vast expanse of art-based inquiry and how this supports infinite methods which guard against the possibility of ever being bound together in a textbook. Art holds a certain anarchy, confusion, and even chaos sometimes, all of which go to the core of its alchemy and freedom (McNiff 1986). Artistic inquiry rubs against the pre-ordained. It cannot know the end at the beginning—nor even the pathway.

The breadth of essays in this book is part of a larger continuity of contributions to the *POIESIS* journal, which, in my view, was unique in its all-encompassing artistic presentation of form and content. *POIESIS* was the only longstanding publication, together with its precursor *CREATE*, in which art took a refreshing lead in the partnership with psychology and other social science disciplines. During a recent process of organizing my papers, I noticed how *POIESIS* was the lone journal that also included many of my paintings—in color—and poems. Thus, the whole of the journal's history and future embodies ABR and not just this book, which deals explicitly with it. I cannot emphasize enough how important this leadership is; how the outward forms of communication need to correspond to the message.

Reversing Polanyi, these expressions might be telling more than we know. Without giving credence to the psycho-diagnostic practices of reading non-conscious statements into everything we do, it can be said that creative expressions and images are like solitary point persons who operate in advance of the reasoning and responding mind and others to follow. This applies to every aspect of ABR, which complements predictability in science, where meaning and even methods of inquiry tend to emanate from what we do without a clear sense at the start as to *what* and *why*. This ability of artistic inquiry to help us discover what we are doing unawares, what we can and cannot see, how we might not be what we think we are, is a primary *raison d'être* for broader application to many disciplines that will benefit from suspending their sense of themselves in order to be renewed.

And perhaps most importantly, the journal welcomed the shadows and darker aspects of knowing that have always been the vehicles for new and important discoveries in my life and work. We all want the angels of insight, but it is usually the demons that start the new work, push at the borders of comfort, and evoke the vulnerabilities of the unknown. The difficult places make it necessary to break apart a familiar structure and find a new direction. Thus I salute the history of the *POIESIS* journal as forming a community of artistic inquiry.

Freedom from uniformity in presenting research

Dealing with and expanding forms of presentation may be one of the most important future tasks of ABR. We have to expand the free and open art space modeled by *POIESIS* to the campuses and institutions that give a face to contemporary research. Rather than depend on research textbooks, we can do what artists have always done—carefully study the works of those who went before us and foster influences among associates today.

If we are permitted to pursue art-based studies within a particular university, most will be required to follow fixed formats for describing and reporting their research. Sally Atkins has articulated this in her essay, "Where are the five chapters?" (2012). There needs to be more push against restraints on expression and standardized forms as Sally and other contributors have demonstrated over the years in *POIESIS*. As someone who appreciates the value of structure and how the simple and direct IMRaD (Introduction, Methor, Results and Discussion) format has benefits and can usually be adapted to support artistic inquiry, I nevertheless believe that it cannot continue to be an absolute prerequisite. Standardized forms may impede the most effective outcomes of ABR. Everything about artistic processes and outcomes is connected to modes of presentation. And as much as I support the use of words and their inclusion, if only as a companion to an art-based study, I know there are things that they cannot grasp nor translate and which are best conveyed through the particular media of artistic expression.

If ABR is given the freedom to communicate and present outcomes in its essential languages (McNiff 2014), we then face the challenges of determining quality according to the values of particular communities of practice, and perhaps liberalizing what is acceptable to them. Because the personal is the way to the universal in artistic inquiry, there will be risks in how the work we show will be received by others who are unfamiliar with this approach to research or unconvinced of its value. These risks are worth taking and they have always advanced human understanding and art.

References

Atkins, S. (2012) "Where are the five chapters? Challenges and opportunities in mentoring students with art-based dissertations." *Journal of Applied Arts and Health 3*, 1, 59–66.

Hillman, J. (1978) *The Myth of Analysis: Three Essays in Archetypal Psychology*. New York: Harper and Row.

McNiff, S. (1986) "Freedom of research and artistic inquiry." *The Arts in Psychotherapy 13*, 4, 279–284.

McNiff, S. (2011) "Artistic expressions as primary modes of inquiry." *British Journal of Guidance and Counselling 39*, 5, 385–396.

McNiff, S. (2012) "Opportunities and challenges in art-based research." *Journal of Applied Arts and Health 3*, 1, 5–12.

McNiff, S. (2013) "A Critical Focus on Art-based Research." In S. McNiff (ed.) *Art as Research: Opportunities and Challenges*. Bristol: Intellect Books.

McNiff, S. (2014) "Presentations that look and feel like the arts in therapy: Keeping creative tension with psychology." *Australian and New Zealand Journal of Arts Therapy 9*, 1, 89–94.

Polanyi, M. (1967) *The Tacit Dimension*. New York: Anchor Books.

23

CRAFTING MAPS, ATTUNING TO FLESH, AND DANCING THE RADICANT

Mobilizing the Expressive Arts and Arts-Based Research to do a Conceptual Translation of "Science as Usual"

Kelly Clark/Keefe, Jessica Gilway, and Emily Miller

Introduction

In 1991, feminist philosopher and social scientist Sandra Harding forwarded her detailed argument about the crucial role feminism had in disrupting what she and others at the time referred to as "science-as-usual." Harding's critique was made in the context of calling for "better science," including "important tendencies to provide empirically more adequate and theoretically less partial and distorted descriptions and explanations of women, men, gender relations, and the rest of the social and natural worlds, including how the sciences did, do, and could function" (Harding 1991, p.1).

Since Thomas Kuhn's landmark text, *The Structure of Scientific Revolutions*, was first published in 1962, historians and philosophers of science, including Harding, have had as a central mission, "outing" science as non-objective, proclaiming every scientist as always already working within relations of power. Postmodern scholars have been especially keen to expose the normalizing and totalizing discourse of science-as-usual, using deconstructionist and other alternative theoretical tools to disarticulate the systems of logic upon which arguments for the "one best way" or "real," or (a favorite in the United States) "Gold Standard" research continue to be based. Philosopher and post-structural educational researcher, Elizabeth St. Pierre (2002) powerfully frames the premise for contemporary postmodern critiques, and does so in the context of the United States government-sponsored agendas for social research. Published specifically in response to the United States government's positivist-leaning agenda to appoint a National Research Council Committee for Scientific Principles for Education Research, whose charge was to produce a set of guiding standards upon which all education and other social research be conducted and judged, St. Pierre (2002) writes:

> This latest attempt to marginalize certain epistemologies and methodologies in order to discipline and control science, to reduce it, to center it, cannot go unanswered. Fortunately, postmodernism is firmly entrenched in educational research, and, like Foucault (1984/1985), postmodernists are always prepared "to begin and begin again" (p.7) their work of decentering, in this case, an oppressive science that produces the "creeping tides of conformity and methodological zealotry" (p.1).

Keen to advance a postmodernist outlook then, social scientists for over two decades have steadfastly challenged durable and deeply politicized theoretical paradigms rooted in logical positivism that assert themselves as the "one best way" to do research. Skeptical of empiricisms that could not account for the complexity of human experience, social science researchers and philosophers since the early 20th century have worked toward clearing the ground for the proliferation of critically oriented perspectives, such as post-colonial, post-human, critical race, feminist standpoint, and queer theories. Spurred on from such post-oriented perspectives, researchers have made great strides in their efforts to expand inquiry design and methods that include alternative approaches to exploring the particularities of social, personal, and cultural life rather than remaining constrained by methodologies that impose unwarranted categorization of what counts as data and its valid representation.

One grouping of alternative inquiry designs that have been set in motion by postmodernity finds its particular force and rhythm at the apex of one of research's most enduring dichotomies—art versus science. Variously defined and highly diverse in application and approach, arts-based research has, for the past two-and-a-half decades, been sweeping across the social sciences. Hailed as "a milestone in the evolution of qualitative research methodologies" (Knowles and

Cole 2008, p.xii.), arts-based research functions as nothing less than a provocation, opening up previously unthought considerations and responses to such common sense questions as "What counts as data?" "How do we display findings?" and "What makes our research valid?" Elliot Eisner (1995, 2005; Eisner and Powell 2002) and Tom Barone (2001; Barone and Eisner 2012) are credited in the United States with having ignited a series of debates about the role of the arts, especially in qualitative research in education. Researchers all over the world demonstrating and/or theorizing the arts as a mode and subject of scholarly inquiry as well as a method of representation have, in the wake of these debates, found ample avenues for growing a diverse field of arts-oriented social inquiry and engaging interdisciplinary audiences.[1] In 2008, the first detailed edited *Handbook of the Arts in Qualitative Research* (Knowles and Cole) was published, marking a watershed moment for arts-based researchers interested in expanding and legitimizing their interests surrounding the use of the arts in social and human inquiry.

Simultaneous with postmodernity's march across the social scientific landscape and the emergence of alternatives such as arts-oriented methodologies, scholars and practitioners in fields formed in the service of understanding and helping people, namely psychology and psychotherapy, have been engaging in their own field-clearing efforts. Working within the context of postmodern critiques in order to disrupt the heavily policed margins of dominant psychological models for human development and healing, revolutionary new human services fields have emerged, challenging the entrenchment

---

[1] See especially Barone and Eisner 2012; Cahnmann-Taylor and Siegesmund 2008; Clark/Keefe 2009; Finely 2003 and Knowles and Cole 2008, for developmental perspectives on and comprehensive overviews and examples of the arts in qualitative research. For earlier discussions shaping the arts-in-inquiry movement and the debates surrounding mergers between social scientists and artists see Leavy 2015; Barone 2001; Eisner 1995, 2002; Sandelowski 1994, and Richardson and St. Pierre 2005. Tom Barone, Elliot Eisner, Karen Finley, Maggie MacLure, and current and former members of the Canadian-based Centre for Arts-Informed Research (www.msvu.ca/en/home/research/centresandinstitutes/CAIRT/default.aspx) have explored with vigor the contentious and fecund space where aesthetics, embodiment, and communication of social meaning overlap. See also Irwin and de Cosson 2004; Springgay, Irwin and Kind 2008, and the A/R/Tography homepage (http://artograhyp.edcp.educ.ubc.ca), where comprehensive lists of relevant publications, conferences, communities of scholars, and other resources are compiled.

of modernist Western worldviews that hold fast to a priori categories of what it means to be human and to experience reality on the basis of a fundamental split between mind and body, culture and nature, self and the material world. The field of expressive arts therapy is one such revolutionary arrival (Atkins and Appalachian Expressive Arts Collective 2002; Atkins and Eberhart 2014; Knill, Levine and Levine 2005; Levine and Levine 1999, 2011; McNiff 2004; Rogers 2000). For more than three decades, founders of this approach have been putting to work lessons learned from postmodernist arguments about the role of art-making, discourse, power, and the material world, including the body, in analyzing the very premises upon which understandings of and pathways for healing the human condition have historically been formed.

It is at the interstices of the parallel movements of arts-based research and the field of expressive arts that this article is situated. The three authors of this article have each studied expressive arts principles and practices, and all are arts-based researchers.[2] Conversations about our independent as well as collective engagement across these two domains have helped us see where they touch, where a mutual set of aims and purpose could be generative of a whole host of new possibilities (see especially Clark/Keefe and Gilway 2016).

This article stands as one manifestation of that possibility and has as its aim a response to the *POIESIS* journal's editor, Stephen K. Levine's (2012) question, "Is the kind of knowing that happens in the arts different than the kind that happens in scientific inquiry?" The work invites readers to consider the limitations of thinking and doing "science as usual," of holding to only commonsense conceptualizations of what counts as research, evidence, validity, and the like. It does so by bringing into dialogue the two perspectives of expressive arts and arts-based research. Each of these perspectives are mobilized to conduct a conceptual translation of a specific set of terms—data, analysis, and representation—that, taken together in the conventional sense, congeal and constrain what we have come

---

[2] All three authors earned a post-masters Certificate of Advanced Graduate Studies through the Expressive Arts Therapy program at Appalachian State University in North Carolina. Each have also conducted studies and published work that blends arts-based research and expressive arts perspectives and techniques (see, especially, Clark/Keefe 2006a, 2006b, 2009, 2010; Gilway 2015; Miller 2014).

to understand and experience as expressive arts informed social scientists. A translation-in-waction ensues, whereby the three authors each take a turn at describing and illustrating specific ways in which they enfold an expressive arts social science into their research process. This translation commences with Emily and her taking-up of the term "data" through the powerful and groundbreaking work of a/r/tography boards. Kelly follows with her discussion of what happens to "analysis" under what she has begun to refer to as somatographic circumstances; that is, a set of dispositions and an approach that leans heavily into the twin concepts of attunement and *poiesis*.[3] Jessica takes on the term "representation," translating its meaning beautifully and for good through poetry and her enactment of dancing the data, or what she calls "choreopoiesis." The chapter closes by returning to Levine's provocation to consider what differentiates knowing through the arts and knowing via scientific inquiry.

Emily's "data" in translation: Mapping "woman," "craft," and the influence of metanarratives with (c)a/r/tography boards

Conventional wisdom surrounding the term "data" implies a collection of objective truths later analyzed and eventually presented for academic consumption through traditional representation. The use of expressive arts as a means of data collection challenges these traditional notions. The clear lines between data collection and data creation begin to erode. Our reality is constructed and held hostage by metanarratives, necessarily bereft of complexity. To collect data in the midst of a grand narrative serves only to reproduce the narrative. The postmodern condition requires that we reject and deconstruct these hegemonic narratives (Lyotard 1984). In order to peek outside our singular metanarratives, we engage fresh methodologies for data collection and analysis to map our research territory. Researchers must find ways to sort out the alter-modern web of experience, which does not easily

---

3   The following section of the present chapter appears in a slightly revised and much expanded form in a 2014 special issue of the journal, *Qualitative Research*. The citation for the article is titled: Clark/Keefe, K. (2014) "Suspended animation: Attuning to material-discursive data and attending via art-making during somatographic inquiry." *Qualitative Inquiry 20*, 6, 790–800. DOI: 10.1177/1077800414530263.

lend itself to inquiry (Bourriaud 2010). I use the arts as one such alter-modern tool of inquiry to map a research territory that doesn't readily collapse into research questions and binary analyses. Knill's (2005) expressive arts therapy technique of decentering alternative world experiences in which we leave the "logic of daily life and enter the logic of imagination" (p.83) is akin to entering the arts-based inquiry liminal space in which we "perceive patterns in new ways, find sensuous openings into new understandings, fresh concepts, and wild possibilities" (Neilsen 1998, p.274).

As researchers explore questions, we create a world of data specific to our own ways of thinking. Before we even begin to collect data, we enclose our research with the language we use (Bowers 2010). The word, "woman," for example, is connoted with all the shackles of history and drips with root metaphor. In order to move beyond the trappings of metanarrative, I use an adaptation of Knill's (Knill *et al.* 2005) architecture of the therapeutic experience toward a post-structural engagement with the arts which broadens the inquiry field. Toward these ends, I create a/r/tography boards centering on individual subjects, questions, and issues, yet not separate from my research or even my research identity as a whole. Many new insights, threads in the tapestry of my research projects, become available through these boards.

Briefly stated, a/r/tography is one of the many arts-based research methodologies that, as our introduction notes, have been emerging in the past decade. A/r/tographers inquire into social phenomenon through artistic and aesthetic means (Springgay, Irwin and Kind 2008). A/r/tography boards emerged for me out of desperation. I had set about trying to complete a piece of writing and was experiencing difficulty in sustaining a/r/tographic thought. I would characterize a/r/tographic thought as a type of thinking that is engaged through a web-like, shifting, impermanent structure of data collection/creation. Processing my inquiry project through an a/r/tographic lens enabled me to shift out of a mechanistic, Newtonian, truth seeking, binaristic structure of data and analysis. I felt it was easier to sustain a/r/tographic thought if I had something in my line of vision that helped prime my mind for thinking via webs and multiplicities.

Figure 23.1 A/r/tography Board. Miller 2011, mixed-media collage on Masonite board.

I began with a piece of Masonite propped against the wall next to my writing station. I pasted a/r/tographic language to the board (e.g., entangles, rhizomatic, interstitial, blurs, liminal, troubles, and so forth). The board facilitated my suspension of knowing and thereby sustained a non-conclusive web-like mode of thinking and analysis. Data and analysis are not quite separate in this process. The board is a practical reminder to meander through my topic. I wrote and pinned things to the board at the same time. As I ran across language, I did Google image searches for corresponding images. I encountered ideas in my writing and looked for ways to express them on the board. The writing slipped over into the board and the board slipped over into the writing. The pieces began to reverberate and allow for a multiplicity of meaning and form, which is appropriate for postmodern fracturing and reforming, deconstruction and reconstruction. The board created a post-structural window through which I could cast off the metanarrative lens that so often frames my data and analysis, my world.

After finishing the piece of writing and the a/r/tography board, I created a second piece of writing in which I explored what the board had to offer my research project. The process became heavily worded and cognitive at this point. I began to analyze how the images and language took shape on the board, what the symbols meant for my subject. The knowledge which sprung from that first a/r/tography board shifted my way of knowing the world, reframed my research project, created new lines of flight, and connected disparate notions. The a/r/tography board became a map, a cartographic representation of the issues I explored. This artistic process helped yield knowledge that could not have emerged from traditional scientific methods in which we can only study what we think we already know.

Qualitative researchers take great effort to recognize subjectivity in data collection and analysis. Arts-based inquiry provides a path to bypass personal narratives about the nature of the world. Arts-based research methods don't abandon subjectivity, but instead, amplify it in such a way that we tap into a suspension of knowledge. We put our knowing on the shelf and move into an epistemology that does not rely on a linear narrative of knowing. We cease to privilege cognitive thinking and in so doing bypass the narratives which frame our reality. This disruption of a linear or grand narrative enables us to supersede or at least account for the history-laden metaphor of language in poststructural analysis. Further, arts-based research creates avenues for the merging of research identities, for multiplicities.

A/r/tography boards enable a more adequate cartography of our position as nomadic subjects so that we may be able to think with/in and outside the hegemony of metanarrative discourses, "modes of representation and forms of accountability that are adequate to the complexities of the real-life world" (Braidotti 2006, p.7). Arts-based research moves data collection into the realm of data creation and in so doing, enables the possibility of change, a flight from the limited narratives that construct our reality.

Kelly's "analysis" in translation: Attuning to material-discursive data and attending via poiesis during somatographic inquiry

It is well known that in much traditional social scientific research, coding functions as the cognitive tool by which researchers analyze or think through previously collected data. In a range of interpretive traditions, analysis involves identifying "chunks" of mainly narrative or survey response data that have been determined to be salient, discrepant, or meaningful in some way. Researchers engage in a progressive process of sifting, sorting, categorizing, and defining, with the aim of making comparisons, establishing connections, generating themes, illuminating findings, and otherwise converging on a set of explanations as to what a given data set means. The advent of highly sophisticated computer-assisted qualitative data analysis software (CAQDAS) has reinforced social scientists' ability to code, categorize, and synthesize large sets of narrative data swiftly. This has, I believe, had the perhaps unintended effect of increasing researchers' tendencies to rely on findings evidenced along lines of textual frequencies, eclipsing the powerful yet less verifiable analytic move of exploring data for its partially ineffable, deeply contextualized as well as aesthetic saliencies or strengths (a point Jessica powerfully returns to below). For the past 17 years, I have been experimenting with analysis practices that eschew my own habits of data reduction and synthetic representation, instead working to place emphasis on the sensorium or the fleshy register of data and its proclivities to engender divergence in my efforts to think and express while in its grip. In 2010 (Clark/Keefe), I began referring to these analysis practices and their productions as somatography;[4] a methodology grounded in an intense attunement to the deep noticing and noting of the bodily, other material, as well as discursive elements of subjectivity and to the *poiesis*, or creativity, of expressive emergences. With an affinity for the principles and practices of decentering from an expressive

---

[4] In 2006, two German researchers, Stefan Beck and Jörg Niewöhner (2006), used the term "somatography" in an article published in the journal *Biosocieties* to describe what they viewed as three sets of issues compelling the need to develop investigative strategies for 'symmetrical' investigations across epistemic cultures. Briefly stated, these issues included a) looping effects or influences of differentiated pathways between, for example, medical diagnosis and what they describe as "selfhood," b) advancements in the understanding of epigenetic regulation, and c) the incorporation of the social into medical domains more generally. Their chief interest in this work was in calling for further investigations into the importance of integrating the perspectives of medical/socio-cultural anthropology and science and technology studies. While I remain very intrigued with their agenda and share their desire for more transdisciplinary studies that move us away from either over-essentialized conceptualizations of the body or the absence of biological markers and agency in social explanations, my use of the term somatography seemingly departs from Beck and Niewöhner's on the basis of one key point: I am not invested in epistemic practices and aims which continue to re-install the dominant conceptualization of unitary "identity," which equates consciousness, rationality, and individualism as the engine for human development.

arts perspective, analysis practices from a somatographic perspective involve mobilizing body-based and arts-informed techniques that help researchers follow, trace, ride or otherwise come into deep relation with the palpating forces of the data themselves. More rather than less divergent in their aims, somatographic analyses seek to transpose the ego-indexed representational impulse circulating through the conventional analytical question "What do these data mean?" into a relationship with data that is instead grounded in the question "What do these data do?" Data and the process and relations by which it becomes meaningful is extended and attended to via *poiesis*. Borrowing from philosopher and expressive arts theorist Stephen K. Levine's (2012) investments in the term, "*poiesis* implies the possibility of new beginnings and, in particular, of the possibility of the arts playing a central role in what is to come" (p.7). Through foregrounding *poiesis*, both in principle and in practice during somatographic research, I begin to see the work and worth of translating the conventional term "analysis" away from its habitual moorings as something signifying the cognitive act of categorizing to instead mean a term signaling the creative thresholds through which the data are becoming expressive, a translation I believe is worth pursuing.

In practical terms, somatographic analysis has involved:

- attuning to material-discursive data (data of bodily, spoken, and other natural as well as cultural features emerging in the field of inquiry) through deep noticing and visual/textual noting

- attending via *poiesis*, or creativity, to data's provocations and the inquiry process itself through making art.

I am trained as an ethnographer and often begin fieldwork by doing observations of the phenomena of interest, utilizing a split-page approach as Glesne (2011) and others describe. This means I "split" my field log page in half vertically (I most often use a 9"x12" sketch book), noting on the left-hand "descriptive" side, concrete details about who is present, what activities are underway, how the physical space appears, and so on. Resisting the impulse to begin making connections or links to what I think I see and know, I hold open and eventually begin to enter the right-hand "analysis" side of my split page by tracing the data's influence. More specifically, on the analysis side of my field log, I follow an embodied register of what the data are doing, making textual and visual notings (through, for example, gestural drawings, tonal variations, handwriting, and so on). Mark-making follows the bodily as well as voiced features and the effects and affects of discursively material subjects—of me in relation with others and in relation to the cultural, physical, and socio-ecological flows in the inquiry event. The image below (Figure 23.2) provides an example from my field log of what emerged under analytical conditions while conducting a recent research project among a group of university undergraduate art students (see Clark/Keefe 2012). The guiding question for this project was; how is it to be in the process of becoming artists and becoming educated?

Figure 23.2 *Artists' Statements Antagonisms* emerged during observations of students giving an oral presentation of their artist's statements; an iconic and notoriously demanding exercise of encapsulating and sharing aloud what a given artist's intentions are for a specific body of work. In my field log/sketchbook, I worked to follow the event of students' presentations. In other words, in a preliminary analytic stance toward attuning to what the data were doing, I engaged in tracing through line and form, the sensation of how students' attempts to articulate their written "statements" related to their largely ineffable art practices and beliefs were becoming an entangled set of corporeal and inter-corporeal performative antagonisms for them and for me watching/listening to them. Mark-making on the analysis side of my split field log page while in this dynamic inquiry fold involved getting out of the way of recognizing and categorizing what each student was saying and instead meeting through analytic art, making the "how it was" to be-coming into meaning.

Attuning during observations grew more intense as I began attending to the data during later analysis via more elaborate art-making. Working with all collected somatographic data (narrative and visual noticings, reflective memos from dream, emotional, and other physiological response data, etc.), I began to gravitate to specific art media because of their physical possibilities for creatively meeting and holding open a space for the form and force of (in the case of this artist statement fieldwork event) speech-centric bias, transient precariousness, and the picked and stitched-passageways of language's ordering effects on art and life's multiplicities. I was drawn to and began tearing specific pages from three texts (Gawain's (1978) *Creative Visualization*;

DeSalvo's 1996 memoir, *Vertigo*; and Northrup's (1998) *Women's Bodies, Women's Wisdom*). These pages were then manipulated and pasted onto 9"x12" drawing paper. Nepalese rice paper skin arrived as the most sense-able layer to then enact a series of thresholds through which further material/bodily incitements and alterations could emerge and upon which other drawn forces and rhythms (such as the "eyeball" image at the center of the larger image) could assert themselves.

The challenge of analysis in somatography then becomes making the active body-with-mind passageways that are the phenomenon under study observable. Observable not in the sense of achieving an objectivist's gaze, but in the sense of something a researcher-artist is able to share by way of occupying a gap between acts of certain translation; between what is known and what is becoming known, where things aren't so clear. I view this as akin to what Knill, Levine, and Levine (2005) describe in their accounting for artistic making, as is understood within the framework of a Dionysian *poiesis*:

> The role of the artist or poet is not to impose a pre-existing form upon senseless matter but to allow material to find its own sense. What is primary is what is given, a chaos of meanings, which demands assistance in order to come-into-form. (p.40)

Somatographic analysis as an act of engaging the arts; it challenges and subverts conventional wisdoms about the researcher's role in making valid connections and passing along systematically arrived at "truths." Indeed, intentions in a *poiesis*-induced analysis are far and away from reductionist tendencies that lead to stable representations of what we have, after all, come to know. It is analysis as a co-implicative and deeply relational process for creatively holding data's material-discursive nature and incitements, buffering the humanist impulse to rush to judgment, and for enlarging the imagination of what could be rather than what is.

CONCEPTUAL TRANSLATION OF "SCIENCE AS USUAL"

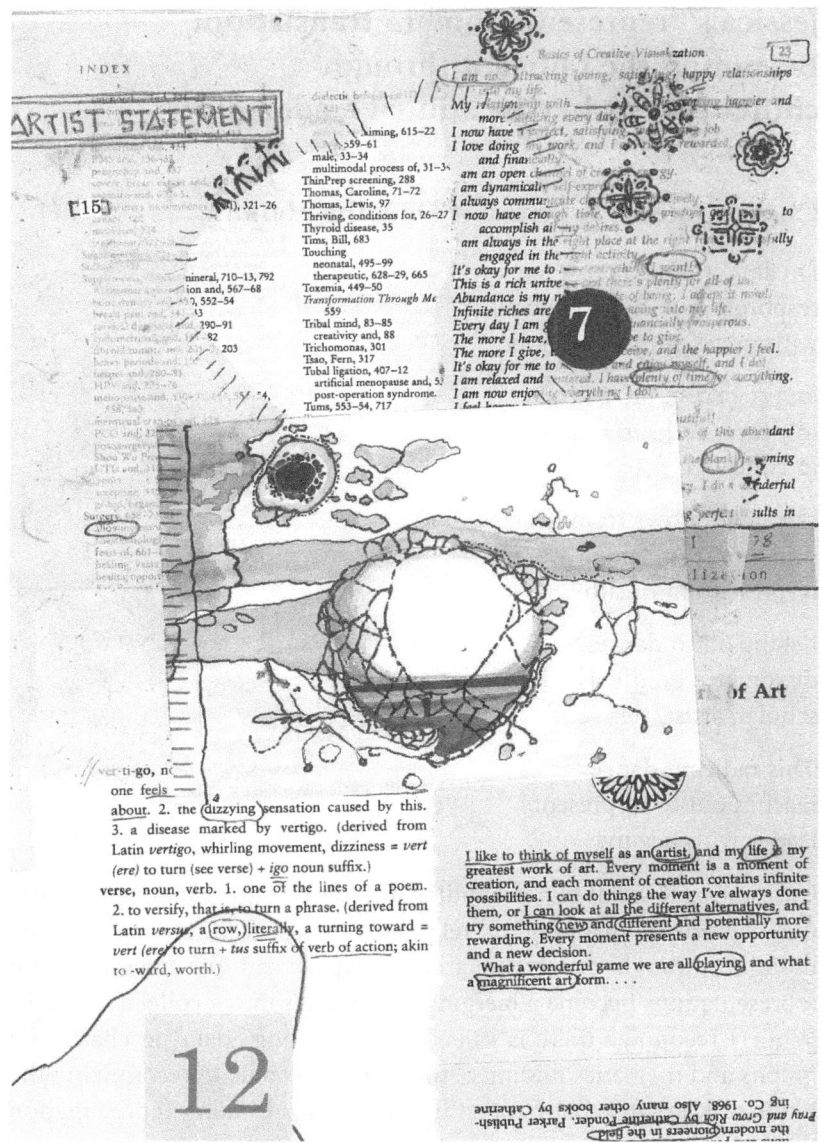

Figure 23.2 *Artists' Statements Antagonisms.*
Clark/Keefe 2010, 9"×12", mixed media on paper.

Jessica's "representation" in translation: Becoming the radicant through choreopoiesis in educational leadership

Choreopoiesis: A Series of Dancing Haikus

Dream, drum, dance, then ask
responding to heart and soul
with grace, smile, and hope

journeywork, my path
to peace, and sustaining self
in collective space

research? grows from heart/
soul work. Affirming we/me,
re-presenting breath

risking all to dance
dissonance boldly as
scholar, artist, self.

This radicant dance
reaches out to re-present
leader with beauty.

Conventional wisdom surrounding the term "representation" implies the convenient mapping of relationships between variables. When thought through expressive arts principles and practices, research representations become a merging of variables into a collective whole. While I recognize there is value in representing "data" in charts and graphs and thematic "findings," there is equal value in recognizing the kinds of knowing that happen in the arts. In thinking representation through the arts, we grant ourselves the unique opportunity to re-present our own and/or our subjects understanding(s) of the work as it unfolds, unfurls, and elaborates itself into multiple, creative iterations of a collective journey. Through this re-envisioning of re-presentation, a translation occurs where the collective (subject/topic/researcher) "translates itself into the terms of the space in which it moves" (Bourriaud 2010, p.51). This is the creative, embodied work of a radicant leader.

What space does this re-envisioning of representation move in? For me, it is a creative, arts-oriented space; a movement space, an embodied space, a collective space, and a generative space where the artful journeywork of scholarship takes root. In this space, I am in the process of becoming radicant artist/researcher/leader, setting my forms of nomadic scholarship/leadership into motion—spinning, dancing and twirling—and using expressive figures and figurations that are continually emerging from my inquiry. Thinking with Bourriaud (2010) invokes the radicant as the researcher who finds themselves situated as an artistic, ecological "individual…(who) resembles plants that do not depend on a single root for their growth but advance in all directions on whatever surfaces present themselves by attaching multiple hooks to them, as ivy does" (p.51). In conceptualizing myself and my scholarly, leaderly, artistic work through the image of the radicant, what I am in the process of better understanding emerges less as clear, scientific, data-driven representations of something I recognize or know concretely, and more as representational provocations because as Bourriaud (2010) attests, the aims of the radicant are to "generate journeys by which [the data and me inextricably] elaborate themselves as subjects even as the corpus of their work takes shape" (p.53). This iterative, ongoing elaboration of the collective, self, and work is what I begin to conceptualize here as the journey of choreopoiesis, an arts-oriented, emergent, generative, and embodied form of research representation that centers in on what happens when we use the movement of physical bodies and their depictions, words and arts-informed figurations to creatively think representation anew.

Translation of the term "representation" commenced for me as a series of haikus that were created in reflexive response to using movement as a form of re-presenting my own understanding of the role that educational leaders find themselves playing in the current socio-political landscape. School leaders, such as school principals or directors, are traditionally represented in Western nations in a highly conventional way. Ubben, Hughes and Norris (2011) frame the conditions by which school leaders are expected to operate as follows: "First, principals must be accountable for the academic progress of all of students entrusted to their care. Second, they must facilitate the social and emotional development of all students" (p.3). However, through both a conceptual analysis of the term "leading subject" (Clark/Keefe and Miller 2012) and from my own experiences as an educational leader, I have discovered that a small, but thoughtful group of arts-based educational leaders (like myself) literally and figuratively find themselves dancing dissonance and avoiding the temptation to ascribe to such binaristic thinking that is prevalent in educational institutions as: right/wrong, responsibility/accountability, good/bad, manager/leader, inspirational entity/director, artist/scholar/leader.

Therefore, as I enact the radicant in search of creative surfaces to attach my conceptual hooks, poetic inquiry and the emergent poem, such as the one used to open this exploration, have often arrived as a freeing form for representing my analysis. According to McNiff (2009), "The poem is a glimpse catcher, holding onto something that would be lost" (p.216). As a practicing educationally leading subject and researcher, I often find myself at a verbal loss and physical deficit to convey my experiences. I find myself literally without words, and physically without action. Then, by holding steady McNiff's (2009) image of the "glimpse catcher," I am able to translate, through a variety of intermodal, arts-oriented lenses, my analytical thinking into an affectively different form of representation. Furthermore, the cultivation of meaningful representation through poetry helps me re-present the embodied and partially ineffable essence of the struggles I face as "leader" on a daily basis.

Alongside, intertwined in, and entangled with my poetic inquiries and emergences, over the past six years I have experimented with how to use creative movement and dance as expressive arts-based forms of research representation, or new creative directions or surfaces where conceptual anchoring can occur. In my radicant efforts towards rethinking representation, both musical arrangement and interpretive dance were utilized as diffractive and generative tools for better understanding, dislodging, and shining light upon the tensions between the different philosophical perspectives on what it means to be in the process of becoming educational leader. By exposing these tensions, this work explored the value of transposing a positive, emancipatory shift in educational leadership in juxtaposition to the maintenance of the principles and practices of educational leadership that "science as usual" actively promotes. The use of expressive modalities, such as dance and movement, as representational tools helped me to uncover the intersection between the scholarly discourses about, of arts-based research and the practical realities of utilizing a creative, arts-based research approach to elucidate my own subjective leadership journey. This intersection was, and still is, the place where the scholarly tensions that emerge in dialogue with each other are animated, brought to life, and then danced into light.

In practical terms, representation of what I had been studying by way of dominant discourses of "leadership for excellence in schools" (Ubben *et al.* 2011) emerged in a set of choreographed movements intended to reverberate with the discourse's paternalistic and colonial nature. These elements of analysis-through-movement were then elaborated and put in direct bodily dialogue with feminist and critical theorist leadership discourse—which together emerged as a type of choreopoiesis, an enactment of radicant representational research practices. This embodied, productive dialogue at the intersections aided me in self-reflexively deconstructing my own leadership/leading subject narratives in relationship to once again what "science as usual" says definitely about traditional leaders and leadership practices.

Engaging in the choreopoiesis meant taking musical scores from one genre—Mozart's Symphony #38 in D Major (Prague)—and physically and artistically listening to it call for the tones and rhythms from other diverse genres, such as Celtic (The Chieftains) and African/Afro-Caribbean drums and vocals, rendering a discordant, dissonant, and vibrant choreographic score as a creative emergence from the interaction. Then the dialogical dancing between the musical discourses became more heated and tensioned as the tempo picked up and the movement piece progressed, with the piece ending with no visible point of romantic closure or resolution; rather the viewer knows only that the discordance and dissonance were danced and feels them bodily and affectively resonating and reverberating throughout.

I used and continue to use movement as a way to work through the practical and scholarly questions I have encountered and to translate the multi-modal, multi-layered analyses that I have conducted around the discourses of educational leadership, its purposes, its intentions, its goals, its motivations, its politics into generative and productive research representations. In the multiple iterations of this choreographed work, movement, dance, and the accompanying poetic transliterations served as radicants, thinking with new directions and surfaces for representational meaning-making and thinking. The combined use of dance, music, poetry, and photography creatively animated discourses that are disparate and often do not come into contact in meaningful ways, unless we engage in choreopoiesis, and use the arts as translational, representational tools to productively bring difficult dialogues to light. One might even argue that disparate discourses are intentionally kept at a distance from each other to prevent these rich and generatively danced discussions from occurring. The feelings of irresolution, rupture, and fissure that inspired my work still persist, as the purpose was and never is resolution. Rather, in thinking with the arts through choreopoiesis, the only way out seems to be to move and to move into deep affiliation with the ruptures we feel, as we anchor ourselves in body and thought to a place where a third way leaks out and a new pathway for the journeywork we call life and inquiry begins.

Opened endings

In Chapter 2 of Levine and Levine's (1999) edited volume, *Foundations of Expressive Arts Therapy*, Paolo Knill writes:

> Realities and their distinctions are a matter of the historical and linguistic discourse we are in. Any distinction, however, does not necessarily make the experiential effect of one reality more "real" than the other... It is in the degree of opening to each other in communal engagement versus aloneness that makes all the difference, as the world coming forth will always be also hidden and concealed. (p.41)

The very important and complex set of ideas and challenges that Knill invites with these three sentences lead us to the belief that our experience of reality, our ability to distinguish one thing or effect from another, is at least in part due to the narratives, the various discourses we encounter and their very real material effects. Knill also helps us understand that as much as we recognize the world (and ourselves in it) as "reality," there are always already excesses, hidden elements, concealments, and secrets to our experiences.

In this work, the discourse of "science-as-usual" is placed in productive relationship with expressive arts and arts-based research discourses. In so doing, we see a powerful translation of data, analysis, and representation ensue, opening each term so that we may better, and through art-making, see its hidden elements and ride on its possibilities, its empowering secrets and excesses. Bringing the perspectives of expressive arts therapy and its practices into dialogue with arts-based research methodologies and approaches has meant, for us, a deep desire in communicating a mutual set of aims and purpose; namely that we need to work together whenever possible, to press open the discourses in which we find ourselves, explore the meanings they have come to hold for us, and then co-construct and put to work in an intermodal language of imagination to see and experience how they (the discourses of science-as-usual and their very material effects) and we in the process could be more positively and productively otherwise.

References

Atkins, S. and Appalachian Expressive Arts Collective (2002) *Expressive Arts Therapy: Creative Process in Art and Life*. Winston-Salem, NC: Parkway Publishers.

Atkins, S. and Eberhart, H. (2014) *Presence and Process in Expressive Arts Work: At the Edge of Wonder*. London: Jessica Kingsley Publishers.

Barone, T. (2001) "Science, art, and the predispositions of educational researchers." *Educational Researcher 7*, 30, 24–38.

Barone, T. and Eisner, E. (2012) *Arts Based Research*. Thousand Oaks, CA: Sage.

Beck, S. and Niewöhner, J. (2006) "Somatographic investigations across levels of complexity." *Biosocieties 1*, 2, 219–227.

Bourriaud, N. (2010) *The Radicant*. New York: Lukas and Sternberg.

Bowers, C. (2010) "The insights of Gregory Bateson on the connections between language and the ecological crisis." *Language and Ecology 3*, 2, 1–18.

Braidotti, R. (2006) *Transpositions: On Nomadic Ethics*. Cambridge: Polity Press.

Cahnmann-Taylor, M. and Siegesmund, R. (eds) (2008) *Arts-Based Research in Education: Foundations for Practice*. New York: Routledge.

Clark/Keefe, K. (2006a) "Degrees of separation: An ourstory about working-class and poverty-class academic identity." *Qualitative Inquiry 12*, 6, 1180–1197.

Clark/Keefe, K. (2006b) "Grandpa Mitchell: A poetic and visual expression of love and loss." *Headwaters: Appalachian Journal of Expressive Arts Therapy 3*, 7–8.

Clark/Keefe, K. (2009) "Between antagonism and surrender: Using art to dwell more resolutely in irresolution." *Creative Approaches to Research 2*, 1, 22–35.

Clark/Keefe, K. (2010) *Invoking Mnemosyne: Art, Memory, and the Uncertain Emergence as a Feminist Embodied Methodology*. Rotterdam: Sense Publishers.

Clark/Keefe, K. (2012) "Becoming artist, becoming educated, becoming undone: Toward a nomadic perspective of college student identity development." *International Journal of Qualitative Studies in Education 27*, 1, 1–25.

Clark/Keefe, K. (2014) "Suspended animation: Attuning to material-discursive data and attending via art making during somatographic inquiry." *Qualitative Inquiry 20*, 6, 790–800.

Clark/Keefe, K. and Gilway, J. (2016) "Attuning to the interstices of arts-based research and the expressive arts: An experiment in expanding the possibilities for creative approaches to inquiry." *Learning Landscapes 9*, 2, 159–180.

Clark/Keefe, K. and Miller, V. (2012) "Transpositions toward Becoming Leading Subjects." In C Gerstl-Pepin and J.A. Aiken (eds) *Social Justice Leadership for a Global World*. Charlotte, NC Information Age Publishing.

DeSalvo, L. (1996) *Vertigo: A Memoir*. New York: First Feminist Press.

Eisner, E. (1995) "What artistically crafted research can help us understand about schools." *Educational Theory 45*, 1, 1–6.

Eisner, E. (2005) "Persistent tensions in arts-based research." Keynote address, QUIG Conference, Athens, GA.
Eisner, E. and Powell, K. (2002) "Art in science?" *Curriculum Inquiry 32*, 2, 131–159.
Finely, S. (2003) "Arts-based inquiry in QI: Seven years from crisis to guerrilla warfare." *Qualitative Inquiry 9*, 2, 281–296.
Foucault, M. (1985) *The History of Sexuality: Vol. 2. The Use of Pleasure* (Trans. R Hurley). New York: Vintage Books. (Original work published 1984).
Gawain, S. (1978) *Creative Visualization: Use the Power of Your Imagination to Create what You Want in Your Life.* Navato, CA: Nataraj Publishing.
Gilway, J. (2015) *Transpositional Spaces and the Process of Becoming-Educator: A Cartography of International Student Teaching Experiences.* Diss. Boone, NC: Appalachian State University.
Glesne, C. (2011) *Becoming Qualitative Researchers: An Introduction*, 4th edition. Boston, MA: Pearson.
Harding, S. (1991) *Whose Science? Whose Knowledge? Thinking from Women's Lives.* Cornell, NY: Cornell University Press.
Irwin, R. and de Cosson, A. (eds) (2004) *A/r/tography: Rendering Self Through Arts-Based Living Inquiry.* Vancouver, BC: Pacific Educational Press.
Knill, P., Levine, E. and Levine, S. (2005) *Principles and Practice of Expressive Arts Therapy: Toward a Therapeutic Aesthetics.* London: Jessica Kingsley Publishers.
Knowles, J. and Cole, A. (2008) *Handbook of the Arts in Qualitative Research: Perspectives, Methodologies, Examples, and Issues.* Los Angeles, CA: Sage.
Kuhn, T. (1962) *The Structure of Scientific Revolutions.* Chicago, IL: University of Chicago Press.
Leavy, P. (2015) *Method Meets Art: Arts-Based Research Practice*, 2nd edition. New York: Guilford Press.
Levine, E. and Levine, S. (2011) *Art in Action: Expressive Arts Therapy and Social Change.* London: Jessica Kingsley Publishers.
Levine, S. and Levine, E. (1999) *Foundations of Expressive Arts Therapy: Theoretical and Clinical Perspectives.* London: Jessica Kingsley Publishers.
Levine, S. (2012) "Editor's introduction." *Poiesis: A Journal of the Arts and Communication 14*, 7.
Lyotard, J. (1984) *The Postmodern Condition: A Report on Knowledge.* Minneapolis, MN: University of Minnesota Press.
McNiff, S. (2004) *Art Heals: How Creativity Cures the Soul.* Boston, MA: Shambhala Publications.
McNiff, S. (2009) *Integrating the Arts in Therapy: History, Theory, and Practice.* Springfield, MA: Charles C Thomas Publisher.
Miller, E. (2014) *Craftonomics: Homo Aestheticus, Homo Economicus, and Poiesis.* Diss. Boone, NC: Appalachian State University.
Neilsen, L. (1998) *Knowing Her Place: Research Literacies and Feminist Occasions.* San Francisco, CA: Caddo Gap Press.
Northrup, C. (1998) *Women's Bodies, Women's Wisdom: Creating Physical and Emotional Healing.* New York: Bantam Books.
Richardson, L. and St. Pierre, E. (2005) "Writing: A Method of Inquiry." In N. Denzin and Y. Lincoln (eds) *The Sage Handbook of Qualitative Research*, 3rd edition. Thousand Oaks, CA: Sage Publications.
Rogers, N. (2000) *The Creative Connection: Expressive Arts as Healing.* Monmouth: PCCS Books.
Sandelowski, M. (1994) "The Proof is in the Pottery: Toward a Poetics for Qualitative Research." In J. M. Morse (ed.) *Critical Issues in Qualitative Research.* Thousand Oaks, CA: Sage.
Springgay, S., Irwin, R. and Kind, S. (2008) "A/R/Tographers and Living Inquiry." In J. Knowles and A. Cole (eds) *The Handbook of the Arts in Qualitative Research.* Los Angeles, CA: Sage Publishers.
St. Pierre, E. (2002) "'Science' rejects postmodernism." *Educational Researcher 31*, 8, 25–27.
Ubben, G., Hughes, L. and Norris, C. (2011) *The Principal: Creative Leadership for Excellence in Schools.* Upper Saddle River, NJ: Pearson Education.

24

KNOWING NOT-KNOWING
Research as an Art-Analogue Process

Sabine Silberberg

The dilemma has always been there. And it had its way with me.

Several theses and one doctoral dissertation later (that is to say, there has been cumulative exposure to this dilemma), neither the field of geography, nor those of art therapy or expressive arts therapy, made the question of research methodology a straightforward task. Though not the fields, nor the advisors, were the ones prescribing the degree of struggle with finding suitable tools. At the core of the path-finding processes, the same question emerged each time: How may we capture and communicate the vitality, the liveliness, and the essence of lived experience?

During the master's level research processes, I woke up to the consistently present shreds of dissatisfaction after surrendering to suggested traditional qualitative formats drawn upon in social sciences and the therapies field, such as case studies, or assigned phenomenological themes as perceived by the researcher. Discomfort arose frequently with research processes and tools that I experienced as less than dialogical or collaborative, and as not sufficiently available to take note of the emergent; the discomfort was deepened by the suggested necessity to assign meaning to the experience of others. Clearly, every approach allowed flexibility in those regards; however, the stronghold of positivist templates and the underlying seductive call into psychiatric "expertism" had an increasingly unsettling influence on me. When I began to imagine the scaffolding, or first draft, for the doctoral research design, the resulting reluctance to compromise led me down a long exploratory road in search of methodological openings. This time, facing a significantly richer and longer process of inquiry, the search was fueled by an intention to reflect the values and principles that guide my day-to-day work as a counselor in the Day Program of an AIDS Foundation in Vancouver, which would now become the research environment. Essentially, the intentions at the heart of the endeavor, the origin of the motivation for a fine-tuned methodological tool, trace back to particular values, to qualities of respect, resonance, and receptivity toward the project participants.

Are not methodological questions always motivated by concern for the dignity and integrity of the people whose lives and experiences are in focus? I am not resting on the assumption that what led me down the rabbit holes of closer looks was a unique or singular intention to reflect experiences thoughtfully; quite the opposite, all creative arts therapists I know share this concern. It simply was the next step. What had been leading up to this, the previous steps, revolved around a radically client-centered approach to addiction-based work, known as "harm reduction."

The harm reduction approach concerns itself with engaging people living with addiction, and implicitly, with the effects of marginalization. More often than not, living with active addiction is accompanied by the presence of mental health concerns, often marked by poverty, homelessness or inadequate and unsafe housing conditions, and cumulative barriers to social and health services and resources. Within harm reduction literature, people living with and in these challenges, are described as "exquisitely complex" (Little and Franskoviak 2010, p.178), and this pragmatic compassion describes the harm reduction-based attitude toward our clients, whose understandably frequently challenging behaviors we view as adaptive and thereby resourceful. It is this combination, the vulnerability and complexity of clients as a result of the mechanisms of exclusion, which requires the necessarily thoughtful clinical approach, and in tandem, the search for a responsive research framework and methodology as an imperative and extension of care.

To give you a sense of the people, the environment, and core elements of the harm reduction approach: strict abstinence is not the goal of the harm reduction approach, but "to reduce the harmful consequences of drug use and other high-risk activities that cut across the spectrum from safer use to managed use to abstinence" (Marlatt and Witkiewitz 2010, p.591). The focus for support is redirected from prevention of drug use toward prevention of harm, and toward improving the quality of life for people who use illicit drugs, and for their communities.

Acceptance and engagement lie at the core of the approach, and to communicate this acceptance, non-coercive services are provided paired with more equalized power, also known as "meeting people where they're at" (Harm Reduction Coalition 2011). Marginalized populations have traditionally been excluded from relevant care (Tatarsky and Marlatt 2010); here, the list of cumulative challenges is lengthy: of living with HIV/AIDS and Hepatitis C, histories of emotional, physical and sexual abuse and neglect, experiences of abuse and violence in sex work, with times spent in prison, varied gender identities and sexual orientations, and of course the stigma of living with addiction and (un)treated mental health issues—all of these leave most clients with significantly less than hope. It leaves them without the willingness to trust, the absence of a relationship with self-worth, and most often without the capacity/tenacity/audacity to negotiate the high thresholds of supposed support systems.

The intricacies and implications of working with harm reduction principles to guide clinical work are extensive on both micro and macro levels. The implicit human rights agenda rests simply on the fact that all people have a right to dignity, respect, and care, and it challenges the dehumanizing image of people who use substances, frequently described as "weak, criminals, lazy" (Tatarsky and Marlatt 2010, p.120). The political nature of the work entails challenging stigmatization, and the support of clients' strengths and resources through collaboration—therefore, clients' availability and interests lead the process. The alternative—what alternative? Mandatory participation or prescribed treatments are not what work in this environment; clients would not return to the Centre or may avoid the clinician. In more than a decade of experience, I have learned that the path toward connection arrives with acceptance, flexibility, and the capacity to let go of preconceived agendas; humor and play are clinical assets in each moment, for each relational opportunity. Next to transparency and swift boundary-setting skills, clinicians draw just as much on sensitivity and detection of strengths and resources.

The fragility of the emergent—whether relationships, (re)discovery of personal resources, or a renewed sense of self-worth—made abundantly clear to me that the methodology ought to mirror the clinical approach, designed by following what may, or may not, emerge in the relationally oriented process.

What also presented itself was the research dilemma of predetermining what to look for. Unpredictability marks the flow of the moments and encounters, and the work takes on the distinct flavor of improvisation; therefore, a vast array of clinical tools is a definite asset to making engagement meaningful for those involved. All clinicians, be they counselors, nurses, arts or recreation therapists, reemerge as "real people" here, in addition to their role-prescribed responsibilities. This constitutes a significant addition to, if not departure from, traditional healthcare approaches, and a step away from treacherous grounds of authority and "expertism." Connections are valued for the quality of what they have to offer in presence, in the generosity of warmth and listening, and in the impact of support like advocacy, medication management, or other tangible care. The improvisational nature of the work, and the importance of each moment and encounter, bearing the possibility to inform the next, manifests in various ways. Groups are typically run in drop-in formats, and commitments evolve slowly and over time; consistency is an unrealistic expectation, and yet there seems to be a rhythm to the relational patterns, each connection unfolding on its own, and reverberating with the overall environment. Arts-based research in this context? Yes, and what I learned in this process: how else?

My love of photography, in particular as a contemplative practice, sparked the intention for the research project, and after many years of integrating the arts into my work as a counselor here, I knew that I could count on the reliable presence of uncertainty regarding all aspects of the process. As unsettling as that can be to the habitual wish for predictability and stability, it was important to me to remain "true" to these chaotic characteristics of processes, despite the fact that research proposals call for overviews, predetermined tasks, and time lines. As Sullivan observantly noted, the positivist mantra, "If you don't know where you're going, how do you know when you get there?" has not been convincing as a guiding North Star in arts-based research processes (2006, p.19). It does, however, touch on a core dilemma I faced at the outset: how to build a research framework congruent with clinical practice shaped by an improvisational attitude? Matters were complicated by the fact that I chose photography. Processes of marginalization create invisibility, as a side-effect of mechanisms of exclusion (Vasas 2005), and urging project participants to become visible for the sake of research, and potentially risk repercussions as a result of the very real existence of the stigma of HIV/AIDS, as well as of being identified as "an addict," was far from my intention. These very aspects gave the search for a receptive-enough methodology the flavor of an ethical quest. Or, in my own words:

> Shedding light, or illuminating matters, plays a central role in both photography and the dissertation-writing process. Light is associated with attention and presence, and thereby with connection, an act of joining, and a quality of being-with. Light is also used as a metaphor for truth, knowledge and sense-making, and therein lie the challenges for this project. The participants, setting, methodologies and researcher involved with this process share a predisposition toward complexity and the in-between, a preference for nuances and grey zones. Light can be relief and revelation; light can also be intrusive to what is comforted by the dark. The setting here is in the borderland between these two poles. Given the unpredictability of the life-circumstances of the participants in this research, my experience suggests that I enter this process with curiosity, and let go of any outcome expectations. Refining my understanding will require respect, an ongoing availability to adapt to circumstances, and my own "photo-sensitivity." (Silberberg 2012, pp.1–2)

By now I had clarified to myself that, at the core of the search for methodology, I place the respect and care for the people involved. Particularly when collaborating with people living with the effects of marginalization, I intend to fend off superimposition of methodological procedures, aiming for awareness of structures of power, however subtly delivered through "necessary procedures." The emergent, the fragile, the not yet formed or visible is tender and at risk, particularly in the realm of the relational, including the arts. I am concerned about contributing, about obliviously continuing to marginalize, and I fear a deadening by method and the draining of life, and voice, out of the data gathered. After describing the quality of experience in the research environments, motivated by the implicit social justice mandate, and guided by the principles of harm reduction, I embarked on the Cinderella-esque search for a resonant approach, scanning through what might be most relevant to the particular combination of arts and population, prepared to embrace a method-less method endeavor.

Even phenomenological applications made me suspicious, at first. As the default method of the expressive arts, I was concerned that here, too, the operationalization into procedures would override the ambiguous and the nascent. After first allowing excursions into thick, rich, juicy poetic morsels received by deep listening, would I then be called back into the known academic territory of linear processes, designed to excavate hard facts as valid contributions to rightfully established knowledge? My concerns were eased. What I found, among the diverse philosophical strands and applications, were openings into resonance and nuance. Inspired by van Manen's words, "writing creates a space that belongs to the unsayable" (2006, p.718), I accepted the invitation to "research as a poetizing activity" (van Manen 1990, p.13) and extended it beyond the unsayable— to photography, and the potentially invisible. What I found were descriptions of a phenomenological perspective as entering the ambiguous, understanding research to approximate meaning rather than determine it. This desire to move toward the edge of insight, or "darkness as the method" (van Manen 2006, p.719), stimulated my capacity to imagine a responsive photo-based research process designed to shed light on what may, or may not, become visible. Research and the desire to truly understand are viewed as an act of care, and as a serving of what we love. This research method is then informed by attitude, rather than technique, and "as a manner and style of thinking" (Merleau-Ponty 1962, p.viii; van Manen 2006, p.720). While the process allows letting go of rigidity of procedure, the research activities are offered responsively and flexibly as an act of respect toward what is desired to be understood. The phenomenological intention to speak the world rather than *of* it (van Manen 1990), and its call for evocative expression, led me down the path of making space for original voices, for the language and expressions of the research participants themselves—people who say that they find themselves not usually listened to. Rather than abstracting and assigning meaning early in the process, the intended approach was to carry those voices forward, far into the discussion of what had been expressed, both visually and verbally. The exciting possibilities for respect and resonance, brought to the process by intention and attitude rather than by predetermined procedures, created an opening for a methodological accompaniment of the emergent.

Encouraged by phenomenological thoughts in my developing methodological toolbox, I ventured further. With photography at the core of this particular arts-based research process, my intention was to scan the qualitative research realm for related expertise, inching towards an understanding of the edge in the current discourse, and toward finding out what it would have to offer to this particular project. What I found was methodological richness, and at first something that appeared familiar: a suspicion toward the image and its acceptability as a way of knowing (Prosser 1998). The early suspicion and discrediting attitudes towards creative arts therapies from medico-psychiatric disciplines reverberated. In particular, the image is perceived as distorted, and "skewed by the socio-context of 'making,' 'taking,' and 'reading;' and, to sum up, images are so complex that analysis is untenable" (Prosser 1998, p.99). This intrigued and amused me, sparking curiosity about suspicion of the image, but not the word? However, while further discussion reaches beyond the possibilities of this article, the criticism also cuts to the core of aliveness of the photograph, and of the arts. What the image evokes for visual sociologist Prosser is the "irksome complexity of traveling through contested territory" (p.116) in his search for "data uncontaminated by idiosyncrasies" (p.123). Leaving the futile gold-digging for evidence of objectivity behind, and turning back to the image under a differently conceptualizing light, I am finding much resonance with my research intentions in visual ethnography. In particular, Pink distances herself from generalizing "manuals," (2007, p.5) as she refers to writings such as Prosser's, and understands them as subscribing to a dominant discourse in order to be accepted and incorporated. Her research approach follows "the very qualities and potentials that the ambiguity and expressivity of visual images offers ethnography" (p.5), including interdisciplinary connections between ethnography and arts practices. Pink emphasizes that methodologies are developed for and with particular projects, "and, as most good researchers know, it is not unusual to make up the methods as you go along" (p.5). She cautions to not use conventional academic approaches "to obscure and abstract the epistemologies and experienced realities of local people" (p.6). Furthermore, working with marginalized populations calls for "an ongoing process of negotiation, reflection, and experimentation" (House, as cited in Clark, Prosser and Wiles 2010, p.89)—a responsive, and thereby emergent process in order to satisfy qualitative research criteria. This adaptability informed by congruence delivers us right back to the doorstep of harm reduction, and the guiding principles derived for the research process. Working responsively, flexibly, and reflexively are quality criteria for this work, and searching for methodological wisdom for photo-based approaches has taken us here, to the call for art-analogue processes to research.

The photograph, because it is understood as both subjective and objective, is regarded with suspicion (Pink 2007). Its use as a vehicle of evidence, in juxtaposition with recognition of the subjective and imaginative, gave rise to a lengthy discourse; its contingent "truths" led to observations such as Berger's, who viewed the photograph as a "meeting place where the interests of the photographer, the photographed, the viewer, and those who are viewing the photograph are often contradictory" (Berger and Mohr 1982, p.7). This conceptualization of the image as subject to perception was followed by a shift in attention to the process of investing meaning, in short, leading to the question, "*How* does the image mean?" (Weber 2008, p.50). This question is emphasized by Pink's understanding of images as intersections of meaning, which are made known in intersubjective processes—and therefore evoke multiple meanings, which change over time, and are highly context-dependent (2007). Photographs are thought of "as a practice, rather than a representation, as taking part in the world rather than reflecting it" (Crang, as cited in Pink 2011, p.93)—and this dynamic notion of a role of photographs enhances research project possibilities with an invitation toward the emergent—again, an inspiring methodological frame for arts-based research in a harm reduction environment. Finally, I felt prepared to invite six people into a process of being introduced to photography; all of them had voiced an interest in it before.

First, what happened was—a lot of nothing. Yes, uncertainty is a marker of my daily work, however, the particular attention under the magnifying glass of research lenses, and the given time-lines tied to ethics board approval introduced an unnerving element into the process. The fact that no photo was taken for the first three months made me acutely aware again of what I thought I had learned to embrace as one challenge inherent in harm reduction-based work—the terror of letting go of agendas. Once I learned to reframe "nothing" as one expression of what emerged, I was able to renew my appreciation for the improvisational attitude underlying the work. Then, the liveliness of six process narratives unfolded, and the expressions of collaboration and support translated into supporting each person in finding an entry point of interest, with an aim of committed engagement.

The images and accompanying narratives communicate undercurrents of meaning, and, for the first time in my own experience with research trajectories, the congruence of intention, content, and process design was affirmed by the continued involvement of the participants, on their own terms, and within their own rhythms of connection. The images reflected their processes vividly, also varying in expression from flooding a session with hundreds of photos, in contrast to weeks of absence from the Centre. Whether their attention was captured by hunting for the beauty of rich sunset hues, or diary-like photographic renderings of the daily noon hour for months, to utilizing the camera as a documentary tool serving a social justice perspective from the margins themselves—their engagements were acts of taking part in the world, a desire to participate in meaning-making for themselves and others. While my role has been to create conditions by conceptualizing the project, and by collaborating as a partner in creative play, they dared to take the opportunity, to shape it. By this choice, a poetic, personal, and political process was set in motion, one of becoming participators in their lives, while being aware of the effects of mechanisms of exclusion, a stepping stone toward a change in self-determination.

Responsive research design in a process involving people living with the effects of marginalization is informed by an "art analogue" attitude (Knill, Levine and Levine 2005, p.135), each step calling for reflection, for a stepping back, and for a response to a newly changed shape, which in turn shapes the next step, rendering research a creative process by necessity (Silberberg 2012). Limitations and challenges are aspects of shaping, and tools for transformation. This responsive and deeply relational approach, which found its reflection in the continued participation and the practice of visual expressions of the six photographers, affirms the importance of emergence and improvisation in arts-based research processes. The confluence of these elements—the core aspects of harm reduction, the expressive arts, and the research methodologies employed—contributed to the at times nerve-wracking endeavor of sensing the land rather than relying on the maps in the arts-based research. Beyond this, the project seemed not only to add to the lives of the participants, but to mine as well. Our research left me with a renewed and deepened appreciation for their ability to live in the present, to be moved by beauty, and to reframe profound obstacles, only to find humor and play in unlikely places.

References

Berger, J. and Mohr, J. (1982) *Another Way of Telling.* New York: Vintage Books.

Clark, A., Prosser, J. and Wiles, R. (2010) "Ethical issues in image-based research." *Arts and Health* 2,1, 81–93.

Harm Reduction Coalition (2011) *Principles of Harm Reduction.* at www.harmreduction.org/about-us/principles-of-harm-reduction, accessed on 02/20/17.

Knill, P.J., Levine, E.G. and Levine, S.K. (2005) *Principles and Practice of Expressive Arts Therapy: Toward a Therapeutic Aesthetics.* London: Jessica Kingsley Publishers.

Little, J. and Franskoviak, P. (2010) "So glad you came! Harm reduction therapy in community settings." *Journal of Clinical Psychology 66*, 2, 175–188.

Marlatt, G.A. and Witkiewitz, K. (2010) "Update on harm-reduction policy and intervention research." *The Annual Review of Clinical Psychology 6*, 591–606.

Merleau-Ponty, M. (1962) *Phenomenology of Perception.* London: Routledge Kegan Paul.

Pink, S. (2007) *Doing Visual Ethnography: Images, Media and Representation in Research*, 2nd edition. Thousand Oaks, CA: Sage Publications Inc.

Pink, S. (2011) "Amateur photographic practices, collective representation and the constitution of place." *Visual Studies 26*, 2, 92–101.

Prosser, J. (1998) *Image-based Research: A Sourcebook for Qualitative Researchers.* New York: Routledge.

Silberberg, S. (2012) Illuminating liminality: A collaborative photo-based process with people affected by marginalization in a harm reduction environment (Unpublished doctoral dissertation). European Graduate School, Saas Fee/ Leuk, Switzerland.

Sullivan, G. (2006) "Research acts in art practice." *Studies in Art Education: A Journal of Issues and Research 48*, 1, 19–35.

Tatarsky, A. and Marlatt, G.A. (2010) "State of the art in harm reduction psychotherapy: An emerging treatment for substance misuse." *Journal of Clinical Psychology 66*, 2, 117–122.

Van Manen, M. (1990) *Researching Lived Experience: Human Science for an Action Sensitive Pedagogy.* Albany, NY: State University of New York Press.

Van Manen, M. (2006) "Writing qualitatively, or the demands of writing." *Qualitative Health Research 16*, 713–722.

Vasas, E.B. (2005) "Examining the margins: A concept analysis of marginalization." *Advances in Nursing Science 28*, 3, 194–202.

Weber, S. (2008) "Visual Images in Research." In A.L. Cole and J.G. Knowles (eds) *Handbook of the Arts in Qualitative Research.* Thousand Oaks, CA: Sage Publications, Inc.

25

PLAYING WITH AUSCHWITZ

A Liminal Inquiry into Images of Evil

Lisa Herman

At the turn of this century, I visited Auschwitz for the first time. The evening before, wandering in Krakow, I chanced upon a stall selling small, carved wooden images of traditional Hassidic Jews playing instruments. I purchased a Klezmer musician, the one with a clarinet. A few years later in Prague, I bought a Hassidic marionette from an Israeli in the Old Jewish Quarter. He had him dancing in front of the Jewish museum that houses objects gathered throughout Europe by the Nazis to record a vanished race. Some time passed, and then a friend and I made a music video with the marionette in an abandoned building site behind her apartment near Seattle.

I have always been interested in the images of evil events and, in particular, the images connected to the Holocaust. I want to know how they affect non-participants in such events. I want to know more about what we learn from people's representations of our vast creative capacities for cruelty, and about our experience when we engage these images. How do they affect those of us who weren't there? I have come to believe we, the non-participants, need to stay creatively engaged with these (fortunately) mediated experiences in order to help prevent their continuing occurrence. We must not become complacent, believing naively that we have learned our lessons and *it* will not happen again. It *is* happening again.

In order to transmit historical knowledge of evil events to future generations, knowledge that stretches our capacities to acknowledge and remember our human potential for self-destruction, we need to engage embodied attention. We must be, as Jill Bennett notes, affected in a literal sense, "stricken with affect" (2005, p.29). Images—visual art, words held by poetic language, theatre, film, dance, song—provide a wide range of affective access points for non-participants. We must educate to incorporate this important data while staying fully present with all our capacities, educating ourselves to know we will not emerge "unscathed" from these encounters with evil (Gilgun 1995, p.182). Bachelard claims, "It is always more enriching to imagine than to experience" (1969, p.88). Even if it is only sometimes so, we can learn and teach others to encounter evil through imagination, play and the arts. We can play with what horrifies us so that we may engage creatively with it.

It is through the arts that we also remember we are capable of beauty and love. We learn to contain our forays into the "shadow side" in their proper realm of the imagination and bring forth our potential to enhance life. We can choose to use our creative abilities to foster relationship, discussion and diversity. Through the ages, some have contained exploration of their destructive possibilities through the arts. Within this frame, there are those who have learned to bring the shadow into the light and transform hate and despair into cries for recognition and inclusion. Through artful presentation, sometimes these cries have been heard.

My research with the images of evil events speaks to the images that won't leave non-participants alone: the ones that are so powerful that we are left holding them inside of us. When we non-participants "experience" genocide, we are neither the survivors nor the perpetrators nor the bystanders. We are the ones who are affected by the monuments, the front pages of the newspaper, the websites, and we wrestle with our own responses of rage, despair and identification with all those involved. Our research participants are the images. They inform us. I count myself among a third iteration of engagement with the Holocaust, among those whose vicarious experience of evil is a subject for investigation (Herman 2001, 2008). The site of our inquiry into the images is the liminal space between history and our own imaginations. If we want to know more, we know we must develop our imaginative capacities to enter this site. Such research needs a methodology that will allow imaginative encounters with the images to facilitate the inquiry and bring both the event and the response into the public domain for discussion and action. Such a methodology allows play with images in the liminal space between the evil event and our own and others' experience as non-participants.

How do we play with an image?

To appropriately research an image, we need to allow it to affect us. To affect us, we must be able to play with it—to suspend disbelief and enter its world. The image is an imaginative toy, calling for encounter. Something shifts in us when we participate playfully with an image. We the "spectators" (Boal 1995) enter unknown liminal space/time. This is the site where the images live. When we fully engage and play with a powerful image, we come into a moment where our customary ways of thinking and being are challenged, and we must make meaning differently in order to stay present to our experience. We must employ different modes to express what is happening to us, so we turn to the old/new practice of the arts. Artists know that play, allowing new imaginative forms to emerge and be expressed, is the most appropriate way to participate with any image. We take our cue from them.

Lincoln and Denzin (2000) claim that artful findings produce shared experience and empathy. When we engage artfully, we are moved to a liminal state, between us and the other—the image—and the possibility exists that we will be moved by the encounter. Our experience ideally will engender further creative responses that will in turn evoke shared experience and empathy for others. Engaging and performing images of evil through the arts, we are permitted affective states without succumbing to them. We can remember we are in a liminal space and are witnessing a mediated event, while at the same time remaining deeply engaged. We can be moved to pity and fear for what humans have done and also be moved to creative action. Artful presentation of research appeals to us (McNiff 1998). We need to stay engaged and thus experience an "aesthetic response," defined by Paolo Knill as "a distinct response, with a bodily origin, to an occurrence in the imagination, to an artistic act, or the perception of an art work" (Knill, Barba and Fuchs 1995, p.71).

When engaging evil, this aesthetic response is not one of pleasure, but still calls us to attend. Presentation produces a moment(s) of disturbance in time and place—an experience of the liminal—where things presented do not make sense in the way they are normally known, where perceptions are changed. We return to everyday reality knowing we have confronted an event outside the bounds of personal and cultural identity, and we feel a sense of the "uncanny": something was wrong in a distressing way. This is performative presentation, discussed by Denzin and Lincoln as writing "that angers and sorrows the reader, writing that challenges the reader to take action in the world, to reconsider the conditions under which the moral terms of the self and community are constituted" (Lincoln and Denzin 2000, p.1054).

The intent of arts-based research in liminal space is to both engage with and distance from the physicality of the experience. Shaun McNiff calls it a "way of digging deep into avoided depths" (1993, p.8) while helping elude the "shadow power" the images may have over us: the power of unaware influences. It is a way of looking at disturbing images of evil within and outside of us, acknowledging their powerful animated existence. This is a process of recognizing the vitality of the images and realizing, in Arnheim's (1986, p.55) words, that "animation flows from the image and affects the lives of viewers…[and that the] essence of the engagement is not what we do to the image, but what it does to us." I have learned I must gather data with respect and care for the images of evil as well as include and safely contain my own felt responses. I concur with Stephen K. Levine (2000, p.91):

> To base our research in the arts means to engage the imagination in the forming of our concepts and in the carrying-out of the project itself. Not only may the initial inspiration come in the encounter with the image…but the conduct of the research may itself be imaginative. We must have faith that the imagination can inform us, that art is not non-cognitive but that it binds together both feeling and form in a way that can reveal truth.

When we choose to follow a Bachelardian phenomenology of the imagination (1969), our co-participants, the "others," are the images, and they are "allowed to speak for themselves" (McNiff 1998, p.55). This artful engagement is for those of us interested in allowing images of evil to inform us physically and to be able to "get more direct reports from the phenomenon we are studying, asking the subject matter itself to comment on or teach us about itself" (Braud and Anderson 1998).

Affect as a source of knowledge

Artfully playing with images, we find visceral information in liminal space. Whether we take direct accounts from survivors or gaze at a photo, we enter this space of mediated representation and receive our own embodied images. When researchers play authentically with written testimony, photos, music, poems and artifacts that have been generated by an evil event, we move into that same liminal space where writers, visual artists, theatre, dance and music performers access material to create their work. Here, in the space between the event and our imaginations, the images engage us, and we are called to respond through a coherent sensibility and methodology: a playfully felt response. We find that inquiring from our physical being and shaping our experience artfully is appropriate for the development of "moral discourse...and sacred textualities" (Lincoln and Denzin 2000, p.1048). When images affect researchers as a personal, embodied experience, we are moved to take action and create, with the intent of engendering further affect.

The embodied researcher of evil is compelled to make art. Linear discourse is inadequate. Images ask us for artful representation. The researcher cannot truthfully record a physical experience of engagement with the image other than artfully. We need multiple art disciplines as we research, since the images do not come through in one form. They arrive in music and in a felt sense, through theatre and clown. They are found in words in print and words that we sometimes feel in the air that touch our scalp and send chills down our spine or acid in our throat. Sometimes we sense images that arise from the sidewalk and sometimes we sense them through other images that we see and hear on a movie screen. Sometimes they are thoughts that drift through our mind or someone else's words left hanging in a room. When we allow ourselves to fully sense these images in our bodies and minds, we may then write a poem or dance or shape a sound in response. When researching images of evil events, if we collect and shape our data within the container of art, we can find a way, inspired by writers in the Holocaust itself, "to struggle against despair" (Brenner 1997, p.120), a way to create from a sense of hope.

Arts-based fieldwork is conducted individually and in collectives. Like the sculptor in her studio or the theatre troupe in its rehearsal space, the researcher begins with the image(s) she wishes to explore and paints, moves, makes sound, writes, talks... Artful researchers follow the image as it transforms, noticing how we respond in our bodies and our minds. We are "nomadic inquirers," described by St. Pierre (2000, p.267) as she worked on her computer:

I did work in this smooth mental space. I found it occasionally if only momentarily, and I would like to return there to do more fieldwork. I am there now sometimes as I write this, and that is encouraging for one who likes to speed along across the steppes, galloping willy-nilly, hooting back at the deep, somber warnings pulsing from the *logos*.

This researcher allows the image(s) to move her. She does not look for linear engagement. She brings her mind and body into appropriate alignment with her co-participant(s). She allows herself to be guided by these disturbing images as she experiences them with all her senses. She lets herself enter the smooth liminal space and collect with all her capacities the data the images present to her. She pounds out words on the computer, crouches her body into a ball-shape, allows sounds to escape from her belly, as the images inform her. She records her process, shapes the material and performs it for her community (Steinman 1995).

I conclude with the following, a poem culled from my own research playing with Auschwitz.

Digging

Digging dead bodies
Who might prefer to be left

in buried pieces

I yearn to join them sometimes

I keep digging
picking
at old scabs until they bleed
red flames warming no one's heart

We are all decayed
still born to a time of no joy measured
on any known scale.

Why try? What for?

I keep digging deeper obeying unheard orders
from beyond the grave
somewhere out of earshot where there are

still some small shivering strings of sound
Where hands still write.
Mind still questions.
Still digging
Digging digging out of the light

Wet muck closes inside of me
Filling my cavities begging not to know anymore

Digging digging out of control
I cannot stop digging

I will die digging

Note: This article, in a somewhat different version, was originally published online in 2010 as "Toying with Auschwitz" in S. Smith and S. Hill (eds), Against Doing Nothing: Evil and Its Manifestations. Oxford, UK: Inter-Disciplinary Press.

References

Arnheim, R. (1986) "William Worringer on abstraction and empathy." In *New Essays on the Psychology of Art.* Berkeley, CA: University of California Press.
Bachelard, G. (1969) *The Poetics of Space.* Boston, MA: Beacon Press.
Bennett, J. (2005) *Empathic Vision: Affect, Trauma and Contemporary Art.* Stanford, CA: Stanford University Press.
Boal, A. (1995) *The Rainbow of Desire: The Boal Method of Theatre and Therapy.* London: Routledge.
Braud, W. and Anderson, R. (1998) "Alternative Ways of Knowing, Encountering and Collecting Data." In W. Braud and R. Anderson (eds) *Transpersonal Research Methods for the Social Sciences: Honoring Human Experience.* Thousand Oaks, CA: Sage Publications Inc.
Brenner, R.F. (1997) *Writing as Resistance: Four Women Confronting the Holocaust.* University Park, PA: The Pennsylvania State University Press.
Gilgun, G.F. (1995) "Fingernails painted red: A feminist semiotic analysis of a 'hot' text." *Qualitative Inquiry 5*, 3, 181–207.
Herman, L. (2001) *Engaging the Disturbing Images of Evil.* UMI Dissertation Services, Ann Arbor, MI.
Herman, L. (2008) "Toying with Auschwitz." Presentation at the 9th annual conference on Evil and Human Wickedness. Salzburg.
Knill, P., Barba, H. and Fuchs, M. (1995) *Minstrels of Soul: Intermodal Expressive Therapy.* Toronto: Palmerston Press.
Levine, S.K. (2000) "Researching imagination – imagining research." *Poiesis: A Journal of the Arts and Communication 2*, 88–93.
Lincoln, Y.S. and Denzin, N.K. (2000) "The Seventh Moment: Out of the Past." In N.K. Denzin and Y.S. Lincoln (eds) *Handbook of Qualitative Research.* Thousand Oaks, CA: Sage Publications, Inc.
McNiff, S. (1993) "The authority of experience." *The Arts in Psychotherapy 20*, 1, 3–9.
McNiff, S. (1998) *Arts-based Research.* London: Jessica Kingsley Publishers Ltd.
St. Pierre, E.A. (2000) "Nomadic Inquiry in the Smooth Spaces of the Field: A Preface." In E.A. St. Pierre and W.S. Pillow (eds) *Working the Ruins: Feminist Poststructural Theory and Methods in Education.* New York: Routledge.
Steinman, L. (1995) *The Knowing Body: The Artist as Storyteller in Contemporary Performance.* Berkeley CA: North Atlantic Books.

PER-FORMING HOME

Spinning New Scripts for Re-Search

Carrie MacLeod

There has been a mistake again. Someone has double-booked the community room in the basement of the housing complex. As youth arrive en masse, threads of panic run through my body. The newcomer cooking class has taken over and the room is too small to share.

This dislocation couldn't be more ironic—the "Re-Inventing Home" performance project is about to conclude for this youth group who intimately know the consequences of forced migration. Exasperated voices cry out, "Not again!" Finding a new space to rehearse at this late hour seems inconceivable to us all. One of the youngest ensemble members suggests that we move into the entrance adjacent to the laundry room to resume rehearsals. I hesitate as I imagine the chaos of people passing by with loads of laundry. My internal dialogue is quickly interrupted by a lone voice, "Listen to the rhythms of the washer and dryers! This is the back-beat for our spoken word performance!" The discovery is palpable and the whole group rushes over to the humming washers and dryers. Spontaneous dances spiral out from laughter as the sound of spinning laundry gives a new life force to the verses being spoken. As beat-box rhythms filter through spin cycles, poetic riffs are crystallized into a multi-modal performance. The laundry room is transformed into a living laboratory, and we decide to stage our community performance here amidst spin cycles and full loads. Neighbors and families are all invited to witness this homespun narrative in a familiar site. As actors, dancers, poets and musicians take their places, the audience is warmly welcomed next to the washers and dryers in the inaugural performance:

"Cycles of Home"

(Press the spin cycle to begin. Lights fade in.)

Per-forming research

When I became lost in performance, I found my home in research. After years of probing for the "right" questions to color the unprimed canvas of arts-based research, the stage re-claimed what I had been looking for all along. With an awareness of the ethical and aesthetic responsibilities that inform research, I intend to be inclusive, politically correct, action-oriented, and collaborative wherever possible. Binders on anti-oppression research frameworks, methodologies from the margins, and participatory action research curricula line my bookshelf. Despite the pursuit to maintain a sense of integrity from every possible angle, I have often come away with more questions than answers. What was I looking for and where was my gaze coming from? Perhaps even more importantly: Who was looking back at me and where were the questions coming from? During the time that I've worked with people in Canada's refugee protection system, these simple questions have become poignant in a much larger dilemma between invisibility, vulnerability, and voice. Working with inexplicable experiences of violence, trauma or risk cannot easily be captured by an outside researcher. Perhaps this is the fundamental shift that is needed in research. The point is not to capture research but to inhabit it, live from it and for it with all of one's senses. A lived inquiry is one that moves freely in between the search, the searched and the silence. On the other side of silence there are barely audible voices waiting to be heard.

I am challenged to relocate myself in a matrix of knowledge networks that are in flux, especially within transitional newcomer communities. My roles shift between community facilitator, producer, director, performer, spectator, ethnographer, arts-based facilitator, education coordinator, and doctoral researcher. When I recently lived "on site" in a settlement house with families seeking asylum for a year, the daily rhythms of domestic life accompanied these other roles.

Was I too close to home to "objectively" understand the sociopolitical realities of refugees? In between multiple arrivals and departures, an unsettling undercurrent was emerging. Can I contribute to a field of knowledge if I, too, am still looking for a home base for research? To my utter surprise, the research was actually re-searching me all along. While I wasn't looking, I was being found by the findings and shaped by the shaping. I completely underestimated the extent to which I, too, was being pursued by questions that were provocative and performative. A recurring pull towards performance was emerging in the flux of displacement right through the gaze of my own eyes.

Performative happenings consistently take center stage in between shifting identities and displaced ideologies. The impulse for performance among newcomer groups simply happened. Even when performance isn't included in a workshop design at the outset, groups tend to gravitate towards performative frameworks on their own volition. There is a bold insistence on seeing and being seen, and per-forming dreams of home in this ritual frame despite the tenuous status of exile. Inasmuch as performance derives from the Greek root meaning "to furnish forth," "to carry forward," "to bring into being" (Jackson 2004, p.13), it makes sense that displaced communities are drawn to a life force that offers alternative possibilities with clear limitations. Entrances, exits, curtain calls, blocking, lighting, and the action held within the proscenium arch all serve to crystallize chaos. In referring to performance here, I am not viewing it as a discrete discipline for trained actors. I build on Richard Schechner's notion that performances mark identities, bend time, reshape and adorn the body, and tell stories. He calls performances "restored behaviors" (Schechner 2006, p.28) and I will add an active stance that includes a re-storying of behaviors. Day-to-day realities are re-storied in performative realms through a dynamic interplay between form and fantasy. Lives are not passively preserved "as is," but are actively engaging and shaping their own storylines. Heated issues that are inaccessible off stage can be re-located, re-dressed, and made visible on stage.

Performance scholar Lynn Fels builds on this and states that to entertain performative inquiry as a (re)search vehicle is to recognize the risk, the unexpected, the stop, embodied in action and interaction through a performance that opens us to possibility. This happens between the known and the unknown, between the "real" and the "not yet real" worlds (Fels 1998, p.33). Such spaces become highly relevant for those who are forcibly removed from their homes and trapped for indefinite periods of time between borders and cultural boundaries. Bodies caught in up in forced mobility stop, start, wait, move, yield, stop, and wait again. A return to the familiar is never guaranteed. Even without a known place of return, the body can't stop itself from trying to find a home. In this flux, research cannot be another force that steals or takes up space, but ought to create embodied spaces of possibility through the imaginal realm.

While exploring refugee issues in Canada for the past two decades via the arts, I have often positioned myself as the one looking into these spaces instead of one looking out from them.

Such lines of demarcation dissipate when newcomer youth assert that I will be performing with them. This is put forward not as an invitation, but as a collective declaration. They challenge the assumption that my involvement will be at arm's-length, and vehemently reinforce their stance with an interlocking of arms. I am literally and symbolically hooked into their collective plotting. In this moment, I wonder whether blurred roles between researcher and performer will create further complications. Can I let go of the desire to obtain an outside perspective while fully immersing myself in the unknowns of a performance process? Settling deeper into this prospect is unsettling and unfamiliar. Proposed bodies of research are bodies to research, and I am not exempt from being a re-searchable body. Can a director's notes ethically accompany actor and researcher's notes if written by the same hands? The stage serves as a bridge between these roles, as it isn't always clear who is setting the stage for whom. The performance shifts in accordance to where the gaze is coming from. As new sight lines emerge through performative acts, these questions illuminate poignant insights just in time.

Per-forming identities

We begin rehearsals with the simple question: What moves you? We improvise our way into the answers.

(Lights fade in)

(Set spin cycle for one minute. Delicate wash. Four actors enter stage right and four actors enter stage left – each whispering the first words heard upon arrival in Canada. All stop and freeze and continue to whisper at a higher and higher volume until a crescendo is reached. Then all find another position and all become silent. Pause. Each actor enters into the chorus at intervals until a common rhythm is found.)

> Rhythm moves me to you
> But I ain't no-body to you.
> An' you ain't no-body to me.
> But don't you worry
> 'cause we're just on d' move
> tryin' ta find another groove
> We're always on d' move…on d' move
> On d' move….

(Fade out)

The challenges of working with refugees, internally displaced persons, and other vulnerable populations are multi-faceted and cannot be addressed simply by the development of a research methodology (Pittaway, Bartolomei and Hugman 2010, p.240). There are multiple exiles that unmake lives in the aftermath of forced migration. Border crossings are multi-faceted and continuous as linguistic and cultural divides contribute to estrangement. Resettlement does not happen in one culminating moment, but rather involves a series of adaptive responses over time. The poietic act of homemaking is multisensory and begins with a destabilization of binaries between "us" and "them." On a tacit level, the multi-vocal language of performance demonstrates that "exile is not only a double life, but one of multiplicity" (Hamid 1999, p.32). It therefore makes sense that people in exile are drawn to engage in multi-vocal performances. Performance serves as a fluid interface for confronting what is untethered and untold. This is the interface that provokes, challenges, and changes the face of migration one act at a time. When country-of-origin enmities on one side of the border are bound to cultural roots on the other, this performative interface serves as a mediator between diverse worldviews. One of the performers in the youth ensemble boldly tells me, "On stage we can dream with our enemies." Entrenched positions often remain frozen until the "arriving third" appears in another form on stage (Knill, Levine and

Levine 2005, p.136). In breaking the fourth wall of my own limited viewpoints and pre-conceived agendas, misrecognition is re-cognized through a performative lens. Where else can "nowhere" rightfully claim center stage?

To highlight this contingent and contentious nature of home making in displacement, I (re) locate research in places that may not have a strong foothold in the national imaginary at first glance. As such, the nature of this inquiry begs for more than one cursory glance. It involves re-moving oneself out of habitual ways of seeing to gain clarity on what is alive and what is at stake. The ingenuity required to transform a laundry room into a performance space is worth noticing here. There is something irrevocably alive in an unlikely space. Re-centering the margins, while decentering dominant narratives, calls for a reflexive gaze that dares to invert space and disturb monolithic identities. Yet, generating a coordinated response is challenging when mobile lives collide in chosen and random ways. This fear of instability becomes heightened when the very presence of the "other" threatens those who guard the gates to citizenship. Who we are in relation to one another directly influences how we make ourselves at home with one another. This holds relevance when bodies in flight are beholden to someone else's care and hospitality—almost to the point of being indefinitely on loan.

Those seeking asylum tend to adamantly refute the "refugee" label. Although the legal term serves an important role in judicial realms, the associated stigmas of "illegal alien," "bogus refugee," or "human cargo" only contribute to stigmas and isolation. This naming can create a momentum for further dispersals and displacements. This sub-human profiling has become its own inhumane performance that demands closer scrutiny. Youth in particular are particularly aware of this underlying subtext of exclusion. They are keen to recast themselves first and foremost as composers and performers. As world fusion rhythms, urban hip-hop, and spoken word poetry are layered into repetitive feedback loops, their re-sounding identities fill spaces that no one else is filling for them. They test the edges of how and where performance can happen—rehearsing their responses in different sites with varying tones, tempos, and timing. The ways the timbre and harmony fuse in public spaces creates new entry points for collaborations across physical and symbolic fences separating cultures and communities. A shared musicality becomes the common ground for lives commonly sidelined by bureaucratic systems. These lyrical rhythms support Trinh T. Minh-ha's sense that "home then is not only in the eye, the tongue and the nose, but it is also...acutely in the ear" (Minh-ha 2011, p.12). Stepping into the performative realm makes it possible to inhabit "...multiple and simultaneous elsewheres, always a step or more behind or ahead or to the side, watching through open windows being watched, performing [them]selves performing or being performed" (Schneider 2011, p.25). Staging the improbable becomes a window into what is possible. Witnessing one another's stories can still take place without the pressure of reiterating the raw details of traumatic events over and over again. The performance of memory is not only achievable through verbatim narration. Rather, tracing history and tracking the persistence of memories is a process that calls for ingenuity and creativity.

Staging research at home

> (Press spin cycle for two minutes. Actors enter stage left. Lines are delivered in unison.)
>
> > Came here with my ma-ma
> > Crossed the sea to Ca-na-da
> > And forgot one leetle thing...
> > I left me-self in Ahhh-FREE-ca
> > I left me-self in Ahhh-FREE-ca... (Refrain x2)
>
> (Fade out)

Amidst complex social, political, and cultural intersections, an unanswered question remains alive: Is home portable, disposable and/or performable? Performative spaces offer fluid frameworks beyond a fixed past. Narrative arcs can be held within the dynamic range of *poiesis*—"the act of making, and artistic making in particular" (Levine 2011, p.23). The "liveness" in performance particularly thrives on remaking, remixing, and re-storying. A performative inquiry does not promise resolution or restitution, and often manifests as a collision course of identities in the imaginal realm. New contracts and constructions of meaning are forged on stage in ways that may not be permissible off stage. Rigid standpoints shift into pivotal dance points when the locus of knowledge is cast from a place of embodiment. Seemingly fixed dynamics can be re-mixed into new social configurations when the non-citizen "other" becomes visible again. A performative inquiry boldly confronts invisibility and asks why certain voices have been silenced for far too long.

Performative terrain: Multi-vocal negotiations

"What else are we supposed to say to you?"

Youth Workshop Participant, Vancouver

"What are we supposed to say to you?" This question frames me, the researcher, as an authority who is looking for a specific response before an actual encounter takes place. The sincerity of this question catalyzes a newfound urgency to engage in an inquiry that is reciprocal, improvisational, and inventive. Research quickly becomes skewed when trajectories are laden with predetermined outcomes. Research ought to make sense for all involved, and relocating the sites of inquiry involves integrating the rhythms of daily life. In following this thread, we strategically re-locate the after-school rehearsals into the housing complex to accommodate the youth who are expected to assume domestic roles at home. As parents learn English or need to take on odd hours of shift work, youth step into the roles of caregivers, family language translators, and cultural informants. Unexpected interruptions shape each session, as untimely arrivals and departures reflect a larger metanarrative of constant transition and upheaval. In response to this ongoing cacophony, the youth rename the weekly sessions "In the House Jams." We devise roving scenes in the playground, in the parking lot, in the corridors and any community room that is free. We work with the concept of staging "nowhere" and explore the intricacies and power dynamics of "no" place. The scenes are purposefully void of particular references to emphasize that displacement is everywhere and is an issue that belongs to everyone. Everyone belongs to nowhere and there is a ubiquity of dislocation that no one is immune to.

As performance spaces find new ways to translate the past, present, and future, settlement tensions previously addressed in isolation are confronted collectively. We begin to make ourselves at home with one another as we transition from over-strategizing to collective-imagining. Codes for acculturation draw from creative assets rather than projected deficits in this generative space. The performative frame offers key insights into how habitual responses of fear and suspicion can shift when multiple worldviews can be re-viewed. The performative interface ironically unmasks what remains hidden from public view. Fictive Canadian dreams slip through the thin veil of the "fourth wall" as residents stop by to insert their unedited perspectives into the scene. Racial profiling and power hierarchies are provocative suggestions given from onlookers. Nothing is superfluous here, and all that comes to us "in passing" is a gift for the performance. The cadence of our shared human experience becomes recognizable when patterns arise from pedestrian gestures. These interjections ensure that the performers don't get ahead of themselves by missing out on contextual cues. This pull towards performative witnessing is not an accident or a one-time incident. There is an unwavering and unspoken commitment to assembling in this way. It comes from an innate desire to be collectively witnessed in our shared human dilemmas. Performance practices serve a visible community indicator of how we are intricately entwined.

When a member of the ensemble is called to fulfill a domestic task in the middle of rehearsals, there is vehement resistance, and a bold retort followed, "But I can't come! They need me!" Indeed, the performance needs him. Amidst the inverted roles in his daily life, he also needs the anchor of performance. This mutuality is unmistakable. The stage provides its own traces and traction in the constant transience. Belonging is not a hypothetical issue to be discussed, but is a visceral experience to be sensed. Long after the staging of various performances, youth continue to point to seemingly nondescript locations to exclaim, "Look! That's where we performed!" Staging frictions makes it possible to reclaim contested spaces and our place with one another.

Who will bring it all home?

Performance inherently generates a range of seen and unseen researchers. Audiences, too, play a pivotal role as researchers, and their receptive role is as vital as the performative act. The audience–performer relationship creates the grounds for reciprocity and generosity. This is counter-intuitive to research trends that rely on a reductive approach—one that depends on a one-way mode of seeing and perceiving. Hospitable spaces generated between performers and audiences invert predetermined guest and host relations. With improvisation and disruption as an ally, this aesthetics of hospitality can move into a living framework that is relational, reciprocal and visible. In "decentering" (Knill *et al.* 2005, p.11), the locus of research from an expert-client model into an actor-audience relationship, stigmas and knowledge claims are dispersed into many hands and living bodies of knowledge. Responsive research gives flesh to one-dimensional figures. It challenges the censoring of historical contexts or political complexities. The invisibility of the forcibly displaced only further permits an absence of legal rights and lack of public awareness. Ironically, this invisibility and imposed anonymity also increases surveillance and suspicion. Our viewing and re-viewing of migration is contingent on the ground we stand on and from where we cast our individual and collective gaze.

With multiple absences coinciding with displacement, this lived research focuses on how performance is accountable to the "thing gone" (Patraka 1999, p.6). Archiving the enormity of losses after years of forced migration is a formidable task. Mobile lives are often shadowed by unresolved pasts that won't fit neatly into familiar archives. Although performance scores may take an indirect approach to history, the fundamental questions that influence the making of history still remain constant. These questions are not confined to theoretical constructs, but are enlarged through the potential of the performative. The multiple vantage points available through performance make it possible to move beyond homogenized versions of history. Although exile dislocates memories to the breaking point, history still breathes through performing bodies of knowledge when the conditions are right. The staging of memory continues long after the curtain closes. Finding our place with one another in performance is a precursor to finding home.

> (Set spin cycle for one minute. Actors and musicians enter stage right. Fade in.)
>
> I am not me here.
> I am not me there.

Who can I be?
But when the world falls apart –
We are still we...
Yes WE are still WE. (x2)

(Fade out. Turn spin cycle to power off. In silence, the ensemble members return to their places one by one. Once settled, all freeze and face the audience.)

Curtain.

Performance happened. Yes, look! Look both ways.

Our lives happened right here.

References

Fels, L. (1998) "In the wind clothes dance on a line: Performative inquiry – a (re)search methodology: Possibilities and absences within a space-moment of imagining a universe." *Journal of Curriculum Theory 14*, 1, 27–36.

Hamid, N. (1999) *Home, Exile, Homeland: Film, Media and the Politics of Place.* New York: Routledge.

Jackson, S. (2004) *Professing Performance: Theatre in the Academy from Philology to Performativity.* New York: Cambridge University Press.

Knill, P.J., Levine, E.G. and Levine, S.K. (2005) *Principles and Practice of Expressive Arts Therapy: Toward a Therapeutic Aesthetics.* London: Jessica Kingsley Publishers.

Levine, S.K. (2011) "Art Opens to the World – Expressive Arts and Social Action." In E.G. Levine and S.K. Levine (eds) *Art in Action: Expressive Arts Therapy and Social Change.* London: Jessica Kingsley Publishers.

Minh-ha, T. (2011) *Elsewhere, Within Here – Immigration, Refugeeism and the Boundary Event.* New York: Routledge.

Patraka, V. (1999) *Spectacular Suffering: Theatre, Fascism, and the Holocaust.* Bloomington, IN: Indiana University Press.

Pittaway, E, L., Bartolomei, L.A. and Hugman, R. (2010) "Stop stealing our stories – the ethics of research with vulnerable groups." *Journal of Human Rights Practice 2*, 2, 229–251.

Schechner, R. (2006) *Performance Studies - An Introduction*, 2nd edition. New York: Routledge.

Schneider, R. (2011) *Performing Remains: Art and War in Times of Theatrical Reenactment.* New York: Routledge.

Cold Spell   Isabel Hayeur

Two Poems
Margo Fuchs Knill

Now I say
an Amen to death
and to the mossy life
and to the vanishing kiss
and to the diminishing snail-pace
and to the last good-bye
and to this-time and now-time

empty of all beckoning.

*

Life's tucked creatures
crawl out from all fissures
and snuggle leisurely on my bosom

yet today one became entangled
in my aged long maiden braid
and the breeze from a green kiss was enough
to let the not yet through.

LIST OF CONTRIBUTORS

Sally Atkins, Ed.D. REAT, REACE, is an expressive arts psychotherapist, licensed psychologist, ritualist, award-winning professor and researcher. She is an author of both professional texts and poetry, and co-author of *Presence and Process in Expressive Arts Work: At the Edge of Wonder*. Sally is core faculty of the European Graduate School (EGS) in Switzerland and Professor Emeritus of Appalachian State University, where she was the Founding Coordinator of Expressive Arts Therapy.

Shara Claire is an expressive arts therapist in private practice in Toronto. She is currently pursuing graduate work at EGS in Switzerland. Shara was Assistant Editor *of POIESIS* for a decade, and now serves on the Executive Editorial Committee of the new Chinese journal CAET, which aims to blend Eastern and Western perspectives in expressive arts. She also sits on the first elected board of the Ontario Expressive Arts Therapy Association.

Kelly Clark/Keefe is an associate professor at the University of Vermont, USA. Kelly's research brings material feminist and post-humanist theories of affect, art, and identity to bear on a range of overlapping topics including: the physicality of educational subjectivity, stratified versions of schooling, and conceptual analyses of educational leadership. Her work also engages philosophies of *poiesis*, affect, and habit to argue for the usefulness of embodied, arts-informed approaches for researching the complexities of contemporary educational circumstances. She is the author of *Invoking Mnemosyne: Art, Memory and the Uncertain Emergence of a Feminist Embodied Methodology*.

Melinda Ashley Meyer DeMott, PhD, is the Director and co-founder of the Norwegian Institute for Expressive Arts Therapy (EXA). She is professor and core faculty at EGS, Switzerland, and senior faculty member at the University College of South East Norway. She has made three documentary films about EXA with refugees and written several articles about EXA work with trauma survivors.

Herbert Eberhart is a social worker and clinical psychologist, co-author of *Presence and Process in Expressive Arts Work: At the Edge of Wonder*. He is co-founder and the former president of the European Foundation of Interdisciplinary Studies (EGIS) that established the European Graduate School in 1995 and ran it for some years. He worked for 20 years as Senior Professor at Zurich School of Social Work and is active in private practice. He still is fascinated by the interplay of Expressive Arts work and language in concrete therapeutic situations.

Rosemary Faire, PhD, has designed and run courses in tertiary and adult education settings since 1981. Her education and teaching career has spanned the fields of Biological Sciences (PhD in epigenetics), Somatic Education (MA), Music Therapy (GradDip), and Expressive Arts Therapy (CAGS). She also has over 25 years' experience working with individuals and groups in the contexts of personal development, movement therapy, arts therapies, community arts and mental health rehabilitation, including ten years coordinating the MA in Music Therapy at the University of Technology, Sydney, Australia.

Jessica Gilway is a dancing scholar, arts-based researcher, and educational leader who recently completed her doctoral studies and worked as an adjunct professor in the College of Education at Appalachian State University. Her research aims to create multi-modal, layered, and theoretically rich c/a/r/tographies of pre-service teacher subjectivity and identity development, international education and study abroad, sustainability in Kindergarten through Grade 12 leadership settings, contemplative practices, and school gardening practices with Kindergarten through Grade Eight children.

Rowesa Gordon, MA, CAGS, RP, co-director and core teaching faculty at the Create Institute, is an expressive arts psychotherapist in private practice who supervises and consults in this field. Her writing and art-work have been included in professional journals, and her paintings have been shown in Canada, Europe, and the United States.

Judith Greer Essex, PhD, is the Director of the Expressive Arts Institute, San Diego. Judith is a licensed marriage and family counselor, a registered expressive arts therapist, certified journal therapist, member of the international trauma professionals, and a board certified dance/movement therapist. She won the National Poetry Awards in the 7th and 8th grade, and has never stopped loving poetry.

Isabelle Hayeur, born in 1969, lives and works in Rawdon, Canada. As an image-making artist, she is known for her photos, videos and her site-specific installations. Her work is situated within a critical approach to the environment, urban development and to social conditions. She is particularly interested in feelings of alienation, uprooting, and disenchantment. Her art-works have been shown in the context of numerous exhibitions and festivals.

Lisa Herman, MFT, PhD, REAT, is a registered expressive arts therapist, the former Director of Creative Expression and Associate Professor at the Institute of Transpersonal Psychology (ITP), and former Executive Co-Chair of the International Expressive Arts Therapy Association (IEATA). She is core faculty at Meridian University and has taught at the Create Institute (formerly ISIS-Canada) in Toronto, and in California at California Institute of Integral Studies (CIIS) and JFK University. She is a novelist, actor, academician, and a grandmother.

LIST OF CONTRIBUTORS

Elisabeth Hösli, PhD, has been a teacher in multi-cultural classes for many years and a counselor for teachers and supervisor in school development. She teaches at the Pädagogische Hochschule, Zürich. Her book, *I Have Got Something to Say But I Don't Know Your Language Yet,* was published by Peter Lang Publishing, New York, in 2000. Her dissertation at EGS (2014) was titled *Studienreise nach Kosovo – Ein situiertes Lehr-Lernarrangement auf der tertiären Ausbildungsstufe.*

Majken Jacoby, PhD, is a therapist, supervisor, and teacher in the field of Expressive Arts. She is a printmaker, painter, scenographer, puppet maker for puppet theater, and book illustrator, all within the field of Visual Arts.

Margo Fuchs Knill, PhD, is Professor, Dean of the Masters Program, Division of Arts, Health and Society at EGS, and a former assistant professor at Lesley University, Cambridge, MA. She is an Expressive Arts professional, psychotherapist, supervisor, and poetry coach. Margo Fuchs Knill works in private practice and teaches internationally at training institutes. She is a poet, the author of *Wenn das Wort zu Wort kommt, To Day,* and numerous other publications, and the co-author of *Minstrels of Soul: Intermodal Expressive Therapy,* as well as a contributor to *Foundations of Expressive Arts Therapy.*

Paolo J. Knill, PhD, Dr. h.c,. is the Founder and former President of EGS, and Professor Emeritus, Lesley University, Cambridge, MA. He initiated the International Network of Expressive Arts Therapy Training Centers and founded the ISIS (International School of Interdisciplinary Studies) European training institutes. As a teacher and performing artist, he has traveled internationally and published extensively, including the books *Lösungskunst, Minstrels of Soul: Intermodal Expressive Therapy* and *Ausdruckstherapie (Expressive Therapy).* He is co-author of *Principles and Practice of Expressive Arts Therapy.*

Ellen G. Levine, MSW, PhD, ATR-BC, REAT, is a co-founder and faculty at the Create Institute in Toronto and a senior staff social worker at the Hincks-Dellcrest Centre for Children's Mental Health. She is a professor and core faculty at EGS in Switzerland. She is author, co-author, and editor of a number of books in the field of expressive arts therapy, including *Principles and Practice of Expressive Arts Therapy.* Her latest book is titled *Play and Art in Child Psychotherapy: An Expressive Arts Therapy Approach.*

Stephen K. Levine, PhD, D.S.Sc, REAT, is an expressive arts practitioner and teacher. Dean of the Doctoral Program in Expressive Arts at EGS; Professor Emeritus, York University; co-director and co-founder, the Create Institute (Toronto). He is the author, co-author, and editor of many books and articles in the field of Expressive Arts, including *Poiesis: The Language of Psychology and the Speech of the Soul, Trauma, Tragedy, Therapy: The Arts and Human Suffering* and *Principles and Practice of Expressive Arts Therapy.* He was the founder and editor of the *POIESIS* journal since its inception in 1999. He is now co-editor-in-chief (with Shaun McNiff) of the journal, *CAET (Creative Arts in Education and Therapy—Eastern and Western Perspectives).*

Kelly Lycan is an installation- and photo-based artist from Vancouver, BC. Lycan's work investigates the way objects and images are placed in the world and the cycle of value they go through. Her work has been exhibited across Canada, the US, and Europe.

Carrie MacLeod is a scholar, practitioner, and artist with twenty years of experience in conflict transformation, peacebuilding, refugee and immigrant resettlement, leadership, and social innovation. Carrie consults internationally and is faculty at EGS and at the Vancouver School of Expressive Arts Therapy. She has published several articles and contributed chapters to texts in the field of Expressive Arts and Conflict Transformation. Her latest co-edited book is *The Choreography of Resolution: Conflict, Movement and Neuroscience*.

Elizabeth Gordon McKim is a poet, teacher of poets of all ages, international performance artist, acclaimed jazz poet of Lynn, MA, and Poet Laureate of the EGS in Switzerland. She has been co-poetry editor of *POIESIS* along with Shara Claire for many years—an inspiring task, which deepened her appreciation for the diversity and scope of the voices of the EGS Community. McKim's roots are in the oral tradition of song, story, and poem. She is the author of six books of poetry, including *The Red Thread*, and her work has been published in many journals, reviews, and anthologies.

Shaun McNiff is author of *Imagination in Action: Secrets for Unleashing Creative Expression*; *Trust the Process: An Artist's Guide to Letting Go*; *Art as Medicine*; *Art Heals*; *Art as Research*; *Integrating the Arts in Therapy*; *Art-Based Research*; and other books. An exhibiting painter who is internationally recognized in the areas of the arts and healing, creativity enhancement, and art-based research, his books have been translated into many languages, and he has lectured and taught throughout the world. McNiff is the recipient of numerous honors and awards for his work, including the Honorary Life Member Award of the American Art Therapy Association. He was appointed the first University Professor at Lesley University in 2002.

Emily Miller completed undergraduate degrees in English Literature and Psychology with a concentration in Creative Writing, a Master of Arts in English Education, and a Doctoral degree in Educational Leadership with a graduate certificate in Expressive Arts Therapy. Emily's academic work explores art and craft practices as an extension of human well-being within the context of an economic metanarrative. Emily is delighted to be a prolific artist/maker and works with her hands almost every day.

Judy Nisenholt lives in Toronto where she has worked as a women's shelter counselor, child welfare social worker, ESL instructor, and photographer.

Sabine S. Silberberg, PhD, initially trained as an urban geographer, is an art therapist and expressive arts therapist. With a focus on photography, she has worked as a counselor and arts therapist in inner city community-based health and mental health care for almost two decades. She is a core faculty member of the counseling/art therapy program at Adler University and of the Expressive Arts Therapy Program in Vancouver, BC.

Jacques Stitelmann, PhD, is a visual artist and poet, as well as a psychologist, psychotherapist, and art therapist. He is the founder of L'ATELIER in Geneva, an institute for research and training, which he has directed for almost 25 years. He is the author of several books in the field of the arts therapies, including most recently, *Formes et Modalities: Des concepts pour l'art thérapie* (Forms and Modalities: Concepts for Art Therapy).

Per Espen Stoknes is a psychologist with a PhD in economics and Director of Centre for Green Growth at the Norwegian Business School. A serial entrepreneur, including co-founding clean-tech company GasPlas, he's also written several books, among them *Money and Soul* and the recent award winning book: *What We Think About When We Try Not to Think About Global Warming*.

Brigitte Wanzenried, lic.phil.I, CAGS, is an art and family psychotherapist and a painter. She is a teacher and supervisor at EGS and at InArtes in Switzerland.

Peter Wanzenried, PhD, is Professor Emeritus of Education in a Teacher Training College in Zurich. He teaches at InArtes Switzerland and at the EGS. In addition, he has been an actor in Playback-Theater for 25 years, currently in the ensemble *Die närrischen Alten*. He has published *Spielräume für Bildung* and *Unterrichten als Kunst*.

Rebekah Windmiller is a dancer, choreographer, and expressive arts therapist. She holds an MA and a CAGS from EGS and is currently studying in the clinical fellowship program at Gestalt Associates for Psychotherapy in New York City. She is a clinical supervisor at Interfaith Medical Center in Brooklyn, NY, where she works on an in-patient substance abuse rehabilitation unit.

SUBJECT INDEX

a/r/tography boards 286–8
act modality 70, 77
aesthetic analysis 13, 103–4, 106–7, 110, 179
aesthetic condition 92–5
aesthetic dimension 10, 266
aesthetic education
 as learning through arts 177–80
 teaching with aesthetic responsibility 181–3
aesthetic experience 12–14, 45
aesthetic response 12–14, 44, 216, 265–6, 313–14
aesthetic responsibility 12–13, 181–3, 269
affect as source of knowledge 314–16
alternative experience of worlding *see worlding, alternative experience of*
Aristotle 10–11, 263, 265
art asylum 194–5
artistic expression
 and arts-based research 275
 as inseparable from person making it 114
 micro effects of changes in 126
 otherness as inherent to 93–4
 and quality 113, 116, 120
 questions relating to 114–15
 relation to process 94
 resources to use for building individuated 123
 shadow domains of 125, 127
 as transformational act through psychological growth 67
 and use of words 279
 as viewed in relation to qualities unique to 117
artists in community *see Black Mountain College; European Graduate School (EGS)*
arts
 art-oriented therapy levels 45–6
 centrality of 204
 disciplines as disciplines of play 44

encountering evil through 312
helping traumatized refugees 148–56
learning through 177–80
like "soul food" 45, 59–60, 217
practice in therapy 44
in protest 245–6
and ritual 159, 168–73
special role in *poietic* ecology 269
thingly nature of work with 173
see also expressive arts (EXA); quality art; work of art
arts-based research (ABR)
 "art analogue" attitude 309
 and artistic expression 275
 call for assessment of professional language 277
 creating avenues for merging of research identities 288
 creating form or following formats 276–9
 definition 275
 discourse of "science-as-usual" placed with 298–9
 freedom from uniformity in presenting 279–80
 functioning as provocation 282–3
 importance of *POIESIS* journal 278–9
 as infinitely variable 277
 intent in liminal space 314
 major challenge facing 276
 methodological frame finding, in addiction-based work 302–3
 photography as 304–9
 search for 301–2
 per-forming 319–21
 perspective on knowing 284–5
 potential to shape future practice 277–8
 quantity-quality discourse 276
 a/r/tography as methodology of 286–8
 with refugees lived 327

 per-forming 319–21
 reductive approach 327
 researchers 326–7
 responsive 327
 staging at home 324–5
 resistance to 276–7
 variously defined and highly diverse in application 282
arts work
 bridge to everyday life 103–6
 challenge and playfulness 102–3
 examples
  Claire 109–10
  Mrs Reinold 107–9
  Zara Inewsky 105–7
 harvesting 104–5
 importance of relationship 99–100
 integrating 105–6
 language
  adequate 100
  recognizing work and process 103–4
 reasons for working well confirming and revealing resources and significance of surprises 111–12
 encounter with poietic potentiality 111
 "overfilling" or "multiplicity of perspectives" 110–11
 resource-orientation 101
 see also expressive arts therapy
artworks
 Artists' Statements Antagonisms (Clark/Keefe) 293
 Cold Spell (Hayeur) 329
 Degradation and Preservation (Levine) 209
 Nutcase Alarm (Gordon) 97
 Pasture 6 (McNiff) 19
 Rock, from 4 perspectives (Lycan) 273
 Stuhl-leben (Wanzenried) 16
 untitled (Nisenholt) 175
Auschwitz 311–17

beauty
 ability to be moved by 309
 aesthetic perception of 12, 26

— 336 —

SUBJECT INDEX

of algorithms 142
in art-oriented therapy 45
of art work
   as important element 68
   sensory experience of 181–2, 217
   longing for 61
   of mountain setting 200
   opposition with "interest" 266
   from *poietic* ecology perspective 269
   quotations on 133–5, 180, 266
   role of limiting resources 41
   sense of wonder as experience of 265
   as sensible manifestation of appearance 262
   in the various 179–80
   wild, undomesticated side 259
Black Mountain College 196–203, 206
Blake, William 26, 28
body and mind readiness 228
body-mind dimension 39–40
Buddhism
   and deep ecology 248
   Middle Way 25–6

catharsis 10–11
challenges in arts therapy 102–3
change agents
   bridging capability 36–7
   helping others find possibilities for change 265–6
   "ingredients" pertinent to activity of 46
   professional, as universal phenomenon 32–3
   trained to understand role of limiting resources 41
   change and quality 126–7
chiasm and intertwining 83–4, 93–5
children and their parents
   art-making 158–9
   effectiveness of therapy 158–9, 173
   oasis in the playroom 159–68
   ritual and the arts 159, 168–73
choreography
   description of solo dance 138–9
   in in-patient environment
   application of 142–3
   context 140–1
   development of 143–4
   seeping into everyday life 137
choreopoiesis 285, 294–8
community

anchoring in here and now 226–7
as complex and moving phenomena 206
culture 218–19
defined by circles of self-identification 248
evaluating resources and needs of 225–6
living/learning 204
nature of 197–8
regeneration of 238
resilience 213, 219, 238
community art
   as alternative experience of worlding 213–15
   as bridge
   attempts at 220
   the bridge itself 220–1
   need for 219
   as contribution to culture of communities
   entertainment events 218
   relational reflection opportunities 218–19
   as decentering method providing range of play 215–17
   didactic principles
   anchoring community in here and now 226–7
   definition 225
   the I and the we 227–8
   motivation for ensemble work 227–8
   provision of space for individual 227
   psychic readiness 228–9
   readiness of body and mind 228
   two levels of readiness 228–9
   two pillars of attention 226
   where we are in "coming here" 226–7
   where we are in "going to" 227
   evaluating resources and needs of community 225–6
   familiar community scores 233
   feedback culture 232
   guidance of process 229–31
   joining with music 231–2
   meaning of 212
   project
   description of 222–4
   warm up exercise 211–12
community arts therapy
   Council of All Beings 251
   music therapy 253
   "Soundsations" 249–50
   suggestion for radical 256
   trouble songs writing process 254–5

"What are you concerned about?" workshop 251–3
compassion fatigue 157
Council of All Beings 251
creative conflict 206
creative environments 24–5, 27–9
creative imagination 21–3, 25, 27–30
creative leadership 26–7
creative vitality 23
curiosity
   appreciative 99
   example of encouraging 237
   experiential field of discovery motivating 45–6, 217
   motivation through 183, 231

data
   coding 288–9
   collection and analysis 285–6
   material-discursive, attuning to 290–3
   representation 294–8
   somatographic analysis 290–3
decentering
   into alternative experiences of worlding 32, 38–9, 46, 173, 286
   and audience–performer relationship 327
   community art as method of 215–17, 220–1
   concept of 13, 60, 214–15
   as coping experience in restriction situation 41
   from deformed 62
   from egoic concerns to imagination of "Earth" 259
   giving opportunity to leave conflict zone 42
   move into experience within logic of imagination 37
   postmodernist 282
   and somatographic analyses 289–90
   togetherness of client and change agent 60–1
   within workshop structure 252
   see also intermodal decentering
deep ecology 247–8, 251, 258
dialogic encounter, balance of 189–90
diet 41–2

"Earth"
   beauty as apprehension of 269
   as capable of transformation 268

"Earth" cont.
  Heidegger's concept of 264–5, 267–8
  meaning cluster 250
  remaining beyond our power 267–8
  works of art and nature 270
eco-philosophy 258–60
ecological self 248–9
ecology
  as based on automobile 262
  deep 247–8, 251, 258
  depth 258–9
  and imagination 24–5, 30
  poietic 267–71
  taking place within "aesthetic dimension" 266
ecopsychology 247–8
education
  aesthetic
    and aesthetic responsibility 181–3
  as learning through arts 177–80
  balance
    of dialogic encounter 189–90
    of different languages creating realities 190–1
    between process and work 192–3
  Rafael's story 184–7
  seminar in Bosnia-Herzegovina 187–9
  with therapy 189
educational leadership 294–8
entertainment events 218
European Graduate School (EGS)
  centrality of arts 204
  comparison with Black Mountain College 196
  importance of imagination 205
  as living/learning community 204
  as process 206
  research and experimentation 205
  transdisciplinarity, transculturalism and creative conflict 206
  as work in progress 203
experiential learning 44–6, 111
experimentation
  in European Graduate School 205
  sustained 121–6
expression
  attraction of 86–92
  concept of 55–6
  condition of, and field of human being 82–5
  finding form 92–5
  Gestalt theory of 122

group 121–2
see also artistic expression
expressive arts (EXA)
  aesthetic responsibility in 12–13, 181–3, 269
  approach to education 178–80
  and art-making 158–9
  based
    on play 9
    on play of *poiesis* 15
    on *poiesis* 10
  communicating from senses to senses 148
  discourse of "science-as-usual" placed with 298–9
  and eco-philosophy 258–60
  expansion to all relationships based on facilitation 14–15, 63
  expressive mode 54
  as flexible tool 133
  interest in wildness 259–60
  perspective on knowing 284–5
  phenomenological view of art-making 11, 13
  relying on *poietic* mode of understanding 265
  as resourceful in offering alternative world experience 59–60
  shaping and holding in 14
  use as means of data collection 285–8
  use in harm reduction therapy 135
  use of to build relationships 131
expressive arts therapy
  balance with education 189
  in broader socio-political context 244–9, 255–6
  for children and family 158–73
  decentering as technique of 286
  egalitarian and inclusive spirit of 113
  emerging to show adaptability to circumstance 132–3
  experimentation with 125
  gaps within 246–7
  "intermodal" theory of 25, 42, 66
  motivating participants in 123
  music in 122–3
  play as key to 173
  with potential to serve the world 30
  power lying in imagination 30
  quality perspective 113–14, 116, 118–19, 123–4
  as revolutionary arrival 284

role of artistic quality in establishing 119–21
role of quality art in 119–21
  for traumatized refugees
role of therapist 156–7
therapeutic factors 155–6
on verge of becoming mainstream discipline 21
see also arts work; community arts therapy

form
  in artistic making 292
  bound with feeling 314
  constellation of body-in-world as "making" of 83
  creating 276–8
  as driving force of life 117
  as essential to art-making 159
  imagined 25
  Knill's reflections on 55
  and matter 264, 270
  poetic act of finding 92–5
  in *poietic ecology perspective* 268–70

Gestalt 68, 72, 80, 122, 218–9, 264
gestures 113, 118, 123–4, 142, 239, 241, 326
green psychology 247–8
group psychotherapy *see* traumatized refugees in exile

haikus, series of dancing 294–5
harm reduction approach 130, 302–3
harm reduction environment
  aiming at sensitivity to clients' culture 132
  beautiful encounters 133
  beauty as powerful ally 134–5
  beauty of connection 133–4
  breakthrough moments 131–2
  clients' experience of counseling 129
  conveying acceptance 133
  "hallway counseling" method 129–30
  harm reduction meeting expressive arts therapy 130–1, 135
  injection-based addiction 130–1
  meeting people where they are 130–3
  tango metaphor 134
  typical day within 128–9
  use of photography 304–9
harvesting 104–5

SUBJECT INDEX

healing
  ecotherapy 247
  function of creative
    imagination 27–30
  and individual's subjectivity
    246
  language of 277
  rituals 32
holding
  environment 14, 29
  function of therapist 249–50
  quality of relationship 99
  role of 14
human being
  capacity for relatedness 198
  expressive condition of 95
  field of 82–5
  imagination reflected in 69
  impossible to think, without
    art 204
  as poietic by nature 261, 270
  as shaping animal 268
  unending circuit with the
    other and the world 90
humanity, pulse of *see Sierra
  Leone, West Africa*

image modality 70, 76
images of evil
  affect as source of knowledge
    314–16
  how we play with images
    313–14
  and liminal space 312–16
  power of 312
  representations of capacity for
    cruelty 311
  site of inquiry 312
  transmitting historical
    knowledge 311–12
imagination
  active 52, 59
  and alternative experience of
    worlding 35–9
  antithesis 28
  arts as disciplines of 178–9,
    205
  arts helping trauma survivors
    to restore 148–56
  creative 21–3, 25, 27–30
  cultivation 25–7
  and ecology 24–5
  encountering evil through
    312, 314
  entering space of 38–9
  as "faculty of faculties" 23
  fingers as instruments of 243
  and healing 27–30
  images of 258–9
  importance of 205
  as "integrative" intelligence
    21–2, 25, 30
  logic of 36–9, 214, 286

middle realm of 25–8
  as more important than
    knowledge 15
  as not totally controllable 38
  operation 23–5
  power of expressive arts
    therapy lying in 30
  as primary creative
    intelligence 24
  and psychology 24
  three realms of 38
  transmission of 28
  use in conflict resolution
    215–16
  use in explaining modality
    69–71, 77
  use in therapy 59
  vitality of 23
  widening range of play by
    engaging 42, 46
  "zones of" 242
in-patient psychiatric unit
  algorithms 139, 142–3
  choreography within 142–4
  description of 137
  expressive arts therapy within
    140–1
  mural-making 141–2
"in the zone" 25–6
inspiration 10–11, 28, 314
integrating 105–6
intermodal decentering
  explanation of 59, 78–9
  future possibilities 63
  "ins and outs" as aspects of
    214
  potential for surprises 221
  process of, in professional
    conversations 99–112
intermodal learning process 192
intermodal transfer 58, 74–5,
  150–1, 153–4
intermodality
  alternating 79
  Knill's book on 56–7
  Knill's irritation with
    terminology 58
  simultaneous 79
interpretation 36–7, 39
intertwining and chiasm 83–4,
  93–5

Knill, Paolo
  childhood theater activities
    50–1
  development of work 48–50,
    121
  on expressive arts 59–60, 63
  on imagination 58–9
  influence of Expressive
    Therapy program 52–3
  interest in arts and psychology
    52

interest in phenomenology 22
  on intermodal practice 57–8
  learning to play piano 49–50
  on legacy 64
  on notion of expression 55–6
  perspectives
    different 54, 60–1, 64
    shifts in 54–5
  on process and art 53–4
  psychological dialogue 63–4
  on reality 61, 298
  shifts in work and in
    understanding 61–3
knowledge
  affect as source of 314–16
  artistic tool yielding 287–8
  of beauty 12
  of evil events 311–12
  exclusion of arts from 177–8
  and imagination 15
  three forms of 11

language
  artistic 100
  called for assessment of
    professional 277
  creating realities 190–1
  different, balance of 190–1
  of healing 277
  recognizing work and process
    103–4
leadership 26–7, 294–8
liminal space 148, 159, 286,
  312–16
"low skill/high sensitivity"
  principle 123, 126, 182,
  229–30

mediality 66, 69–72, 79
medicine 41–2
modality
  as dimension of *poietics* 73
  expressing three important
    ideas 72–3
  favorite 75
  and mediality 69–72
  as phenomenological concept
    for expressive arts 66
  switching 73–5
  therapeutic use of 77–80
  types
    act 70, 77
    image 70, 76
    movement 70, 76–7
    sound 70, 76
    taste/smell 75–7
    word 70, 76, 78
  work, working and working
    through 66–9
movement modality 70, 76–7,
  124
mural-making 141–2

music
  choreopoiesis 297
  community art example 221–5
  community music therapy 251, 253–4
  joining community art with 231–2
  Knill's career 52–3, 55, 57
  Knill's early experiences 49–50
  McNiff's experience with 121–5, 127
  shared musicality 323–4
  sound modality 69–70, 76
  "Soundsations" 249–50

nature
  aesthetic response and responsibility 265–6
  deconstructing concept of 261
  Heidegger's concept of "Earth" 264–5, 267–8
  human destruction of 266–7
  and *poiesis* 262–3, 270–1
  and *poietic* ecology 267–70
  as product of culture 261
  romantic image of 267–8
  Rousseau's idea of 270
  shaping 261–2, 266
  temporal mode of being 263–4
  treated as "natural resource" 267
  Nietzsche, F. 263–4

oeuvre *see work of art*
"oeuvre orientation" 137
"other person"
  elusiveness 87
  embodying otherness 87
  as partner-in-expression 82–3
  presence of
    impact 86, 89–91
    perpetual 88
    relationship with 89–92
  otherness
    "alien presence" 90
    of dynamics of sensing 93
    exploring through play and art-making 194–5
    of form 92, 94–5
    and imagination 24
    impact of lack of 91–2
    as inherent to artistic expression 93–4
    of materials 70–1
    "other person" embodying 87
    respect for 268, 270
    three realms of 88
  "overfilling" 110–11

performance
  bringing it home 326–8
  "Cycles of Home" 318–19
  happening 327–8
  of memory 324, 327
  performative terrain 325–6
  performing identities 321–4
  performing research 319–21
  rehearsals and improvisation 321–2
  spaces for 325–6
  staging research at home 324–5
  youth keen to recast themselves as performers 323–4
personal enabling 41, 45, 216
perspectives, multiplicity of 110–11
phenomenological concept, modality as 66–80
phenomenological perspective 11, 13, 36–8, 42, 54–5, 61–2, 82–3, 178–9, 194, 263, 305–7, 314
phenomenology 13
philosophy
  conflict with poetry 10, 262–3
  distinction between science and art 177
  eco- 258–60
  and *poiesis* 261–5
  teacher of 199
photography, use in arts-based research 304–9
Plato 10, 177, 262
play
  arts disciplines as disciplines of 43–4, 59, 205
  creating field of 148–50
  and curiosity 99, 231
  encountering evil through 312
  example of effectiveness 159–68
  experiencing as safe and permissible activity 236–7
  as experiential learning 44–6, 111
  exploratory 230
  exploring otherness through 194–5
  with images 313–15
  importance of creating space for 173
  linked to ritual 159, 173
  making way for exploration in 141
  meaning cluster 250
  as means of bridging reason and sense-experience 178
  music 46

  as phase of intermodal learning 192
  phenomenon of 215
  range of
    art-making increasing 156
    challenges increasing 213–14
    community art providing 215–17
    expanding in restrictions 36, 60
    "ins and outs" as aspects of 37, 214
    lacking 34, 58–9
    necessity of increasing 32, 46
    need for a map for restricted 142
    provision of contrasting with situational restrictions 37–8
    widening by engaging imagination 42–3
  restorative back-and-forth quality 158
  therapy for adults 44
  as type of focusing 44
  validation of, as human potential 38
  and youth 236–7
Play of Poiesis
  double meaning of 9
  expressive arts based on 15
playfulness in arts work 102–3
poems
  After (Atkins) 20
  Among (McKim) 274
  Balance (Wanzenried) 193
  Cedar Fire Fragment (Essex) 210
  Change in the Air (McKim) 176
  Choreopoiesis: a Series of Dancing Haikus (Gilway) 294
  Digging (Herman) 316–17
  Iraqi Girl (Faire) 254–5
  Language Creates Realities (Wanzenried) 191
  Poetry connects. (Fuchs Knill) 204
  Poietics of Alterity (Levine) 17
  Practicum on the Eating Disorders Ward: Sonnet 1 (Claire) 98
  Rafael (Hösli) 184–7
  Two Poems (Fuchs Knill) 330
  untitled (Stitelmann) 80
poetry
  capacity to transcend self 204
  as concerned with words 70, 76
  conflict with philosophy 10, 262–3
poiesis
  as "act of making, and artistic making in particular" 324
  and aesthetic responsibility 269
  as always possible 12

SUBJECT INDEX

attending via, during somatographic inquiry 288–93
as based upon medial space of imagination 25
as bringing-forth 261
contribution to ecological thinking 262
definition 62
as discovery, or way of knowing 178–80, 263
dislocation and displacement as precondition of 85
distinction with *theoria* 177–8, 263
expressive arts as based on play of 15
Heidegger's understanding of 261, 263–5
as living experience 205
meaning of 10–12
modality as dimension of 73
nature shaped through 271
Nietzsche's restoration of 263
as opening possibility of something new 179
and philosophy 261–5
research as act of 15
as soul-making 204
and urban redevelopment 270
POIESIS journal 9, 114, 126, 205, 278–9
poietic basis of being 82–95
poietic ecology
no "free lunch" in 268
possible principles of 268–70
and romantic conception of nature 267
poietic potentiality 111
pollination analogy 23
process and work
balance between 192–3
recognizing 103–4
protest art 245–6, 256
psychic readiness 228–9
psychology
field-cleaning efforts in 283–4
green 247–8
and imagination 24, 30
as not at center of art-based work 63–4, 71–2
psychopathology 194–5, 246
psychosis 22–3
psychotherapy
gaps within 246–7
metamorphosis in 245–6

quality art
context 117–19
in expressive arts therapy
discourse on 113–15
role in establishing 119–21
quality and change 126–7
defining 115–17
sustained experimentation 121–6

radicant artist/researcher/leader 294–8
Re-Inventing Home performance project 318–19
reality
art as level of 67–8
concept of 21–3
effective 61, 265–6
imaginary 40–2, 44
influence of metanarratives 285
Knill on 61, 298
language creating 190–1
literal 34, 151, 178, 205
other shapes of 190
relational nature of 198
return to, on encountering uncanny 313
and worlding 34
refugee protection system of Canada
home
cycles of 318–19
finding 327–8
staging research at 324–5
multi-vocal negotiations 325–6
performative happenings 320
performative inquiry as research vehicle 320–1
refugees
challenges of working with 322–3
understanding 319–20
rehearsals
and improvisation 321–2
space for 325–6
role between performer and researcher 321
shared musicality 323–4
refugees in exile *see* traumatized *refugees in exile*
relational reflection opportunities 218–19
relationship, importance of 99–100
research
as act of *poiesis* 15
definition 275
in European Graduate School 205
of images 311–17
location of 323
see also arts-based research (ABR)
resilience 213, 219, 238
resource-orientation 101
resources
confirming and revealing 111–12

evaluating community 225–6
"response" and "responsibility" 12
rites of restoration
and change agents 32–3
examples in western culture 32
personal inability 33–4
phases where alternative experience of worlding is introduced 35
and reality 34
situational restrictions 33
ritual 159, 168–73

science
discourse on 281–5, 296–9
distinction with arts 177–8, 249, 282–3
and imagination 22
importance of creative element in 10
science-as-usual
"analysis" in translation 288–93
"data" in translation 285–8
discourse of postmodern scholars keen to expose 281–5
in relationship with expressive arts and arts-based research 298–9
"representation" in translation 294–8
self-organization 43, 104, 110–11, 216
sense modality 83
sensing 13, 82–4, 87, 93, 95, 224, 228
shaping
in art-making 182–3
in community art 215–16, 220–3, 226–8, 230
concept of 14
existence of other 90–1
and form 92–3, 159, 173
intervention with thingly process of 40
life storylines 320
limitations and challenges as aspects of 309
and living body 83
loop of 88
nature 261–2, 265–71
as phase of intermodal learning 192
pull of 88–9
Sierra Leone, West Africa
ambiguity as guiding creative force 235
challenge to cultivate safe, creative space 235–6
community regeneration 238
drum metaphor 242

Sierra Leone, West Africa *cont.*
  forgiveness 235, 241
  former child soldiers 235–6
  hands metaphor 242–3
  as humanity on edge of survival 234
  reputation as "world's worst place to live" 234
  Truth and Reconciliation Commission (TRC) 240
  war zones to zones of peace 241–2
  youth
    acts of improvisation 239
    communicating cultural norms and values 239
    composing fictional narratives 239
    encouraging sense of curiosity 237
    experiencing play as safe and permissible 236–7
    peace processes from body to page 239–40
    performances 238–41
    restrictions faced by 236
    storytelling 237–8
    truth-telling processes 240–1
simultaneity principle 26
situational coping 41, 45, 216
solution-focused perspective 60–1, 101, 219
somatographic inquiry 290–3
sound modality 70, 76
"Soundsations" 249–50
surprises, significance of 111–12
systems theory 42–3, 110–11, 216, 219, 226

taste/smell modality 75–7
theoria 11, 177–8, 263
theory
  constructivist 190–1
  ecological 24
  Gestalt 122
  intermodal 25, 57–60
  learning 45
  as pre-existing and given to us 11–12
  systems 42–3, 110–11, 216, 219, 226
  transpersonal 42
  worlding 36–7
therapeutic process
  alternative experience of worlding
  decentering as indispensable condition for 38–9
  and logic of imagination 36–8

body-mind dimension 39–40
commonalities 31–2, 46–7
diet and medicine 41–2
different scientific perspectives on 64
interventions
  with thingly process of shaping 40
  with "work of art" (ouvre) 40
personal enabling and situational coping 41
play
  arts disciplines as disciplines of 44
  as experiential learning 44–6
  therapy for adults 44
  as type of focusing 44
  practice of arts in therapy 44
  professional change agent as universal phenomenon 32–3
research suggestions 46–7
rites of restoration 33–5
use of modality 77–80
worlding experiences 42–3
"thin places" 25
thingly
  aspect of media 39–40
  dream, artistic act as 38
  imaginary space in community art 215
  nature of work with arts 173
presence
  of acts or objects 39
  of images 35
research for 46
process of shaping 40
witnessed experience 61
total expression (*Gesamtkunstwerk*) 30
transculturalism 206
transdisciplinarity 206
transpersonal self 248–9
traumatized refugees in exile
  arts helping
  art as container of pain 150–2
  field of play 148–50
  meaning of group 154–5
  stuck with memory of single image 153–4
  context 145
  Elisabeth from Turkey 149–50, 154
  Imir from Syria 152, 156
  Kadi from Kurdistan 151
  Leonard 154
  Mercedes from Chile 152, 155
  nature of living in exile 146–7

Omid from Iran 151–2, 154–5
  role of therapist 156–7
  therapeutic factors of expressive arts therapy 155–6
  types of exile 147–8
  unique project 146
trouble songs 245, 251, 254–6

vision 11, 24–5, 27–8, 202–3, 205, 224–5

"What are you concerned about?" workshop 251–3
White Mountain Graduate School *see* European Graduate School (EGS)
wild ethics 258
word clusters 84, 250
word modality 70, 76, 78
words
  coming out right 88, 91
  creating realities 190–1
  on rocks 170–1
  unable to fully express 149, 279
work
  balance with process 192–3
  describing 103–4
  working and working through 66–9
  see also arts work; expressive arts therapy
work of art
  appearing as formed expression 82
  arts-based understanding of 63
  beauty in emerging 182
  as entity within rituals of restoration 41–2
  giving daily life its dream 181
  as intermodal 70
  interventions with 40
  nature as 261–71
  stringent logic within 36, 214
worlding
  alternative experience of community art as 213–15
  decentering as indispensable condition for 38–9
  and logic of imagination 36–8
  "in and out," "to and fro" of 40
  research suggestions 46–7
  and rites of restoration 35
  experiences 34, 42–3
  terminology 34

AUTHOR INDEX

Abram, D. 258–60
Anderson, R. 314
Appalachian Expressive Arts Collective 284
Arnheim, R. 122, 314
Atkins, S. 20, 279, 284

Bachelard, G. 312, 314
Barba, H.N. 25, 33, 42, 56, 69, 75, 151, 248, 313
Barone, T. 283
Bartolomei, L.A. 322
Bateson, G. 110
Bathanti, J. 202
Beck, S. 289
Bennett, J. 311
Berg, I.K. 101
Berger, J. 308
Bion, W. 69–70, 72
Boal, A. 313
Bodenheimer, A.R. 37, 39
Bourriaud, N. 285–6, 294–5
Bowers, C. 286
Bragg, E.A. 248
Braidotti, R. 288
Braud, W. 314
Brenner, R.F. 315
Brown, M.Y. 248, 252

Cage, J. 52–3, 69, 201
Cahnmann-Taylor, M. 283
Cameron, N. 249
Canadian Harm Reduction Network 130
Canin, J. 249
Chodorow, J. 38
Clark, A. 307
Clark/Keefe, K. 283–5, 289, 291, 293, 296
Clinebell, H. 247
Cobb, E. 24–5
Cole, A. 282–3
Cramer, D. 200

Davis, M. 29
de Cosson, A. 283
de Jong, P. 101
de Shazer, S. 60, 101
Denning, P. 130

Denzin, N.K. 313–15
DeSalvo, L. 292
Duberman, M. 197, 199, 202, 205

Eberhart, H. 60, 62, 99, 110–11, 284
Einstein, A. 15
Eisner, E. 283
Epston, D. 101
Estes, C. 245

Faire, R. 249, 251–2
Felman, S. 153
Fels, L. 320
Finely, S. 283
Fink, E. 34
Foucault, M. 282
Franskoviak, P. 302
Fuchs, M. 25, 33, 42, 56, 62, 69, 75, 151, 204, 248, 313, 330

Gawain, S. 291–2
Gilgun, G.F. 312
Gilway, J. 284
Glesne, C. 290
Gomes, M.E. 247

Hamid, N. 322
Harding, S. 281
Harm Reduction Coalition 303
Harris, M.E. 206
Hawkins, K. 133–4
Hayeur, I. 329
Heidegger, M. 12, 14, 261, 263–8, 270
Henkel, C. 249
Herman, J.L. 155
Herman, L. 312
Hillman, J. 13, 64, 117, 119, 245–7, 277
Honermann, H. 110–11
Hopkins, G.M. 179
House, R. 246, 307
Hughes, L. 295, 297
Hugman, R. 322

International Harm Reduction Association 130
Irwin, R. 283, 286

Jackson, S. 320
Jacoby, M. 63–4, 135, 204

Kanner, A.D. 247
Katz, V. 197, 199–200
Kellen-Taylor, M. 251
Kenny, C. 253
Kerr, T. 130
Kind, S. 283, 286
Knill, P.J. 25, 33, 42, 56–7, 60, 69–70, 102, 111–12, 117–18, 122–3, 134, 137, 142, 151, 180–1, 204–5, 213–14, 217, 248, 252, 284, 286, 292, 298, 309, 313, 322–3, 327
Knowles, J. 282–3
Kriz, J. 62, 110–11
Kuhn, T. 281

Lane, M. 206
Langan, D. 251
Laub, D. 153
Leavy, P. 283
Levine, E.G. 111–12, 134, 181, 205, 209, 213–14, 284, 286, 292, 298, 309, 323, 327
Levine, S.K. 12, 17, 25, 32, 42, 62, 111–12, 118, 126, 134, 181, 204–5, 213–14, 248, 284–6, 290, 292, 298, 309, 314, 323–4, 327
Lincoln, Y.S. 313–15
Little, J. 302
Lyotard, J. 55, 285

Ma'anit, A. 245
Macy, J. 248, 251–2, 255
Marlatt, G.A. 302–3
Marqusee, M. 245
McNiff, S. 19, 24, 53–4, 118–19, 124, 126, 275–9, 284, 296, 313–14
Mentha, D. 111–12

Merleau-Ponty, M. 82–4, 86–7, 90–1, 93, 306
Metzner, R. 247
Meyer, M.A. 148, 150
Miller, E. 284, 287
Miller, V. 296
Milner, M. 69
Minh-ha, T.T. 324
Mohr, J. 308
Moore, T. 198
Moyer, B. 248, 252
Mulisch, H. 36

Neilsen, L. 286
Nellessen, L. 219
Niewöhner, J. 289
Norris, C. 295, 297
Northrup, C. 292
Nunn, P. 253

Palmer, P. 198
Patraka, V. 327
Patterson, T. 200–1
Pink, S. 307–8
Pirsig, R. 127
Pittaway, E.L. 322
Polanyi, M. 275, 278
Powell, K. 283
Prinzhorn, H. 68
Prosser, J. 307

Reynolds, K.C. 199
Richards, M.C. 197, 202–3

Richardson, L. 283
Richter, J.P. 23–4
Ricoeur, P. 13
Rilke, R.M. 60
Rogers, C.R. 99, 198
Rogers, N. 246, 284
Ronk, S. 253
Roszak, T. 247
Rumaker, M. 201

Sandelowski, M. 283
Sarton, M. 200
Schechner, R. 320
Schiffer, E. 213
Schiller, F. 177–8
Schneider, R. 324
Seed, J. 248, 251
Sessions, G. 247
Shalev, A.J. 39
Siegesmund, R. 283
Silberberg, S. 305, 309
Smith, P. 205
Spittal, P.M. 130
Springgay, S. 283, 286
St. Pierre, E.A. 281–3, 315
Steinman, L. 316
Stendhal 266
Stern, D. 68–9
Stewart, W. 131
Stige, B. 253
Stitelmann, J. 66, 80
Sullivan, G. 304
Suzuki, S. 124

Tatarsky, A. 303
Turner, V.W. 91, 132–3
Tyndall, M.W. 130

Ubben, G. 295, 297

van der Hart, O. 153
van der Kolk, B.A. 153
van Manen, M. 306
Vasas, E.B. 304
Ventura, M. 245–7

Wallbridge, D. 29
Watzlawick, P. 38
Weber, S. 308
Wessan, L. 246
White, M. 60, 101
Wilber, K. 248–9, 254
Wiles, R. 307
Winnicott, D.W. 14, 29, 72, 158, 161
Witkiewitz, K. 302
Wood, A. 131
Wood, E. 130

Yalom, I.D. 155, 158

Zettel, P. 131